Without Shame
learning to be me

CONNELLY AKSTENS

Potowomut Press

EAST GREENWICH, RHODE ISLAND

Visit: connellyakstens.com

Potowomut Press
26 Netop Drive
East Greenwich RI 02818
518-796-3521
connelly@connellyakstens.com

Cover and book design: Susanne Murtha
Cover photography: Rachel Tine

Library of Congress Cataloging-in-Publication Data:
Akstens, Connelly—
    Without shame: learning to be me / Connelly Akstens.

ISBN: 978-1-7364379-0-2

Library of Congress Control Number (LCCN): 2020916307

    1. Akstens, Connelly (fka Tom Akstens), 1947—Family. 2. Transgender
    —Biography. 3. Boston—Biography. 4. Cape Cod—Biography. 5. Col-
    lege of the Holy Cross, Worcester (Mass.)—Basketball—Biography.
    6. Fishing—Biography. 7. Folk Music Revival—Cambridge (Mass.)—.
    8. Woodstock (N.Y.)—Music Scene—.

The author has, in some instances, changed names and identifying details to protect the privacy of individuals. The author and publisher do not assume and hereby disclaim liability for any loss, damage or disruptions caused by the contents of this book.

For my parents,

Constantine W. Akstens and Isabel Connelly Akstens

and my grandfather,

Judge Thomas H. Connelly

Contents

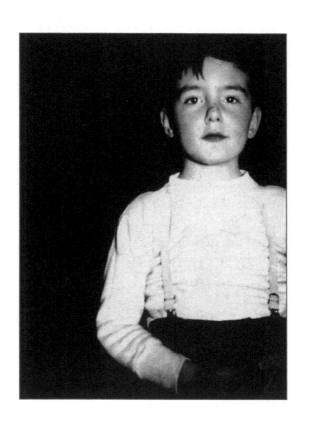

Preface

If you would know me, look in your [own] heart.—Lao-tzu, *Tao Te Ching*[1]

For most of my life, I lived in the shadow of shame. From the age of three or four, I was perplexed about whether I should be a boy or a girl. For a long time, I was afraid that if anyone discovered my confusion about my gender there would be terrible consequences. I would surely be humiliated, maybe even locked up in a mental institution. So I kept myself hidden—hidden in plain sight, if you will. I managed to perform masculinity pretty well: as an athlete, musician, fly fishing guide, professor, friend and lover. I lived my life as best I could, but I made sure that no one ever knew me completely. Otherwise, who would want to be my friend? How would I have a career? Who would love me?

When I was fifty-five, I decided to change that. With the help of my spouse Susanne, the past two decades have been a process of coming out of hiding, letting myself be known and leaving shame behind. That process has led me to write this book.

I'm nobody's victim, and this is not a "Me and My Miserable Transgender Life" book. I've made my own decisions, some of them good and some of them bad. I've been both wise and foolish. I've been both generous and selfish. I've been honest and I've lied. But, taken as a whole, my life has been full, varied and rewarding. Wow—I nearly finished that last sentence by writing, "in spite of my unconventional gender." That's the apologetic mindset that's easy to fall into when you're not like everyone else. But it would be wrong to write that. In truth, I've been surprised to discover as I was writing this book how much my unsettled gender identity has actually made my life richer. More complicated, certainly—but decidedly richer. I hope to share that discovery with you as you read.

My story is anecdotal. That's mostly because I don't understand my life as a sweeping, coherent narrative. Perhaps I just don't think in those terms. Dickens, Tolstoy, Victor Hugo—these were writers who saw life through a wide-screen, epic lens. I can't pretend to have a smidgen of that vision. My inspirations have been more modest. I have read and taught Russell Baker's *Growing Up* many times. Baker was a master of the vignette, the short story within a longer story that had its own, self-contained truth. Vladimir Nabokov's remarkable *Speak, Memory* awakened me to the potential of memoir to define its own form and its own relation to time and truth. Works such as Cervantes' *Don Quixote*, Fielding's *Tom Jones* and films such as *Thirty-Two Short Films About Glenn Gould* have convinced me that life really is episodic and that there are rewards to be had for embracing it as such. And you won't be surprised to discover that books by the master of the anecdote, James Thurber, have been on my bedside table for years.

I've been blessed with many odd experiences, some stunning misadventures and the acquaintance of many quirky people. And whatever I have to say about it, or whatever you may think of it, I'm grateful I can finally tell my story without shame.

Connelly Akstens
Potowomut, Rhode Island
January, 2021

Ursuline Academy first grade class in Boston Public Garden. I'm the tall one. I felt jealous when Francis (third from right) was chosen to play a girl in a skit.

1
Rainbows and Ladybugs

Red and blue bands of light danced on the ceiling. They delighted me. Sometimes they were there and sometimes they weren't. That is my earliest memory.

Where did they come from? Where did they go? When I was quite a bit older, I realized the colors came from the goldfish bowl on the windowsill. When the sun hit the surface of the water at a certain angle, it threw a rainbow on the ceiling. If the window was open and a breeze stirred the water, the rainbow shimmered. Coming to this knowledge gave me satisfaction, but it destroyed the mystery. It was a passage from pure sensory pleasure to the kind of scrutiny and analysis that has always dampened pleasure for me. I've learned that rational thought always seems to expel wonder.

I was born in 1947, the year Jackie Robinson crashed the race barrier in baseball, something resembling a flying saucer wrecked in the New Mexico desert and T-Bone Walker recorded "Stormy Monday." Until I was six, we lived at 61 Park Drive in Boston. The apartment looked over the Fenway, a park designed in the 1880s by Frederick Law Olmsted, as part of his "emerald necklace" network of elegant Boston greenspaces. In summer, Mother would walk me across the street to the park. She'd set out a red plaid wool blanket with tassels (which I still have) and I'd toddle around, stumbling after ducks and pigeons. Together, we'd gather ladybugs from the rosebushes and take them home in a jar full of grass. We poked holes in the lid of the jar. The ladybugs lived on the windowsill, next to the goldfish.

There always seemed to be music. I remember delightful sounds coming in through the window. When I asked her years later, Mother told me that a violinist from the Boston Symphony lived in the apartment above ours and practiced endlessly. My parents didn't play music themselves, but they had an RCA phonograph and radio combination and played records a lot. She told me later that I loved Tchaikovsky's *Nutcracker Suite*, mambo music, Ukulele Ike records, Tommy Dorsey's "Song of India" and my father's favorite jazz song from his youth, Red Nichols' "Feelin' No Pain." Of course, the only thing I knew then was that there were sounds in the air that made me feel happy.

In winter, my mother would take me across the Fenway to the Gardner Museum or the Museum of Fine Arts. At the Gardner, I would dawdle in front of John Singer Sargent's *El Jaleo*, an enormous painting depicting a flamenco dancer and her singers and musicians, until Mother grew impatient and ushered me along. At the Museum of Fine Arts, I liked the

Egyptian mummies and the small effigies of crafters, farmers and seafarers that had been buried with them. There was even a miniature ship and some cows. But most of all, I loved Sargent's *The Daughters of Edward Darley Boit*, another of his huge canvases. It's a portrait of four young sisters, painted in 1882. They are depicted in a large room dominated by two huge blue-and-white vases. The girls seem poised and remarkably present. Mother would tell me later that I would stand in front of the little girl in the left foreground of the picture for a long time, meeting her gaze. When I visit the painting now, seventy years later, I am still struck by the composure with which she looks out of the image. "You used to tell her that she was pretty. She was your first love," my mother told me. That's probably true enough, but I think somehow it was more complicated. I think that in some way I didn't understand, I felt that Mary Louisa Boit was like me and I was like her.

In warmer weather, Mother would walk with me around the corner and down Jersey Street to Fenway Park. In those days, most Red Sox games

Strolling with Mother on the Fenway. I look happy. She looks perplexed. But the matching plaid oufits?

were played during the day. Mother was a great fan of Ted Williams, and I learned at her knee that there was no other player who could rival Ted for hitting, and that he was a wonderful fielder, too. "Just watch him swing," she instructed. "It's poetry." It might have been the first time I heard that word. I also learned that Ted was very brave. From what she said, he had flown a plane in the war and single-handedly defeated the Germans. He was going to give the Communists in Korea a taste of it, too.

My grandfather knew someone who wrote a sports column for one of the Boston papers. The writer was glad to give him passes for his daughter and grandson. Not many people came to the Red Sox games in those days, anyway. We always sat in the press box on the first base side. When a foul ball went over our heads, I would rush out the door, duck under a railing onto a gravel area and grab it. I was too young to know much about the game, but I knew how to hoard baseballs. To make the day even better, I always had a hot dog with mustard and relish and got to go "Whoooooooop" with the rest of the crowd when a foul ball behind home plate rolled down the screen. After the game, my grandfather's friend would take the balls down to the locker room and get them autographed. Ted Williams, of course. Jackie Jensen, Jimmy Pearsall, Dom DiMaggio, Sammy White, Mel Parnell. I had balls autographed by them all. Where they disappeared to, I can't imagine.

I went to Ursuline Academy, a school run by French nuns in a majestic brownstone at the corner of Commonwealth Avenue and Arlington Street, across from the Public Garden. I started school very early, at three and a half, in part because of my precociousness, in part because I was an only child who needed contact with other children, and in part because (as she admitted to me much later) parenting wasn't my mother's forte.

I loved the school. The nuns were very musical and arty; they didn't seem to care any more than I did about arithmetic and other, similarly tedious pursuits. We spent our days singing songs in French and English, acting out little plays, painting and drawing, baking cookies and tarts that we would eat later in the day for our snack, and napping. Mother noticed that all of the finger paintings that came home with me from kindergarten were orange. She was concerned that I was so monochromatic. "I wouldn't worry," the nun told her. "Orange is such a sunny and happy color. Tres joyeux! If it were a gloomy color like purple, I might worry." One day, Mother came to fetch me for some reason and was bemused to find my teacher standing in the middle of the room with the skirt of her habit hitched up above her ankles and all the children gathered around her, scrutinizing. "Thomas just asked me if I have legs," the nun good-naturedly explained.

At recess time, we'd cross Arlington Street to the Public Garden to run around and shake off the lethargy induced by cherry tarts and napping. A very nice, portly policeman would stop traffic at the crosswalk by holding up his white-gloved hand and blowing his whistle. He was Officer Mike, the model for the policeman in the classic children's book *Make Way for Ducklings*. We were honored to have him as our custodian. We were instructed to show our appreciation by piping "Thank you, Officer Mike" after we had safely crossed.

I loved recess time the most in the weeks before Christmas, when there was a crèche with live animals on the Boston Common, near the State House. We would bundle up in our hats, mittens and mufflers and make our way to revere the Christ child—but mostly to pet the docile donkeys and sheep in their pen and feed them hay and carrots. When we got back to school, we'd spend the rest of the day cooking Christmas treats and making ornaments as gifts for our parents. Given the curriculum of Ursuline Academy, it's little wonder that I still rely on a calculator to do long division.

2
Spacemen

When I was a senior in college, I applied for a Rhodes Scholarship. Let history record that in 1968 I didn't get one and that a Georgetown student named William Jefferson Clinton did. Oh, I guess history has already recorded that fact. Well, in any case, my advisor for the Rhodes process told me that I ought to apply for a passport. "You can't get a passport overnight," he declared. "If this works out, you'll need one."

To get a passport, I needed a birth certificate. I asked Mother where mine was. She started a very evasive song-and-dance. She said over and over, "You don't really need a birth certificate. Your baptismal certificate is just as good."

"So you say, but the passport application explicitly says birth certificate. Where's mine?"

"Just give them your baptismal certificate. It will be fine."

It wasn't fine. The application came back. *Missing document: birth certificate of applicant.* I asked my mother again. The best she could do for an answer was, "Maybe someone in your father's office can help."

I gave up talking to her about it. Over Christmas break, I went into Boston to the Public Records Office and got my own copy. Every firstborn male child in my family had been named Thomas for generations. But on my birth certificate, there was no first name. The document said that "Baby Akstens" had been born on February 1, 1947. "That's weird," the clerk at the counter volunteered. "Sometimes we get these because the mother

I loved that coat. It came with a wooden whistle, which I'm holding proudly.

and father were fighting about the name. But they always say 'Baby Boy Cohen' or 'Baby Girl Sullivan.' This one just says 'Baby.' Odd, huh?"

Actually, standing there with my birth certificate in my hand, things didn't seem so odd. A wild cascade of things actually seemed to make sense for the first time. My fascination with the clothes in Mrs. Billings' steamer trunk in the attic of our first house on South Street. My interest in Mother's fashion magazines. My resentment when Francis, a classmate, was chosen to play a girl in a second-grade skit. The jolt of fear I felt when my friend Roland, whose father was a "baby doctor" at St. Elizabeth's, the hospital where I had been born, got angry and taunted me: "I heard my dad tell my mom that when you were born, they didn't know whether you were a boy or a girl." And, most of all, a mysterious medical procedure I endured when I might have been three or four years old.

I was lying on my back. There was a large light over my head, and the rest of the room was dark. Three adults were under the light, looking at me. They had things over their faces. One of them said, "Don't be scared, we're just spacemen."

Just spacemen. *There's* a sure-fire way to alleviate a child's anxiety. *Don't worry, kid, we're just going to take you into outer space.*

The next thing I remember was waking up. I was on my left side and something was restricting me from moving. It sounds impossible in retrospect, but I'm sure no one was there with me. I opened my eyes. There was wallpaper next to the bed. It had pictures of Mickey Mouse, Minnie and Pluto. I knew Mickey and Minnie. I loved Pluto. I felt safe.

To this day, waking up in that room is one of the most emotionally charged experiences of my life. From something Mother let slip years later, I know was operated on at Children's Hospital in Boston—perhaps twice. The word "intersex" was never mentioned (it simply wasn't in those days). She suggested evasively that it had something to do with "bleeding in your underwear." She said something to the effect that she hoped I wasn't thinking about it anymore, but if I was, I shouldn't ever have to think of it again because everything was fine now. Or did she say "fixed now"?

3
Fa

The family story went like this: When I was a toddler, Mother tried to teach me the word "grandfather." She said the word, pointed to him—seated in his favorite wicker chair on his beloved "veranda" in Falmouth Heights—said the word again, pointed to him once more and so forth. Finally I got the message, toddled over to him, grabbed his leg in a bear hug and yelled the only part of the word I could: "Fa!" From that day until the day he died, he was "Fa" to all of us.

To the rest of the world, he was "The Judge." Mother often shopped for vegetables at Ten Acre in Falmouth, which had a wondrous doughnut machine in the window just like the one in my favorite book, *Homer Price*. As she was picking through the beans and tomatoes, Mr. Lovell the grocer might say: "We've got some nice corn—picked just this morning—The Judge will like it." Or if we encountered casual acquaintances of Fa's (Dr. Spock and Helen Hayes among them), they would always offer their "best regards to The Judge."

Fa told me that his grandfather had been a horse trader in Galway, Ireland. With pride, he claimed that his ancestors had been "Galway sluggers"—outlaws who would sneak down from the hills above the bay on moonless nights to "slug" sheep with their shillelaghs and drag them back to their cottages for meat in the winter. In any case, there is some mystery about how this son of an Irish stevedore from Copp's Hill in the North End of Boston became a judge who was regarded for both his compassion and his toughness. It also seems remarkable that Fa's brother Pat became postmaster of Boston, and that his sister Margaret was a graduate of Portia Law School and became one of the city's leading labor lawyers by 1915—in an era when professional women were regarded with blatant contempt.

Even as a youngster, Fa had a combination of smarts, handsomeness and charisma. He caught the eye of Marian Lawrence, who would become a doyenne of Boston Brahmin society and the mother of "Chub" Peabody, All-American football player at Harvard and governor of the Commonwealth. She wrote in her autobiography about seeing Fa at a dance:

> Tom Connelly was there, and he was terribly nice…I can hardly refrain from telling him he is the most attractive personality I know.[2]

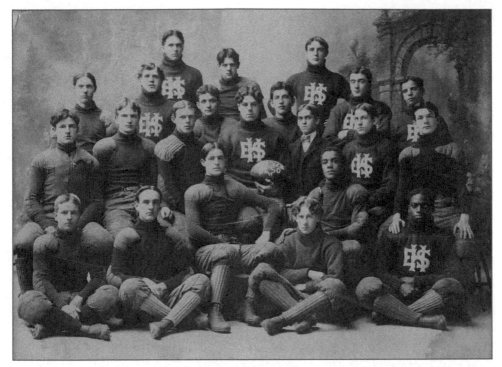

Fa (top row, right) with the 1899 English High School football team

But romance between a Beacon Hill society girl and an Irish kid from the North End was unthinkable in those days.

Fa had been a renowned athlete. He was a star player on the North Bennet Street Nine, a youth baseball club that regularly beat prep school teams like Groton. But he really excelled at football. He was captain of the Boston English High School football team for two years, 1900 and 1901. These were the days of the punishing "flying wedge" offense. Football was brutal—much closer to rugby than today's game. The deaths and crippling injuries to players would cause President Teddy Roosevelt to take action in 1905 to reform the game. Fa's team picture from 1899 shows a bunch of kids who are wiry, confident and itching for a brawl. It's a mix of Irish faces, Italian faces and Black faces. Very tough kids.

In those days, Boston English was right next door to Boston Latin, the city's public college preparatory school, whose alumni include Samuel Adams, Benjamin Franklin, John Hancock, Ralph Waldo Emerson, Leonard Bernstein, George Santayana and…need I go on? English has a quirkier list of notable graduates: J. P. Morgan, Leonard Nimoy and Louis Farrakhan. By and large, Latin School kids went to Harvard or Tufts; kids from English mostly apprenticed to a trade or went to work on the docks.

Which is what Fa did when he graduated. Like his father, he unloaded cod and halibut from Grand Banks schooners on the old fish pier. The closest he came to college was on fall weekends, when he traveled to Amherst to play football as a ringer for "Mass Aggie"—the forerunner of the University of Massachusetts. He got train fare, two nights with board in a lodging house and twenty bucks under the table. Apparently, this was not such an unusual arrangement in that era—Yale's notorious James Hogan and Stanford's William Morley are more famous cases of paid ringers. For his part, Fa contributed to the Aggies' regular thumpings of Connecticut, Amherst, Williams and Rhode Island (46–0 in 1903). He claimed that he never attended a class. True or not, he was evidently given a diploma after four years, and then studied law nights at Northeastern University Law School.

Somehow, he landed a job as chief of staff to Governor David I. Walsh. When Walsh left the State House in 1915 to go to the United States Senate, he gave Fa the choice between the comparable appointment in Washington or a spot on the bench in Boston. Fa prudently took the judgeship, which in the Commonwealth of Massachusetts was a lifetime appointment.

Fa (right) with Governor Walsh, aboard USS *Chicago*, Boston Harbor, 1914

Fa was ensconced in an imposing new courthouse in Brighton in 1925, where he sat for more than thirty years and where his portrait by Jacob Binder still hangs. I loved watching him preside over the court. After the morning sessions, I would play in the jail cell that ordinarily held criminal defendants. I marched around with the court officer's long white baton, imposing order on imaginary murderers and gangsters. I banged the gavel and yelled for order in the court. In short, I was a rambunctious brat. For lunch, Fa would order in enormous sandwiches of baked Virginia ham and dry, aged Swiss cheese from Moskos, a Greek restaurant in Allston. The sandwiches always came on caraway rye with lots of pickles and tangy mustard "for The Judge."

An unbiased observer might conclude that Fa was a bit of a crank. He never drove a car. He insisted on a shave with hot towels and Dickinson's witch hazel at the barbershop every morning. He sent his uncashed Social Security checks back, addressed directly to President Dwight D. Eisenhower at 1600 Pennsylvania Avenue. He'd scrawl across the front of the check: *I did not work my entire life to be on the dole!* Dating from his time with Senator Walsh, he had a grudge against the Kennedys; whenever the opportunity presented itself, he would make known his opinion that "Joe Kennedy is a conniving, social-climbing, philandering bootlegger." Mother put some perspective on this when she pointed out that Fa himself had employed a bootlegger during Prohibition, a French Canadian fellow who trafficked in the finest Scotch whiskey. She recalled the wooden crates in the basement, the bottles nested in excelsior packing. In fact, one of Fa's great pleasures in the 1920s was his regular wintertime junket with a few judicial cronies on the Crescent Limited to New Orleans, where the Eighteenth Amendment was honored more in the breach than the observance. They played cribbage and bridge all the way down on the train, ate oysters at Antoine's and crab at Galatoire's for a couple of days, and then played cards all the way back, each with a suitcase of carefully wrapped bottles of Cuban rum.

But, as a child, I was unconscious of these eccentricities. I loved Fa more than any other person in my young life, and he doted on me shamelessly. When my parents badgered me with their demands for good behavior and good grades, Fa would gesture me to his side, put his big hand on my head and say, "You're doing alright boy! Let me sing you a song I used to sing when I was your age:

> I went down to L Street to take a little swim,
> And I wasn't very dirty when I first jumped in

Sing! Don't worry." This infuriated Mother to the point of tears.

In grade school, I would look forward all week to Friday night. My parents and I would have dinner at Fa's house—usually lobster, with peas and turnips in winter, corn and beans in summer, or piles of asparagus in spring—and always Fa's favorites: pickled Harvard beets and Major Grey's Chutney. Fa's housekeeper, Minnie—a wiry Scots lady who had been forced to work as a fly tier as a child—would help to get the dinner and then leave to visit her sister until Sunday afternoon.

My parents would leave after dinner, and then the fun would start. Co-conspirators against their orderly, sensible world, we'd raid the kitchen and pop popcorn and make tall Dagwood sandwiches on rye with horseradish mustard and sliced dill pickles. Lots of pickles. Fa would pour himself a robust tumbler of Bonded Old Fitzgerald and open a Pepsi for me. We'd turn on the TV in the sunroom and settle in for the Friday night fights. As Fa got further into his bourbon, his commentary on the fights would get more raucous: "Look at that bum. Hit 'im again! You're boxing, not waltzing, you bum! Don't let him off the ropes, dammit! He's down! He's up! He's down again! He's out!" And then at the end, when Sugar Ray Robinson or Archie Moore had defeated the foe, Fa would grab my small right hand in his and exclaim: "Shake the hand that shook the hand of John L. Sullivan!" I found the whole thing thrilling.

Fa died when I was eleven. He spent weeks in the hospital with his head in a gruesome traction device. When we went to visit, he would beckon me to the side of the bed, put his large hand on my head as he always did, and say, "You're doing alright, boy!" But there was no singing anymore. Mother later told me that I "ran through the house screaming like a wild animal" when she told me he had died. I have no recollection of that at all.

At his funeral, the crowd at St. Ignatius church in Chestnut Hill overflowed onto the steps and the sidewalk. Senator Saltonstall, judges, bishops and other bigwigs were in the front of the church with the family. But in the back were several hundred of the ordinary people of Brighton. Some of them had been brought before his bench on charges such as vagrancy, larceny, battery, public drunkenness and "L & LC" (lewd and lascivious cohabitation).

As we followed the casket from the church, some men I now realize looked like they came out of a Damon Runyon story (I imagine they had names like "Lefty" and "Fingers") came up to my mother with their hats in their hands and shook her hand earnestly. "God bless The Judge, Missus. He could have sent me up for three to five, but he let me off with two years probation."

This man, who loved good food, a good drink and a good rumble, had a big place in his heart for me, and for people he called "the downtrodden." Among his effects when he died were several books on the Holocaust

Portrait by Jacob Binder

and the founding of Israel, and on the desegregation of schools. There was also a copy of an article he had written on alternative solutions to what was known in those days as "juvenile delinquency": "Sending a boy to prison is sending him for an advanced degree in crime." It was a theme he knew well. "When I was about your age, I stole a pickle from a pickle barrel on Hanover Street. If I'd been caught, I would have been sent to reform school," he once told me. "But I could run faster than the cop," he added with a wink.

The Greatest Show on Earth

When I was four or five, I was enchanted by the circus. I had a book about the circus and an Emmett Kelly clown doll. My friend Roland had a toy big top with clowns, a ringmaster and some animals, including lions and tigers that lived in an elaborate cage on wheels. When Roland told me that the real circus was coming to town, I pestered my parents to take me.

Father was involved in some big legal case, so he was off the hook. Mother had dreadful allergies. She was particularly vexed by dust, hay and animal dander. I imagine that her vision of the seventh circle of hell might well have been an afternoon at the circus. Nevertheless, she rose to the occasion. After all, how could she refuse to take her darling only child to the circus? The plan was that she and I would go to Boston Garden, see the afternoon show, and then meet Father in town for dinner.

I don't remember much about the circus itself, except that it was very bright, very noisy and people were always busy doing things. Whatever was going on, I loved every minute of it. My mother didn't. She suffered through it with some Benadryl and a pile of Kleenex, and she recalled the ordeal for many years.

We met Father at some restaurant near the giant teakettle on Court Street. We went upstairs to a table. I remember there were big murals on the walls portraying Pilgrims and Indians. While we were waiting for our dinners, Father asked me how I had enjoyed my trip to the circus.

"It was super!"

"What did you like best?"

"The elephant went to the bathroom and a man picked it up with a shovel!"

5
My Brief Life of Crime

Before she went back to graduate school, my mother spent quite a lot of time visiting older ladies. When I was little, I often got dragged along. Mother would take a small gift of some kind, wrapped in colorful paper and finished with a bow. The ladies would have lunch. And they would talk. A lot. Lunch was the good part—I remember the lobster salad, potato chips and cucumber sandwiches with mayonnaise and pepper. But as the talking droned on, I would wriggle and squirm in my seat until I would be told to "go play."

Marie Greene had been a friend of my grandmother's. She had an imposing shingled house with a sunroom bay window that overlooked the channel entrance to Falmouth Harbor. A luxurious lawn stretched from the gardens toward the road by the water. In later years, I discovered a photograph from the 1920s of my grandfather, in white flannels and a straw boater, at a lawn bowling party. Marie's house was in the background of the picture. But those grand days had long since passed. A croquet set and a few bent wickets were all that remained. Usually, I was sent out to knock the ball around with a mallet while the ladies talked.

One rainy day, however, I was ushered into another room and given a book. I was a hotshot reader for my age, but the book didn't have any pictures and I was soon bored. Snooping around the room for something to do, I found a little green figure of a cat. It charmed me. I played with it for a few minutes and when I heard Mother coming, I put it into my pocket.

Mother found it when she emptied out my pockets that evening. She wasn't happy with her discovery: "Where did you get this?"

"Miss Greene's house."

"Did she give it to you?"

I looked down at my shoes. Suddenly I felt hot and sweaty.

"You just took it?"

I stared at my shoes.

"You know that's wrong, don't you?"

I stared at my shoes.

"Well, we are going over to Miss Greene's and you are going to give this back to her and apologize. Right now."

The five-minute car ride seemed to last an hour. By the time we parked at the house, I was shaky and tearful. Miss Greene was waiting for us in her wicker armchair by the bay window. "Miss Greene, I'm sorry that..." I began, and burst into tears.

The old lady took my hands in hers and told me that we all do things that we regret and that we ought to learn from our mistakes. Then she told me that the cat was made of jade and her brother had given it to her when she was a little girl—at about my age.

In some Jackie Coogan movie, the old lady would have given the cat figure to the child, which he would (of course) cherish to this day and always (of course) remember when he looked at it that—you know the rest. Pass the hankies and roll the credits. But Miss Greene was too wise for a cheap Hollywood ending. She took back what was rightfully hers. I didn't get to keep what I coveted, because I had done something wrong to get it. But she gave me a lesson that I took to heart. I've never needed a little jade cat to remind me.

6
Was It Something I Said?

My Uncle Thomas was a very distinguished, serious gentleman. A graduate of Holy Cross in the '20s, he had earned his medical degree at Tufts Medical School and taught cardiology there. I never saw him in anything other than a three-piece Brooks Brothers suit, a gold watch chain and a stiff collar and tie. He was a man of few words, but commanding presence.

One Thanksgiving when I was about six, Fa was ill, so Uncle Thomas presided over the family dinner, a gathering of twenty or so. Uncle Thomas sat at the head of the table. I was on his right, a place of honor. The turkey arrived, splendidly brown, bursting with stuffing and surrounded with a garnish of roasted apples and cranberry sauce. There were big, steaming bowls of potatoes, peas and gravy. All of my favorite foods together in one place! I couldn't wait.

But Uncle Thomas was in no hurry. Methodically, he sharpened the carving knife with the steel. Then he eyed the bird and began to cut. The slices were perfect. The platter piled higher and higher until finally, Uncle Thomas determined that there was enough turkey for the entire clan. Then he turned to me and asked the traditional Thanksgiving question: "Thomas, would you care for white meat or dark meat?"

I was beside myself with anticipation. I could barely respond, but I remembered that I had heard some kid say something on the playground earlier in the week that made the older kids laugh. I liked to make people laugh, so it seemed like a good thing to say. Politely, I responded, "I'd like some of both, please, Fuckface."

A profound silence descended over the gathering. Then a muffled gasp. Then some nervous tittering among my older cousins. "Quiet!" Uncle Thomas commanded them. I was perplexed. No one seemed to think what I had said was funny.

Abruptly, my father grabbed me by the shoulders, hauled me out of my chair, marched me into the kitchen, gave me a serious talking-to, grabbed a bar of soap and washed my mouth out with it. I spat and sputtered. I drank some water to try to get rid of the taste, but the soap bubbles went up my nose. Finally, I was allowed to go back to the table and have dinner, after a suitable apology to everyone for having said "a stupid thing."

Without any ceremony, I was given a plate. All that beautiful turkey, stuffing, mashed potatoes, apples, cranberry sauce, peas and gravy. And it all tasted like Pears Soap. Ugh.

7
Mrs. Billings' Steamer Trunk

When I was six, we moved into a dilapidated Georgian mansion on South Street in Brighton. It was close to my grandfather's house on Gerald Road. Otherwise, the house didn't make much sense for a family of three. The place was enormous, with pillars, a grand portico, two parlors, a vestibule, a library, a butler's pantry with a dumbwaiter down to the larder in the basement, and a third floor with maid's quarters and two big storage rooms. I understand now that my parents bought it as an investment. They planned to rehab the place, sell it after a few years and move on.

I remember vividly the day we moved in. I stood on the porch, watching men carry things into the house from a big yellow-and-green van. I thought the men were very smart because they had a ramp that ran out of the back of the van and directly onto the porch. No stairs. Adults could be very clever.

The South Street House in 2019; the grand porch and three chimneys have been removed.

We settled in. My parents spent the summer painting, hanging new drapes and having furniture reupholstered. When the work was done, they threw a big dinner party to celebrate our new home. Mother hired a lady to help her prepare the food. They planned and worked for days. Flowers in vases came the morning of the party. A man and a woman arrived wearing uniforms. He set up a bar in one of the parlors while she arranged the table in the dining room. Hors d'oeuvres appeared on trays. I was told sternly not to touch them. It was the first chilly evening of the fall, so Father decided to turn on the heat. The guests were arriving as the thermostat kicked on for the first time since we had moved in. There was a rumble in the basement, then a bang that shook the house. Black, sooty smoke billowed out of the registers in the floors. Fearing an explosion, everyone ran for it. The fire department came. I thought it was thrilling. None of the adults seemed to share my glee at all the excitement.

In the meantime, I had made a discovery. The house had been owned by two older women known locally as "the Billings sisters." Evidently, they were rich and a bit eccentric. The storage rooms on the third floor were loaded with their possessions, left behind when the house had been sold. In one alcove, there were hundreds of books. I made a collection of the ones with pictures, some of which I still have. *The Last of the Mohicans* with

the wonderful N. C. Wyeth paintings of Indians. A book about the Seven Wonders of the World with engravings of the Pyramids and the Colossus of Rhodes. A book called *Voodoo Fire in Haiti* that had woodcut-style illustrations of some very exotic goings-on. One of them intrigued me; in it a naked goddess appeared to be bathing in the moonlight with her arms over her head. I also tried to puzzle out the pictures in the Rockwell Kent *Moby-Dick*. In one of them, the whale seemed suspended against the starry night sky. What was going

on? Whales swam in the ocean, not across the sky. I began to learn from that image that not everything is literal. I began to learn that there is another dimension—whether verbal or visual. Call it poetry.

There were also dining chairs, sunlamps, boxes of blankets, a wicker hamper full of picnic stuff, mirrors, old records, tennis racquets, crewel-work footstools—and a steamer trunk.

On the side of the trunk were stenciled the letters "E. C. Billings. Boston." Stood on end, it was as tall as I was. I undid the latches and it opened up to form a little portable dressing room. The right side had a rod, with clothes on hangers and a compartment at the bottom for shoes. The left side had drawers with a shelf above for hats and such. It was filled with

Mrs. Billings' things. Without thinking even for a moment, I started to put on some of the clothes. My feet were already too big for her little shoes, but I could wear her dresses, gloves and camisoles. I leaned a mirror against the wall. I put on this, and then that, looked in the mirror and changed it all again. I whirled until I was dizzy with delight. I returned to the attic many times in the six years we lived in that house. Gradually the zippers on the dresses and buttons on the blouses became too tight to fasten. It didn't matter much. Just knowing those things were there comforted me. It took me fifty years, but I finally overcame my shame enough to tell a trusted friend about these experiences. His response was both terse and wise: "You must have been a very creative child."

Yes, I experienced delight and found comfort in that attic, but about the same time I began to have a recurring dream that troubled me for several years. In the dream, a little girl stands in front of a brick wall, smiling. Suddenly the wall collapses, burying her. I'm sure the little girl in those dreams was me. But, more than six decades later, I'm still puzzled about her annihilation. Did it represent some subconscious desire to be rid of the feminine part of me? Or did it express my fear of the awful things that would happen to me if I were discovered?

Fear and shame kept me from confiding in my parents about any of this, but they must have known what I was doing. A six-year-old child doesn't put things back in their proper place; the stuff must have been scattered. But they never reprimanded me. They could have said on any Saturday, "We're cleaning out the attic," and the trunk and its contents would have disappeared. But they didn't. From time to time I'd try to cover my tracks by running around in a cowboy outfit, capguns blazing. But I'm sure I wasn't fooling them any more than I was fooling myself.

Still, my parents' anxiety about my gender explorations must have been building. One afternoon after school I was in the backyard, playing with two of the neighborhood girls. They were teaching me to skip rope. They held the ends of the rope and did a singsong thing while I tried to jump in time. I was having fun and laughing when Father came down the driveway. He yanked my arm and thrust me up the back steps and into the kitchen. "What are you doing?" he demanded. I said I was skipping rope. "That's for girls. I don't want to see you playing with girls. Ever." He stomped out of the kitchen. I stood there and tried not to cry. Crying was for girls, too. Wasn't it?

8
Catty

For as long as I can remember, I've loved to fish.

Father did, too. Before he had a boat of his own, he would rent one from a Portuguese guy on Waquoit Bay who had a few sixteen-foot Delano skiffs with five-horsepower, green Johnson Sea Horse outboards. For a few bucks, you got boat, motor, a can of fuel, a soggy boat cushion, a pair of oars in case the motor crapped out and a bailing can (you'd need it).

Off Father would go in a cloud of oily blue smoke, and he'd usually come home at the end of the day with a cooler of fish gutted, iced down and ready to fillet. I would admire each fish, touch it reverently and smell its briny odor. I begged to go with him.

When I was five or six, he started taking me along on some of his excursions in nicer weather. We'd pack bologna sandwiches for ourselves and squid and sea worms for bait—all in the same little plaid Skotch Kooler. We caught an amazing variety of fish. Scup, fluke, black sea bass, tautog, sting rays, dogfish, eels, scary-looking goosefish, sea robins and puffers—and once a striped bass of ten pounds or so. I loved the flamboyant sea robins. Father told me they walked on the bottom of the ocean with their "feelers." I laughed until I was giddy when the buck-toothed puffers squeaked and croaked and blew themselves up like spiny balloons when you tickled their bellies. When we threw them back, the balloons floated for a moment and then *zip!* they were gone. I was always fascinated by the mystery of what was on the end of the line this time. *What was down there, anyway?*

A sixteen-foot Delano wasn't much of a boat. A flat bottom, Amesbury-type skiff made of wood lapstrakes—sort of a whaleboat stripped of all its sea-keeping virtues and cut in half. She was intended to be a functional workboat for protected bays, and she wasn't a match for the afternoon southwest blow on Vineyard Sound. Especially when powered by a five-horsepower stinkpot.

But nothing deterred my father. After he had graduated from soaking bait to casting wooden plugs with what the gurus at the Red Top Bait Shop in Wareham called a "poppin' rod," we sometimes went west, around Nobska, through Woods Hole and along the north shore of Naushon. Other times we went east as far as Cotuit. And sometimes we crossed the sound to the Vineyard. I remember refilling the gas can in Menemsha; Father told me the dark man at the gas dock was "a real Indian."

Once we motored past the Gay Head cliffs and the lighthouse and out to Nomans Land—an excursion that, on some days, would challenge a modern twenty-four-foot center-console fishing boat with a two-hundred-horsepower motor. The ocean swells were big, but we motored on. I was scared but I was even more scared to show it. My father was almost giddy with the adventure of the open ocean. He handed me the bailing can and told me not to worry; he had "seafaring blood" from the Finnish sailors and fishermen in his mother's ancestry.

Until I was eight or so, I felt more at home on the placid pond at the end of my grandfather's road. Inspired by my friend Robbie's tale of catching a catfish and having it for dinner, I set out on my first solo fishing expedition.

There was always a rowboat tied up at the end of the path. I wasn't supposed to use it. With my rod, a can of worms, a Coke and a peanut butter, jelly and Marshmallow Fluff sandwich, I climbed aboard the boat, grappled with the oars and somehow got myself a few yards offshore. I dunked my worm and waited. Then I ate my sandwich and waited some more.

The afternoon wore on. I was wondering how someone on Martha's Vineyard could be an Indian. Indians were in the movies—out west, where Roy Rogers, Hopalong Cassidy and the rest of the cowboys were. There weren't any cowboys on Martha's Vineyard. Were there?

My first worm had drowned and turned gray, so I put another worm on the hook, dunked it and waited some more. And then I felt something tugging on my line. The ancient fascination: *What is it?* I reeled and reeled and there was a catfish! I lifted him into the boat, and promptly got stung on the hand by one of his barbs. Who knew that a catfish could sting you? There was a bucket in the boat. I filled it with water and lowered the catfish in. He seemed pretty content. I was wildly excited.

Grabbing the oars, I thrashed my way to shore and ran back to Fa's house, water splashing all the way. There was still bit of water left in the bucket when I ran up the back steps and into the kitchen. "Look!" I yelled. "I'm going to have it for dinner!"

Mother explained that I was not going to have it for dinner. Company was coming for dinner. I had to get cleaned up right away. And what were we going to do with this damned fish, anyway? My father had a solution. As I pretended to scrub behind my ears, he filled the clawfoot bathtub.

"He has a name," I called over the sound of the water. "His name is Catty." Then, ceremoniously, we lowered Catty from the bucket into the tub. He seemed none the worse for wear from his journey, and immediately began to swim in lazy ovals around the tub.

"Mum, *wow*! Come look at this!" She did, and both of my parents agreed that Catty was the most beautiful catfish in the world, much too beautiful to have for dinner and that, in the morning, he would go right back to the pond to rejoin his other "catfish friends." Even at that young age, I think I was skeptical of the notion that catfish actually had friends—which reminded me, I had to run to get Robbie and show him my *own* catfish. But the doorbell rang downstairs as the guests arrived. "In the morning," I was told.

During the night, I checked on Catty three or four times. Each time he was still swimming in lazy ovals. I wondered if he was getting hungry. "Get into bed and stop bothering that fish!" came my father's voice through their bedroom door.

"I think he's hungry," I ventured.

"He is *not hungry*," came the voice. "Get into bed and stay there."

In the morning, my parents found me asleep on the bathmat. When Father awakened me, I stuck my head over the edge of the tub. Catty was still swimming in lazy ovals. We got the bucket and scooted him in. He thrashed around a bit but settled down as we carried him out to the station wagon for his trip back to the pond and a joyful reunion with his catfish family, friends and finny well-wishers.

"Robbie!" I remembered. "I've got to show Robbie!"

My parents indulged me. We stopped at Robbie's house. I ran up the back steps and pulled him away from his breakfast. "You've got to see my catfish!"

Robbie sauntered to the back of the station wagon and looked in the bucket.

At age eight, Robbie was already a seasoned angler. "Mine was bigger," he said.

9
Home Sick

When I was in the early grades, I loved staying home sick from school. The days seemed long and luxurious, lying in bed, propped up with extra pillows, soothed by Vicks VapoRub, entertained by Mister Potato Head and comic books and fed on chicken noodle soup, saltines and ginger ale. Then, as it grew dark outside the window, Father would come home from work. Mother would be in the kitchen. I could hear their muffled conversation. Smells of cooking filled the air. As if by a miracle, I would revive and decide I was well enough, after all, to come down to dinner and polish off half a chicken, a baked potato, two servings of green beans and a sizeable wedge of Boston cream pie. The wonders of modern medicine be praised! But my hope would be that when Mother took the thermometer out of my mouth the next morning she might shake her head and say, "Still a hundred and one. You'd better stay home another day."

My companion was the radio. Bob and Ray had a bizarre, improvised comedy program on WHDH. Most of the time—perhaps because of my fever-induced delirium—I had no idea what they were talking about, but I loved the fast pace and the wild word games. It seemed that anything could be anything else and anyone could be anyone else in the phantasmic world of Bob and Ray. In retrospect, the *Bob & Ray Show* was a foundation for my later excursions into the worlds of Genet, Dalí, Artaud, Borges, Jonathan Winters and *Firesign Theatre*. But all I cared about then was the pleasure of two people inventing characters, voices and dramatic situations purely with the power of their imaginations. In the afternoon the WCOP *Hayloft Jamboree* would come on, with Eddie Zack and his Dude Ranchers and Betty Hutton, the Queen of the Hillbillies. They played and sang wonderful cowboy and mountaineer songs. In between, Big Brother Bob Emery had his show on WEEI, with lots of stuff for kids and his catchy theme song at the end of the show, "So Long, Small Fry." Given all this and chicken noodle soup, too—why would anyone want to go to school?

Father seemed to have another agenda—that I ought to be using this time to become acquainted with literature, rather than absorbing a lot of "drivel" and "poppycock" from the radio. He appeared one morning with a book. "I want you to read the first forty-nine pages and tell me about what you read after dinner tonight." Like it or not, he had determined that I would improve my mind while I was confined to what he derisively called my "bed of pain." I looked at the book. *Treasure Island*, by Robert Louis

Stevenson. There was a wonderful picture on the cover of three pirates, with a cutlass, pistols and the Jolly Roger. I liked pirates. I opened the book and started to read. It was a story about a boy who got involved in all sorts of thrilling and dangerous adventures. I liked it very much.

I have the book in my hand as I write this. I recall vividly, more than sixty years ago, opening the book to the endpapers. There is an astonishing illustration of seven pirates leaning forward and pressing on with sinister determination along a beach, in search of treasure. The sky in the picture, for some reason I am still at a loss to understand, is yellow. Perhaps to catch the attention of a child, such as I was, or perhaps to convey a sense of menace. The volume Father had given me was the edition illustrated by N. C. Wyeth and published in 1911. The book had belonged to my mother's brother David when he was a boy. I took away from my experience of the book a lifelong appreciation for Wyeth's illustrations. When he painted a pirate, damn it, it was a *pirate*.

I don't remember what I told Father about the book that evening, but I do know that I did finish it in a few days. I was proud. It was the first real book I had ever read. *Treasure Island* stays in my imagination. Long John Silver. Cap'n Flint the parrot. *Pieces of eight! Fifteen men on a dead man's chest. Yo-ho-ho and a bottle of rum.* And the boy's "dark and bloody sojourn" on Treasure Island, where greed destroyed men's lives.

10
Just Ducky

When I was about eight, my father's farmer client offered us a "nice fat duck" for Easter. That sounded good to my parents—a fresh, farm-raised duck would be a welcome change from the standard fare of a baked ham with cloves stuck in the top. We would be away for the first part of the weekend, but the farmer would leave the duck in our garage Saturday afternoon. No problem.

We got back from the Cape Saturday evening, unloaded the car and were sitting around the dining table with some sandwiches when my father remembered the duck. "Better get it into the refrigerator," he advised. I was dispatched to the garage to get the duck. I opened the garage door and turned on the light. A burlap bag was flopping around the floor. Frantic quacks were coming from the bag. The duck.

I ran for my parents. "The duck's alive. He's in a bag."

They went to investigate. My mother thought it was the funniest thing she had ever seen. Thirty years later, all I had to do to get her laughing was to say, "Remember the duck?" My father saw less humor in the situation and started to talk seriously about the need for unambiguous language in communication and the responsibility to treat animals humanely. Mother listened patiently, and finally said, "I'll get some Cheerios and a bowl of water. Then we'll let him out of the bag and close the door." That was the only plan we had, so it had to be a good one.

When we opened the door in the morning, we saw that the duck had made a hell of a mess. Clearly, we had to come up with another strategy. Monday morning, Father had to go to work, and I had to go to school. So Mother went to the lumberyard and explained that we needed materials to build a pen behind our garage for a duck.

"Why do you want to do that, lady?" the lumberyard guy inquired.

She didn't really have a good answer. On the way home she stopped and bought three giant-size boxes of Cheerios. The duck seemed to like his Cheerios very well, even if he did leave a prodigious mess afterward.

At any rate, the materials arrived in the afternoon, and when Father got home from work he and I hurriedly built a duck pen with a little shelter. It was a nice one, too. But we didn't take much time to admire our work, because we wanted to acclimate the duck to his new home before he fouled the garage floor any more than he already had. We carried the duck, flapping his wings like mad, behind the garage and deposited him in the pen. He was crazed for a moment, flapping and squawking. Then we lowered a bowl of Cheerios into the pen. He started to shovel the cereal down.

I named him "Ducky." "Donald" somehow seemed too obvious, even to an eight-year-old. I would carry on an imaginary conversation over and over—"How's your duck? He's just Ducky!"—until my parents would command me to stop. From time to time, we'd fill the wheelbarrow with water and Ducky would have a grand old time, flailing his wings madly and throwing water all over us. Most of the time, he just ate. Box after box of Cheerios. He got pretty big.

One day, a police officer came to the door. Mother and I stood side by side in the doorway. He looked as if he had something urgent and official to say. "Miss Connelly, do you have a white duck?" It didn't matter that my mother had been married for ten years and had a child; in the eyes of the Brighton cops, the daughter of The Judge would always be Miss Connelly. She allowed that we did. "Well, he's causing trouble. He's running around in the middle of Chestnut Hill Avenue, disrupting traffic." The duck had escaped! "You'll have to do something right away. Or we'll have to do something ourselves." *Would they shoot Ducky?*

I jumped on my bike and rode hard for Chestnut Hill Avenue, just around the corner. Horns were honking. Voices were raised. There Ducky was, scampering among the cars and then flying a few feet when anyone tried to approach him. Ducky could fly! That's how he had escaped! I knew what to do. I rode for home, ran up the back stairs, grabbed a box of Cheerios and returned to the scene of the fracas. I poured a pile of Cheerios on the pavement, and Ducky made a beeline for his favorite snack. The cop grabbed him and carried him down the street and back to the pen, to mocking laughs and cheers. "Got anything to cover the top of this cage?" he asked. I ran for the roll of chicken wire and the cop improvised a cover. I gave Ducky another bowl of Cheerios. He seemed to have forgotten his escapade already and shoveled them down as if the whole thing had never happened.

11
Hurricane

Fa's summer house was a hundred yards inland from the beach at Falmouth Heights. One evening, when I was six or so, we walked along the three-foot seawall to Maravista, a sandy bump that nudges into Vineyard Sound. A dozen thick, dark wooden pilings stuck out of the sand.

"Why are those logs in the sand?" I asked.

Fa explained that there had been houses there and that in the big hurricane of 1938 they had been swept out to sea and all the people drowned. Nothing was left but the pilings—and, as the story goes, one very wet cat, clinging for dear life to the top of one of them. For weeks, my dreams ran away with themselves: visions of houses floating out of sight, people on the rooftops. Sometimes, in my frightened dreams, the people on the rooftops were us.

I was already anxious. At school that spring, we had been given a fold-over card with slots for coins. The card had a picture of a pretty girl of about my age, leaning on crutches. She had ugly braces made of metal and leather on her legs. The card was an appeal for something called the March of Dimes. We were instructed to take the card home and get the adults in our family to fill it with dimes to help defeat polio, a terrible disease that could leave us crippled like the girl in the picture. "If your legs hurt, tell your mother right away," the nun urged us.

In August of 1954, Hurricane Carol hit the Cape with little warning. I overheard Fa discussing our options with Mother. It wasn't much of a discussion. She was for leaving immediately for Boston. Remembering the pilings and my dreams, I wanted to go.

"Like hell," Fa declared. "Open the upstairs windows an inch so the glass doesn't blow out, go out and get some candles, a lot of ice, a dozen lobsters in seaweed, and two dozen ears of corn. We can cook on the gas stove. And make a big pitcher of whiskey sours. And lemons—we'll need them for the lobsters and the sours. We're going to ride this thing out."

That night, the house came alive, moving, trembling and moaning in the wind. When hundred-mile-per-hour gusts lashed the rain against the windows, it sounded like a shovelful of gravel hitting a brick wall. The power went out. We huddled in the living room, wrapped in blankets. As a candle flickered, Fa told us the scary story of the Great Boston Molasses Flood of 1919, when a storage tank burst and lots of people drowned in millions of gallons of the sticky stuff. Then he dozed off in his chair as the wind roared.

Shortly after dawn there was a violent, ripping crack. And then another. I sprung to the window in time to see the roof of our garage fly through the air and crash into the park across the street. *Would the roof blow off the house?* I ran downstairs. Fa was in the kitchen, pouring coffee. "We should have gotten some goddamn doughnuts," he grumbled. "The next time we'll remember to get a dozen doughnuts. We'd better write that down."

When the tide came up later that morning the streets flooded, but the sun came out and the wind subsided. It was over. A rowboat went by the house. Two men in white Civil Defense helmets rowed up to the veranda and asked if we were okay. Then the junkman came up the road on his weekly rounds, coaxing his horse and wagon through two feet of water. "'Mornin', Judge," he called out, cheerfully. "A fine good mornin'. I've got a radio here that's worth five dollars, easy. But seein's how the power's out, I'd let it go for two."

12
The World's Greatest Lawyer

Father was a partner in a major Boston law firm. He had been an actor and debater in college; his idol then had been the suave, somewhat effeminate English movie star Leslie Howard. A photograph of my father in his freshman year at Holy Cross shows him emulating Howard's hairstyle and posture. The young man in the picture has a debonair smile. He radiates charm, confidence and intelligence. He was, in fact, quite brilliant. Sometimes, in joking moments, my mother would call him "Mister Smarty Pants 165"—a coded reference to his IQ.

He loved opera—especially Strauss' *Die Fledermaus*. He read the existentialist Martin Buber and the Jesuit mystic Teilhard de Chardin for relaxation. He took Mother to New York to hear Dylan Thomas read his poetry and to see Richard Burton perform in *Hamlet*. He was an intellectual adventurer. He was also a type 1 diabetic.

Unaware of his illness, he had played football in high school. One day he didn't come home from practice. Neighbors joined the family to search for him. Finally, at first light, they found him unconscious in a field. He recovered in the hospital, but his disease could only be managed by the guesswork methodology of the day.

Father as a college freshman, 1934

As a high school senior, Father would look across the valley from his family's little house on Lawrence Street to the stately Victorian Gothic spires of Holy Cross, only a half mile away. He would imagine himself reading in a comfortable armchair in the library or debating world affairs with classmates over coffee. He loved drama; perhaps he would even have a chance to act! But the family had six children and his father was in failing health. If he had to quit his arduous work as a railroad inspector, it would be up to my father and his brothers to provide. College seemed out of the question. Then he heard about a competitive examination for a scholarship to the college across the valley. When he went to take the test, he was dismayed to see a room full of aspirants, because there was only one scholarship. He won it.

Father (center) as a gangster in a college production of *Waiting for Lefty*

Father excelled at Holy Cross. He was president of the varsity debaters and the dramatic society and had lead roles in several productions. He graduated with highest honors in 1938 and then breezed through Boston College Law School on another scholarship. He lived at the corner of Newbury and Clarendon Streets in Boston, in a garret apartment at the top of one of the most picturesque buildings in the Back Bay. My suspicion is that during his law school days and the early years of his law practice, he did not lead the life of a monk. He was thirty-two, and she twenty-nine, when my parents married.

Although he gave up his dream of the theater for a more secure career in law, Father never lost his flair for the dramatic. His favorite plays and films were courtroom dramas: *Witness for the Prosecution*, *Twelve Angry Men*, *Inherit the Wind* and *To Kill a Mockingbird*. As a lawyer, the courtroom was an outlet for his theatrical side.

Whenever I had a day off from grammar school, I would accompany Father to work. I would carry his briefcase as he went to court, dressed up like a little adult in my gray flannels, navy blazer and bow tie (Father's bow tie was his courtroom trademark). Then we would have a "grownup lunch" in the downstairs grill at the Parker House, a lawyers' hangout in those days.

On one of those days he had a case for one of his firm's regular clients, the Hood Milk Company. The case gave him a perfect opportunity to ham it up for my benefit. A woman claimed that she had discovered a dead mouse in a bottle of Hood milk. She had given some of the milk to her child, who became sick. Father told me she was "looking to cash in." The woman had kept the mouse in her freezer for evidence. That turned out to be her fatal mistake. Her attorney was in custody of the frozen mouse, and my father had petitioned the bench to have the mouse x-rayed. The woman's lawyer brushed it off as a stunt. When it came time to cross-examine the woman, Father produced the x-ray. He brandished the sheet of film in his hand as he intoned, "I have in my hand x-rays of the mouse in question. These x-rays clearly and indisputably show that the mouse's neck had been broken. Do you actually expect the jury to believe that the mouse somehow sustained a broken neck as it fell into a bottle of milk? No. Of course not. I submit that *you* (he paused for dramatic effect) *willingly and intentionally* took a dead mouse from a trap and put it into the bottle of milk yourself!" Another dramatic pause. "Your honor, I see no purpose to be served by the further questioning of this witness." He turned his back contemptuously on the stupefied woman as her attorney called "Objection!" The judge banged the gavel for a bench conference. After a few minutes of muffled discussion, the case was dismissed.

I was amazed, and very proud. My father must be the greatest lawyer in the world. Only his wisdom and skill as a defender of justice had stood between this dishonest woman and the success of her dastardly scheme.

I was surprised afterwards when the lawyer for the woman joined us at our lunch table in the Parker House. He and my father were laughing together as I was munching my potato chips. "Oh my God, Connie," the other lawyer chortled.

Little adult with bow tie

He imitated my father, *"I have in my hand x-rays of the mouse in question.* Did you see the judge smirking? I thought the jurors would laugh out loud. Just too damn funny!" Funny? The thwarting of a sinister attempt by a cheat and a liar to exploit the judicial system for ill-gotten reward was no laughing matter. Or was it? That day, I began to graduate from my simplistic, Superman-inspired view of good and evil in the world.

In high school, Father had spent summers as a short-order cook at Olympia Park on Lake Quinsigamond. He told me he loved the nonstop action when the place was busy, and the mental gymnastics involved in keeping a dozen meal orders straight. For the rest of his life he loved to cook, especially big breakfasts. I remember my parents working together after dinner to do dishes and clean up as the radio played in the kitchen. Sometimes, they would dance around the kitchen to the music. Unlike most men of his era, Father did laundry. He'd grab a mop as readily as a lawnmower. His motto was the old saw "Many hands make light work." *Let's pitch in and get it done*. And unlike some on my mother's side of the family, he was no snob. He met everyone on equal terms. As a lawyer, he had learned that everyone has a story to tell, and that the way to connect with people is to listen. He'd roll up his sleeves and dirty his hands with anyone. Saturdays at the South Street house were usually devoted to plastering, painting or plumb-

Father cooking up the 'cue

ing. Father strove to outwork Pat, his hired handyman. Pat was an older Irish gent with a thick brogue. Father always cooked a big lunch for us on those days. "It might be the only good meal Pat has all week," he confided. Most of the other partners in his firm probably spent their Saturdays in the bar at the club.

Father was compassionate but, as is often the case with brilliant people, he could be uncompromising in matters of the intellect. I knew I was in for a grilling when I got a B in European History my first semester in college. "B? In a history course? Could you explain to me how anyone gets a B in a history course?" He really couldn't imagine. "You read the books, study and write the papers. You do what it takes to get an A. It isn't complicated." In fact, my professor had a nervous breakdown in the classroom one day, babbling about airplanes flying over Ohio and dropping secret messages that needed to be decoded immediately to avoid Armageddon. The unbalanced professor had disappeared, along with his grade book, and had been replaced for the last month of the term by a graduate student from Brandeis who, it seemed, gave everyone a B to solve the mess. I explained the bizarre set of circumstances. "So?" Father asked.

After my parents sold Fa's house in Falmouth Heights, they bought a little Cape Cod-style house on the Buzzards Bay side of the Cape, on Scraggy Neck. They paid $18,000. The house wasn't much. The two acres of property and two hundred feet of beach were the real attractions. We tore up rotten decking, ripped out underbrush and made a lot of trips to the dump. Father and I developed a new hobby—dump picking. We'd get up early and go to the local dump with a station wagon full of debris and junk. Scraggy Neck is in à very affluent area, and the stuff that other people threw away was testament to conspicuous consumption. I never bought a bike; I'd make a Frankenbike out of the front wheel from one, the rear wheel from another and the frame from a third. I found a brand-new set of Walter Hagen golf clubs that still had the price tag on the bag and a Zenith shortwave, ship-to-shore radio that worked perfectly. We never bought a lawn mower or outboard motor. Like the mowers, the outboards generally only needed a new spark plug or starter cord to run perfectly.

One of the motors was a real honey—a virtually new, shiny black 7.5-horsepower Mercury. We brought it home, put the lower unit in a trash can full of water, choked it and pulled the cord. *Vroooom!* We couldn't believe our good fortune and resolved to find a little bay boat to hang it on. It didn't take long. Driving along Red Brook Harbor Road a few days later, we saw a trim twelve-foot wooden skiff in someone's driveway: FOR SALE. $50. Fiberglass boats had taken over; woodies went cheap. We stopped, looked her over and Father wangled the guy down to $35.

The next morning we mounted the engine, launched her off the beach and hopped in to take her for a spin. Our crazy dog, John XXIV, was still a member of the household, and he announced with a bark that he would come, too. We were in high spirits and hauled him aboard. We got about fifty yards from shore when the dog decided he would rather be in the water than in the boat. He stood on the middle seat, put his front paws on the gunnel, trembled, whimpered and made as if he would hurl himself overboard. At the same time, Father and I stood up and reached to control the dog. Water poured over the gunnel. We shifted our weight to the other side. The dog followed, barking insanely. He lunged over the side with a huge splash and started to swim for shore. More water poured in. We were swamped, but still barely afloat. We sat there, shin deep in water. "Oh shit!" Father exclaimed.

"The motor's still running nicely," I observed. We looked at each other for a moment, and then laughed as we had never laughed together before.

Father's parents, Eufrosina and
Motiejus Akstinas

13
An Enigmatic Woman

Mother was a complicated person. She was fiercely loyal to her friends but capable of very harsh judgment of their choices in life. She was a psychologist who worked compassionately with clients with mental disorders and multiple handicaps but had little patience for exploring the inner landscape of the psyche. She was a great people watcher. She could invent fanciful and amusing stories about someone she had seen in the dentist's waiting room or the vegetable market that would have everyone around the dining table in stitches. But there always seemed to be an unnerving, condescending edge to those stories.

Mother in grade school

She considered herself independent but traded her independence away for security in marriage. She was dedicated to her career in social work until she was twenty-nine as, year after year, her friends married and started families. She told me once that she felt isolated and had to "get with the program." Presumably, I was part of that program. She protected herself by sending out coded warnings; once she told me that she had seen "the most incredible thing you could imagine. Some little fag was trying on a woman's blouse in Bloomingdale's. My God!" Decoded: *Don't you ever dare to talk to me about whatever's going on with you and your gender. Just don't.*

After I was born, she had some disorder (hepatitis, I believe) and she and I were separated for six weeks. Perhaps we just never bonded as mother and child usually do. I don't think I ever heard her tell me that she loved me, and I don't remember that we ever hugged each other.

After she had been diagnosed with cancer in 1978, I went to visit and took her to see *Close Encounters of the Third Kind,* a film I had found uplifting. *It will take her out of herself,* I thought. The film was at the Circle Theater in Brighton. Almost thirty years earlier, when I was four, she had taken me to the same theater to see *Cinderella*. When the evil queen began to mix magic potions and transform herself into a witch, I climbed over Mother and trotted up the aisle. She thought I had to go to the bathroom. In fact, I was terrified. I ran through the lobby, out the door, down the hill to Beacon Street and along the trolley tracks. When she finally caught up with me, I was reprimanded, not comforted. I tried to joke with her about that episode while we waited for the film to start, but she didn't seem to remember. I found *Close Encounters* even more captivating the second time around. Mother just sat in silence until the aliens came on the screen. "My God," she whispered, "I've got clients who look like that."

My grandmother had died the year I was born. When she was in her sixties, Mother confided to me that she had been carrying a burden of guilt for thirty years. When her own mother died, she told me, "I just didn't care the way I knew I was supposed to care. I really tried to care. I wanted to be able to cry. But I just couldn't." I'm sure the well of resentment that blocked her feelings was very deep, and I know of at least two things that made it so.

Mother had been an exceptional student at Girls' Latin School in Boston. She told me that she loved it there, spending her days with other brainy girls from all over the city who had been chosen to attend the country's first public college preparatory school for young women. She had been accepted

Mother at Woods Hole, 1946

to Radcliffe and literally had her bags packed to go across the Charles River for orientation week when her mother had what she called a "conniption fit." After talking with some whiskey priest, my grandmother had decided that if her daughter went to Radcliffe she would lose her religious faith, her virginity, her moral compass and her self-respect—all in the first day. From day two, there would be a relentless, downhill slide into alcoholism, drug addiction and white slavery. Grandmother absolutely refused to allow it, and she badgered Fa, who was ordinarily mightily strong-willed, into going along. It didn't seem to matter that her cousin Rufina had graduated from Radcliffe without becoming an addict or a prostitute, or that Mother had spent four years at Girls' Latin in a secular environment with classmates and friends from every ethnic and religious background in the city. My grandmother was on a mission to protect her daughter from perdition. Mother would live at home and go to Emmanuel, a small Catholic women's college near the Fenway. That was the final word.

She spent four angry years at Emmanuel. But there were a few things to laugh about. One was her close friendship with Mary McGrory, with whom she had also gone to Girls' Latin. McGrory was a merciless wit who went on to become a confidante of JFK and to win a Pulitzer Prize in the Watergate era as a political columnist. At Emmanuel, Mother and McGrory would play the new word game called Scrabble—in Latin, no less—and drink oceans of coffee to while away the hours between classes. In their graduation yearbook, Mother was described as "gingery," "mettlesome" (a word I had to look up) and a "raconteur of great gift"; McGrory as "strangely quixotic."

"Gingery...mettlesome...a raconteur of great gift..."

Another source of levity at Emmanuel was one of her English professors, a learned nun with an M. Litt. degree from Oxford or Cambridge. The woman was extraordinarily well read but completely batty. She would describe to the class the mystical union she had with the poet Coventry Patmore. Evidently, she would have visitations from Patmore in the middle of the night, when she was in a dream state. One can only imagine the shenanigans that must have gone on, since Patmore had died in 1896. Patmore, incidentally, was the author of "The Angel in the House," a poem that is despised above all others by contemporary feminist theorists.

Another nagging thorn was Grandmother's reaction when Mother got engaged to Father. Mother had endured some sort of failed romance with Eddie Logan, a dashing army officer and the son of General Logan, after whom the airport in Boston is named and whose bronze statue as a World War I hero is on the Esplanade by the Charles River. General Logan had been Mother's godfather. Grandmother had enthusiastically approved of that union and had been distraught about the breakup. She was vehemently opposed to my father, certainly in part because he was a Lithuanian from Worcester. When she discovered that Father was diabetic, she forbade the marriage, because she "didn't raise her daughter to be a young widow." (The irony that military officers such as Eddie Logan often leave young widows was seemingly lost on her.) Mother was nearly thirty. She knew what she was getting into and told her mother to go to hell, evidently in no uncertain terms. Mother and Fa made all the arrangements for the wedding; my grandmother refused to go...but, fearing scandal, relented at the last minute.

For all the resentments she carried, Mother could be surprisingly tolerant. Her own taste in music ran to Harry Belafonte singing "Jamaica Farewell." But in high school, when I'd play my Little Richard and Ray Charles records as loudly as my little KLH suitcase stereo could possibly play them, she'd say, "Well, I don't understand your music, but then again, my parents didn't understand when I played my Benny Goodman records. I don't want to be a stodgy old bore, so tell me who these singers are and what this music is all about." In return, she told me stories of going to the Totem Pole Ballroom at Normubega Park when she was a teenager and a "college girl" to dance to Goodman and Artie Shaw, and to swoon along with her other friends to the Tommy Dorsey band and their young vocalist, Frank Sinatra.

Mother, who had come from such an insular Boston Irish background, had African American, Asian and gay friends from her work who came to the Newton house for parties and visited us for weekends at Scraggy Neck. She particularly liked George, the brother of her friend Isabel, who owned a bookstore. In the '70s, George would appear from time to time with a new companion. She complained to me, "I wish George would settle down. I don't know why people like George can't just get married and adopt children. It's so unfair." One day, Isabel and she went to Roxbury with some of their Black friends to buy some sort of West African garments. I happened to arrive at the house for some reason that evening, and there they were in the sunroom, drinking martinis in wildly colorful tribal robes with matching hats. The outfits were stunning on the Black women. They were simply outlandish on the two suburban White women who were usually dressed impeccably in stylish but conservative fashions from Bonwit Teller and Peck & Peck. As I stood in the doorway, Mother asked, "Well, what do you think?" I could only smile and say, "Amazing!" There was something innocent and charming about Mother's attempt to cross racial boundaries and be, as she called it, "with it."

When I was sixteen, Mother decided to pursue her master's degree in Counseling Psychology at Boston College. She wanted a professional career and, given my father's precarious health, it was a strategic decision. Her goal was to finish in a year and get to work. My parents hired a live-in maid so that Mother could devote all of her time and energy to her studies. Our first maid was Margaret, an immigrant Irish girl of about eighteen. Margaret was a vivacious redhead with a ready smile; to my sixteen-year-old eyes, she was quite captivating. My parents noticed my interest in Margaret, and she was soon replaced by a grandmotherly Jamaican lady named Mignon.

When I asked her about her lovely and musical name, she told me that her mother had been the cook on a large estate in Jamaica and had named her after her employer's favorite main course when they had dinner parties, filet mignon. Mother took five courses a term at BC, finished her master's degree in a year with a 4.0 average and had her choice of several job offers. To celebrate, she threw herself a big dinner party and Mignon got to prepare her namesake dish.

Mother with Fa at fourteen months

I can't leave these thoughts about Mother without recalling one moment of gentleness and tenderness between us. We were in the window seat of Fa's big bay window at the Cape, quietly watching a dramatic cloudburst. I must have been about six years old. Mother unexpectedly said, "Hoppin' dolls. Watch them. Hoppin' dolls." I was puzzled and asked her what she meant. She told me that when she had been a little girl, she had sat in this same window seat, watching the rain. Her mother had come to sit with her and had told her to watch the "hoppin' dolls"—the rain drops as they hit the pavement and bounced up a few inches. "I was a child once, too, you know," she said. At least for that moment, I felt as if she knew me.

14
Weirdos

I've always loved teaching James Joyce's short story "Araby." The language is rhapsodic and extravagantly sensual. Reading the story, I hear the sound of leather and metal when the narrator says that the stableman "shook music from the buckled harness." It's also intensely visual. As the beautiful young girl in the story moved, "the soft rope of her hair tossed from side to side."[3] I can see the girl, radiant as she stands in the only light on the dismal street, turning her silver bracelet idly around her wrist while the younger boy struggles to talk with her. For fifty years, I have identified with the boy in the story—and "identified" is not a word I use casually. I know that when I was his age, I felt the pang of isolation and the fervent desire for love.

My students, however, have generally been of another mind about "Araby." They are at a loss to understand how the young boy is allowed to set off, alone and at night, on a trolley to go to a bazaar somewhere across the city. "His parents should be reported to Child Protective Services," they declare. Well, the boy's parents do not actually appear in the story; it seems that he is being raised by an aunt and a drunkard uncle. And, of course, there was no such thing as Child Protective Services in 1905 when the story was written. In any event, to help offset my students' assumption that everything must be judged by present standards and values, I sometimes tell them about my own excursions into the city, by myself, when I was about the boy's age.

When I was twelve, we moved out to a vaguely Spanish Colonial house on Commonwealth Avenue in Newton. I loved the South Street house and was sorry to leave it behind—and with it my cat Whitey and Mrs. Billings' steamer trunk and its treasures. One of the many changes brought about by this move was a posted list of chores that I was to do every Saturday morning. The list changed with the seasons: sweep off the back stoop, pick up the yard, take out the trash, brush the dog, rake the leaves or shovel and sand the driveway. In exchange for the faithful completion of these duties, I was given an allowance of a dollar at lunchtime.

Every few weeks, I would plan an outing to spend some of my riches. After lunch, my mother would say, "Dinner's at six. Don't be late," and I would hop on my bike and head to the Riverside train station in Newton Center. I'd board a train and ride it to Park Street and rush up the steep stairs to visit my three favorite places in the city. One was Eric Fuchs' model train store. HO-gauge trains chugged and smoked their way along the walls of the shop, went through tunnels, narrowly missed collisions with other trains traversing bridges and tooted their whistles as they came to crossings. There were livestock cars with tiny cows, observation cars, flatcars carrying logs and my favorite—the caboose. I could watch their marvelous choreography for hours. From there, I was off to Jack's Joke Shop near the Boston Common for a supply of what were the essentials of early adolescent life in those days: handshake buzzers, hot-pepper gum, whoopee cushions and plastic vomit. Then I'd get a hot dog with all the fixins at Joe and Nemo's and catch a train home. I reveled in a sense of grown-up independence.

One day as I was leaving, Mother gave me the usual admonition about dinnertime, and then added, "Watch out for weirdos." She didn't elaborate. Even though I had no idea what she was talking about, her warning made me uneasy. As I rode the train into Boston, I scrutinized the passengers. Was that guy, reading his paper in the seat by the door, a weirdo? I guess he did look kind of *weird*, somehow. I'd better be on the lookout. At the train store, I began to sense something *weird* about the older man behind the counter who had always been so friendly and helpful. His pleasant smile now appeared like a sinister leer. The guy at the joke shop seemed decidedly *weird*. He was always doing magic tricks for the customers and demonstrating devices that made rude noises. Suddenly, his hijinks seemed very creepy. The hot dog guy at Joe and Nemo's seemed the *weirdest* of all. He had a heavy, dark unibrow, simian hands and peered menacingly over the cash register. Everything and everyone in Boston had become scary.

When I got home late that afternoon in an obvious state of agitation, Mother asked me what was wrong. I told her that I was frightened because I had seen a lot of weirdos on my excursion. She didn't take the opportunity to explain to me about child molesters; she just tried to reassure me by saying that there were really only a very few weirdos in Boston and that while I ought to be cautious, I really didn't have to be so worried. "Just be careful when you're by yourself and you'll be alright." Rather than probe the issue further, I took her words as comfort and began plotting whether to put the plastic vomit in Brian's locker or on Murph's desk Monday morning.

15
Who Pulled the Plug?

Whenever I really screwed up, my mother's lament was "Why can't you be more like Richard?" Richard, my classmate, seemed to be a model young gentleman. He was intelligent, industrious, studious, talented, athletic, handsome, virtuous, considerate, loyal, reliable and trustworthy. Forgive me if I've left anything out. From an adult perspective, Richard had the whole package of attributes. Unlike Richard, I was inclined to daydreaming and mischief.

In spite of my inadequacies, Richard and I were fast friends. When we were given a seventh-grade writing assignment for a descriptive essay on our town hall, we decided to do the fieldwork part of the project together. We rode our bikes to Newton City Hall on a crisp October Saturday morning. We spent an hour or so scribbling in our notebooks about the building and the grounds. Richard's essay was nearly complete. I was at the stage of "Made of bricks. Has a tower with a clock in it. Some leaves on the ground." I was utterly uninspired. As Richard polished his prose, I wandered over to the duck pond to check for frogs and salamanders. I was turning over rocks to see what was lurking underneath when I noticed a sluiceway with a wooden board that kept the water in the pond.

"Hey, Richard!" I called. "Look at this!"

Abandoning his notebook on the grass, he came over and began a learned explanation of the hydrodynamics of sluiceways. I cut him short. "Let's pull the board out and see what happens!"

Richard resisted. "We'll get in trouble. The water will go out of the pond. It will be our fault."

"Come on, let's do it!" I urged. "We can always just put it back."

Perhaps Richard had been longing to do something devilish all his young life. For whatever reason, he surprised me by grabbing one handle while I grabbed the other. On the count of three, we pulled. The board lifted out of its metal track. The water gushed out of the pond with great force. It washed Richard's notebook downstream.

"Oh no!" Richard cried and ran after it. He hustled back with the sodden essay and declared that we had to put the board back in place immediately. We tried, but the flow of water was too powerful. Soaking wet, we decided to abandon the project and run for it. He jumped on his bike, I on mine. We rode to our respective houses. Mother was used to me coming home a mess; all she said was, "Don't track water and mud all over the place." I learned in school on Monday that Richard's mother had quite a few questions about why he was coming home with soaking wet pants. But he assured me he hadn't cracked under interrogation. Had Richard actually *lied*?

That week the local paper had an editorial about the draining of the duck pond at city hall. The article called for increased surveillance and harsh penalties for vandals. The title of the article was "Who Pulled the Plug?"

16
The Blue Slip

In the fifth and sixth grades, my friends and I often had what these days are called "sleepovers." We were caught in that frightful, wonderful space between childhood and the dawn of adulthood. We'd camp out in pup tents in the backyard or sleep in bunk beds in someone's basement. We'd play Monopoly and trade baseball cards. We'd strum ukuleles and sing "On Top of Old Smokey" (or its parody, "On top of spaghetti, all covered with cheese/ I lost my true lover, from having to sneeze"). We'd talk in whispers about what it would be like to kiss a girl. After a platter of late-night cookies and some musings about the vastness of the universe, we'd go to sleep.

One of my friends had an older sister. She might have been fifteen; I was eleven or twelve. Somewhat like the boy in James Joyce's story "Araby," I idolized her. One night as we were getting ready for bed, she came home from some sort of party. She monopolized the bathroom for quite a while. When I saw the light go out in the hallway, I took my pajamas and toothbrush in hand and headed for the bathroom. As I was changing into my pajamas, I saw that a light blue slip was hanging on the hook. I touched it. It was still warm. Her slip. Without questioning what I was doing, I put it on over my head and let the straps settle on my shoulders.

The nylon against my skin triggered sensations that even today are easy to recall but difficult to describe. It was as if the entire surface of my body had suddenly sprung to life. When I moved, the slip moved, giving me the delightful pleasure of being touched lightly in many places at once. Without fully understanding what was happening to me, I had my first erection. Hurriedly, I took the slip off, hung it back on the hook, and got into my pajamas.

I lay awake long into the night, feeling that I had done something wrong, something very shameful. Yet I couldn't wait to do it again.

17
The Beetle Cat

Even though I was discouraged from playing with girls, it had somehow been ordained that I would be pals with Maureen, the daughter of one of my mother's friends. "Why don't you go bike riding with Maureen?" or "It's windy today, I'll bet Maureen would like to go to the park and fly your kite." But Maureen was a fussy girl, given to tantrums and sickliness. While Maureen pouted and sneezed, her older sister Annie took me under her wing.

Annie's family had a Beetle Cat that was moored with the rest of the Beetle fleet in Falmouth Harbor, between the Catholic chapel and MacDougall's boatyard. The summer I was thirteen and she likely eighteen, Annie taught me the basics of sailing. "It's easy," she would say. "Just steer with the tiller, pull in on this line called the 'sheet' until you feel the wind in the sail—and off we go!"

I loved the sensation of moving through the water quietly, with just a gurgle from the stern where the transom and rudder troubled the water. Had I been a few years older, I would have loved Annie, too. But I was just a kid and she was, well, a young lady. I put aside any fantasy that Annie and I would someday get married and go sailing off in a big boat like the ones we glided past in the harbor and concentrated instead on her instructions: "Bear away a little. Pull in the sheet a little more. We're going faster now, see?"

I'm just a tyke here at Falmouth Heights beach, but I'm quite sure that's Annie in the middle. The Beetle Cat adventure would be years later.

The Beetle Cat is a wonderful craft. Designed in 1921 in New Bedford and handcrafted to this day from white pine, oak and cedar, the Beetle is beamy, stable and has a pronounced weather helm. Speed is not one of her virtues, but with the centerboard up she can ghost in less than a foot of water; board down, she can sail a close reach in a stiff southwesterly breeze on Buzzards Bay or Vineyard Sound without drenching the crew. She's unballasted, so she will float even if completely swamped. She's an ideal boat for young sailors.

After we had been out a few times, Annie surprised me. "You can sail her now. Take her out anytime you want." I could hardly believe what I had heard.

One Saturday, my parents went to a wedding in Worcester. They had evidently decided to trust me alone at home for the first time. They gave me very explicit instructions. I could stay home and read. I could go to the beach, but only directly there and back. My lunch was in the refrigerator, on a plate covered with waxed paper. "Have fun!" they told me as they left.

Actually, the day they had planned for me didn't sound like very much fun. I had already hatched a scheme. Mother and Father had been out of the driveway about two minutes when I jumped on my bike and raced to the harbor. I grabbed the sail bag out of the locker and held it over my head, as I had seen Annie do, as I waded out to the Beetle. I hopped aboard, rigged the sail, cast off and headed to the mouth of the harbor. The channel at Falmouth is narrow and bounded by two jetties. But if you start as far west in the channel as you can, a starboard tack in the prevailing southwest breeze might just slide you through. It did. I trimmed sail and set course for the Vineyard. As close hauled as the Beetle would allow, I sailed directly for West Chop and beyond it to Oak Bluffs, my destination. The breeze was stiffening up. I could feel the helm quiver. I was making good time. I was very excited with my adventure.

My parents and I had gone into Oak Bluffs a few times in our sea skiff, docked and wandered around. I'm sure they liked the town for its colorful nineteenth-century gingerbread cottages on Trinity Avenue. I liked it because it had a hot dog stand with lime rickeys and a duckpin bowling alley upstairs. My plan was to have a hot dog, drink a lime rickey, bowl a string of duckpins, sail back to Falmouth and beat my parents home. I would put one over on them.

I steered determinedly past East Chop Light and made the harbor at Oak Bluffs. As I was tying up at the dock, an older man asked, "Hey, kid. How long you gonna be?" I told him an hour, and headed up the hill to my destination. The hot dog was tasty in its grilled bun and the lime rickey was cool in its tall, frosted glass. I bowled my string, but as I finished up I began to get anxious about getting home on time. I ran down to the harbor, jumped aboard, raised the sail enough to catch some breeze and shoved off. A southwesterly gust shot me out of the harbor. I jibed, with a loud *twack* of the sail, and made for the lighthouse. As I rounded the point, I was making good headway. Nobska Light and Falmouth were in sight, about four miles away. If the southwest breeze held up, as it always seemed to on August afternoons, I should make the harbor in an hour and be home in time to run down to the beach and get enough sand in my sneakers to make a good cover story.

But then, about halfway across the sound, the wind died. I sat, becalmed. It's a feeling of abject helplessness that all sailors know. In this case, the helplessness was mixed with my rising sense of panic. *What if I don't get home before them? How will I explain this? They'll never let me out of their sight again!* I tried to paddle the stern around so the Beetle would catch any puff on a broad reach, her best point of sail. I pumped the sheet. Forget it. There was nothing to do but to sit. The water was glassy calm. The sun felt hot. A motorboat went past and people waved. Their wake tossed the Beetle around. To make things worse, the tide was moving me east, away from my destination.

After a while, ripples appeared on the surface and I could feel the air beginning to move. Then the breeze started to freshen, but this time from the east. I caught a puff, got some headway and pulled the centerboard. I was running before the wind, which was stiffening by the minute. Soon there were whitecaps. At their best, Beetle Cats don't go very fast, but I felt as if I were at the helm of *Cutty Sark* or *Flying Cloud*, rounding the Horn in one of those old pictures, with "every inch of canvas hung."

In short order, I made the jetties of the harbor, jibed with another loud *twack* and passed between them as pretty as you please. I made for the mooring, tied up, struck the sail and stowed it in its locker and raced home on my bike. I hadn't been in the house for five minutes when my parents pulled into the driveway. I tried to calm myself down, to prepare for the

With a vintage Beetle Cat, about fifty years later

---

17 The Beetle Cat

interrogation that was sure to be at hand. But they simply came in and started to go about their business. Mother began to put away a few groceries they had picked up and opened the refrigerator. There was my lunch, still covered with waxed paper. "You didn't eat your lunch?" she inquired.

"Guess I wasn't hungry," was my lame reply.

"You're *always* hungry," she observed, archly. But mercifully, she let it drop.

Shortly before my father died during my last year in college, we had a long lunch together at one of his favorite restaurants. I didn't realize how sick he was, but I'm sure he did. We lingered in the booth over coffee for a long time, and he told me stories. When he was fourteen, he said, his parents and sisters had gone with some other adults to a wedding. He was given strict instructions to stay at home and do homework. "That didn't sound like much fun," Father confided. He waved as his parents drove away with their friends, but he had a plan—and it didn't involve homework.

He had watched very carefully as his father drove the family's new Model A Ford. He had been dying to try it himself. So he hopped into the driver's seat, pushed the spark control up, pulled out the choke, pushed down the clutch and pressed the ignition. It started. Carefully, he moved the gears until he found reverse and backed the car out of the driveway. *This is easy*, he thought. He decided to take it for a spin. He drove haltingly around the neighborhood. The next thing he knew he was driving smoothly on Lake Avenue, and then on Route 9, moving along with the other cars. He saw a sign: TO BOSTON. He kept going. "I couldn't *not* keep going. I wasn't scared," he explained. "I was more curious than anything else." But he did get scared when he realized he was actually in Boston, driving on Huntington Avenue. People were out doing their Saturday shopping. A lot of people, and cops were directing traffic. *What if someone sees I'm just a kid driving this car?* He panicked when he got to Copley Square. There were even more people, buses and cars. How was he ever going to find his way home? Carefully, he retraced his steps and got back on Route 9. Around Brookline, he saw another sign: TO WORCESTER. When he got to White City in Shrewsbury, things started to look familiar. He followed Lake Avenue, drove up the hill and pulled into the driveway. He was trembling with exhilaration.

About five minutes later, he heard a car pull into the driveway. His parents and sisters came into the house. His father went to the icebox to get a beer. "Connie didn't eat his lunch," his father announced. "Didn't you see I left you a nice lunch?" his mother asked him. He dodged her question: "Guess I was too busy to get hungry."

The next morning, his father went out to warm up the car for the Sunday trip to church. It wouldn't start. He fiddled with the spark and the choke. It still wouldn't start. Then he checked the gas. The tank was dry. Furious, he went inside. He picked up the phone and called the police. "Someone siphoned the gas out of my car last night!" he told the cops. "A man's car isn't safe in his own driveway!"

Father shook his head as he concluded his story. Perhaps in disbelief that he'd ever done something so crazy; perhaps in wonder that he'd finally revealed himself to me as something less than perfect. We smirked at each other and then laughed from the belly up.

Fifty years later, I still regret that I didn't tell him my own version of the story, my story of Annie's Beetle Cat and my clandestine voyage to the Vineyard while he and Mother had been off at a wedding. But I know why I didn't. In that moment, I realized that he wanted to leave me with a memory of him that was different from the rather starchy character he had played for so long. He did. I didn't want to take away from that. I also know that, just as he was finally free from the need to set himself up as a paragon for me to follow, I was free from seeking his approval or his forgiveness. Still, I know that if I had told him the story, he would have loved it. Father and son. Two renegades. As it was, we finished our coffee and rode back to the house without talking much, but perhaps as close as we had ever been.

18
John XXIV

When we moved to South Street in Brighton, we adopted a female cat named Whitey. She was a useful creature in the drafty mansion my parents had bought. She prowled upstairs and down, slaughtering mice and bats. She had a litter of kittens in the basement coal bin. When we spied on her brood, she carried them one by one up to a closet on the third floor. I had great fun playing with her tumbling kittens as they grew. I loved Whitey's independence and her mysterious sense of purpose. And she purred me to sleep at night.

I was less enthusiastic about dogs. Our first dog, a cocker spaniel named Nicky, had been a slobbering, moronic creature. Nicky had been trained to do his business on newspapers when he was a puppy. Somehow, he never got beyond the newspaper stage. When we walked the dog in the Fenway in the morning and evening, we had to take a few sheets of the *Boston Globe* with us. Nicky would whine and prance around until we set the newspaper on the grass. Then he knew what to do.

We moved out to Newton when I was thirteen, and Whitey was left behind with the new owners of the South Street house. They were happy to have an animal billed as a "champion mouser." I asked my parents if we could get another cat at the SPCA. They had a different agenda. They declared that "a boy of your age should have a dog." I imagine this had something to do with their anxiety about my gender confusion. By this time, Mother had caught me wearing a pair of her earrings while I was doing my homework and had noticed my interest in her copies of *Glamour* and *Mademoiselle*. They probably hoped that a dose of canine bonding, à la Rin Tin Tin and Rusty on television, might cure me. So we got a dog, not a cat.

My father had a dairy farmer as a client, and one Saturday we drove out to his farm to select from a litter that seemed to be a strange mix of different shapes and colors. My father's choice from among the rambunctious youngsters was a wild-eyed, hyperactive creature who sparred aggressively with his brothers and sisters. "He's strong and healthy," Father observed. The farmer assured us that the pup would be a good one, since his mother was a farm dog.

"How about the father?" my father asked.

"Couldn't say," the farmer replied with a knowing smirk.

On the ride home, the pup seemed on the verge of frenzy. He rushed from side to side in the back seat, drooling. Father assured me that he was just unused to riding in cars and would settle down. He didn't. When we got home, we fixed up a cozy dog bed in the downstairs laundry room, complete with a ticking alarm clock. "It's comforting for a puppy," Father explained, "like his mother's heartbeat." I listened to the clock. *Tick, tick, tick.* It didn't sound like the *ta-dum, ta-dum, ta-dum* of a heartbeat to me. The pup yipped all night. "It's okay," Father assured Mother and me. "He just misses his mother. He'll grow out of it."

"When?" Mother asked pointedly.

We had a family conference at breakfast about naming the dog. We were stumped. There was a newspaper in the breakfast nook, open to an article about Pope John XXIII, who was extremely popular at the time. "Let's name him after the pope!" I suggested.

"That's just bizarre," my mother said.

"Probably some kind of sacrilege," Father added.

I argued that they had promised me that this was going to be my dog— and I reminded them that I had really wanted a cat and not a dog to begin with. So all things factored in, I should be the one to name him. To avoid running afoul of the ecclesiastical authorities, I would call him John XXIV.

"Jesus Christ!" cried Father in exasperation.

"Did someone recently mention sacrilege?" Mother observed. We all laughed.

John turned out to be completely insane. It was as if he was compelled by incomprehensible forces to do things that were irksome to humans. He yipped. He nipped. He knocked a leg of lamb off the counter and dragged it across the kitchen floor. More than anything else, he ran away.

In this era before leash laws, families would let their dogs outside to do their business in the morning, then call them in for breakfast. We soon learned that John was a free spirit and didn't like to come when called. When he was young, I would go searching for a few minutes and find him sniffing around in a neighbor's yard. No big deal. But soon, he started to disappear in earnest. We'd get a call from Needham or Framingham: "Do you have a brown dog?" We'd drop what we were doing and go to bring him home. Kind of a big deal. Then one Saturday morning as we were loading the car for the Cape, we got a call from New Hampshire: "Do you have a brown dog?" The lady was very nice and said she couldn't let him in the house because she had cats, but she'd give him a pork chop to keep him around. I thought that was pretty funny. My parents failed to see any humor in the situation. They thought that a detour to New Hampshire on the way to the Cape to pick up a wayward dog was very big deal indeed.

"Worst thing we ever did was to get a collar and tag for that dog," Father grumbled.

We had a family conference about John XXIV's future that night, as he slept off his adventure and digested his pork chop by the fireplace. I talked my parents into giving him one more chance before he went back to the farm.

A few weeks later, Mother was getting ready to go to off to some function with Father when he got home from work. As she bustled around, the phone rang. The dreaded words: "Lady, do you have a brown dog?" It was the stationmaster from Park Street station in downtown Boston. John must have wandered over to Newton Center, hopped on a Riverside train and gotten off at Park Street. "You better come and get your dog right away, lady. I'll be nice and hold him here for an hour. I'm not supposed to. He should go right to the pound." Mother was frantic. I didn't drive yet and Father was already on his way home. Crazy as he was, we couldn't let John be sent to the pound. The stationmaster had an idea. "I could send him home in a cab. But it'll cost ya." Mother capitulated and gave him our address. I was dispatched to the front of the house with a ten-dollar bill in my hand.

It was a blisteringly hot day, the kind of deadly still August afternoon that is building toward an inevitable thunderstorm. I sat in a patch of shade and waited for the cab. After a while my father appeared, trudging up Commonwealth Avenue in a sweat with his jacket slung over his shoulder. He was surprised to see a cab pull up in front of the house. *Who could be arriving in a cab?* As he walked over to investigate, the driver got out, went to the rear door on the passenger side and opened it. John XXIV sprung out, bounded across the lawn and greeted me joyfully. Father stood there stupefied as I paid the driver six bucks. The next morning, we took John back to the farm.

19
A Small Dance at the Ritz

When I was in the seventh grade, Mother decided I ought to master the social graces. Accordingly, I was enrolled in a dancing school that gathered at the Longwood Cricket Club in Brookline on winter afternoons. Station wagons from Newton, Wellesley and Weston jockeyed for position in the driveway of the club, discharging grumpy-looking young ladies and gentlemen who arrived as if dressed for a party.

Our instructors were an impossibly buoyant couple who never stopped smiling and never stopped moving. Swooping and fluttering, they herded the fidgety boys toward the clutch of giggly girls at the other end of the room. A hi-fi played the music our parents had danced to at the Norumbega Totem Pole and Symphony Ballroom in the '40s, music we rejected for the Everly Brothers, Fats Domino and Chubby Checker.

"Moonlight Serenade," "Stardust," "Moonglow" and other moody evocations of nocturnal romance drifted through the room as our instructors paired us off. I was a very tall boy; Jane Curtin was a pretty tall girl. I was gawky; she was gangly. We were a match. As I had been instructed, I would bow slightly from the waist, extend my right hand (*Remember, Thomas! Palm up!*) and solemnly intone, "Good afternoon, Jane. Might I have this dance?" (*Remember, Thomas! Say "might," not "may."*) Jane would grimace and place her white-gloved hand in mine. Off we would go, shuffling across the floor. "*Guide her, Thomas. Guide her,*" the male instructor coached me, and moved my right hand more firmly around Jane's waist. Jane stiffened. She was not a girl to be guided. She despised me.

This unfortunate pairing continued until Jane disappeared from the class and was replaced as my partner by a girl named Marilyn. Where Jane had scowled, Marilyn smiled. Where Jane had stiffened, Marilyn yielded. When the intermission came, she perched demurely on the edge of her chair while I asked, "Would you care for a cookie and some punch, Marilyn?" (*Always use the young lady's name when addressing her, Thomas.*) She replied that she would be delighted. We munched, sipped the fruity concoction known to us in other, less formal circumstances as "bug juice" and made small talk about our respective school bus trips to Old Ironsides, the "rude bridge" at Concord or the Gardner Museum. As we talked, I began to like her and she seemed to like me. Amazing.

I helped her on with her coat as we were leaving—and with her matching hat. "My mother makes me wear them," she offered apologetically.

"They're mink. Everybody thinks I'm snobby." I assured her fervently that I didn't think she was snobby at all. "You're really nice," she replied. Young love was on the wing.

At dinner that night, I told my parents all about Marilyn. I thought they would be pleased that I had made a new friend at dancing school. I was wrong.

"I know her mother," Mother said. "She rich and she's loopy. She zips around town in a Maserati convertible and wears a sable coat."

I struggled to find something positive to say. "Marilyn has a nice coat, too. A mink coat. And a hat that goes with it."

"A mink coat! A thirteen-year-old girl should *not* have a mink coat!" Mother thundered.

In the weeks that followed, there seemed to be a cloud over our dancing, chatting and munching. "My mother knows your mother," Marilyn told me. She didn't elaborate. She simply frowned and her frown made my young heart sink. *Romeo and Juliet* begins with a prologue about "a pair of star-crossed lovers." I had been reading the play in school. I decided that Marilyn and I were at least star-crossed, if hardly lovers. Our union had been doomed by some irrational animosity of our families.

Things ended when her mother intercepted a mushy letter I sent to Marilyn while she was "summering" in Marblehead. Her mother sent the letter to mine without comment. In the letter, I had told Marilyn how much I missed her and that I wanted her to be my girlfriend. After a long and anxious deliberation, I had signed it, "Love."

Mother put on her psychologist hat and explained, quite gently, that I was too young for "emotional involvement." It hurt—and it hurt even more to go to dancing school in the fall and to see Marilyn paired off with some other gawky kid. But time healed that wound quickly enough.

Then, in the spring of my senior year in high school, I got a fancy engraved invitation in the mail. I was invited, it said, to "a small dance at the Ritz" in honor of Marilyn's debut into society. Some of my other friends who had endured dancing school got the same invitation. It sounded creepy, but my friends urged me to go. Actually, it was kind of fun to get all decked out in black tie—sort of a James Bondish fantasy—and to cruise down Commonwealth Avenue toward the Ritz-Carlton and toss my keys nonchalantly to the kid who was parking cars.

The "small dance" turned out to be an epic blowout, a party for the ages. Marilyn's mother had booked the entire hotel. Bo Diddley played upstairs for the young crowd; Lester Lanin's society big band played in the ballroom downstairs for dancing. There were mountains of caviar and

Bo Diddley handed out these souvenir photos the night of the party.

smoked sturgeon that rivaled the Romanovs' table. Chilled lobsters, oysters, beef fillet, racks of lamb, artichokes, piles of asparagus, exotic fruits and pastries filled a dozen buffets. There were open bars on every floor, and servers prowled all night with French champagne. Bo Diddley rocked on. Lanin's band swung, if discreetly. The food and booze kept coming, in a display of endless excess. The party roared on until dawn. Some of the revelers went across Arlington Street to the Public Garden and did the Great-Gatsby-wading-in-the-fountain-in-the-park-in-your-tuxedo-and-evening-gown thing.

At one point toward morning, I actually saw Marilyn. She had a tuxedoed beau on each arm and a soused smile on her face. "Hello, Marilyn. Gee. Fantastic party."

She looked at me glassy-eyed, quizzically. It took a moment. "Oh!" she exclaimed. "Oh! Hi!" And then her escorts whisked her off into the night.

Snapshots I

Money in the Streets

Until we moved to South Street in Brighton when I was six, Mother and Father and I would walk on summer nights from the apartment on Park Drive to a little ice cream shop on Jersey Street, not far from Fenway Park. I loved ice cream and I have been told that on these excursions I was giggly and squirmy with anticipation—annoyingly so. Somewhere, there's a typical "cute kid" picture of me in front of the shop, wearing most of my ice cream cone.

I remember Father bending down, reaching toward the ground and then, with a big grin, showing me a quarter he'd just found and putting it into my pocket. It seemed as if this happened every time we walked out for ice cream—always on the way to the ice cream shop, and always on the left-hand side of Jersey Street.

I wonder now if it was a trick. Did he plant a coin under a loose paver or in his shoe just to make our little walks more exciting? Perhaps. But I still smile when I think of Father's uncanny knack for finding money in the streets. To this day, I keep my eye on the sidewalk when I walk up Jersey Street to a Red Sox game—always on the left-hand side of the street, naturally, because that's where the money is.

The Foot-o-Scope

One of my father's many firmly held convictions was that shoes that fit properly were the key to a healthy and prosperous life. "You can't concentrate if your feet hurt," he'd say.

The annual back-to-school excursion to John's Shoe Store in Falmouth for my new Buster Browns or Poll Parrots involved the whole family. Mother would pick out the styles. Father would supervise as I tried them on and dutifully paraded up and down the length of the store as he questioned me about the state of my toes and my arches. The process was tedious and always seemed to take place on one of the most beautiful days of late summer. On those days, I was itching to get home, run to the beach and feel the warm sand between my bare toes.

One year—I was likely in the second or third grade—we went for the annual fitting and there was something new. John's had installed a Foot-o-Scope x-ray machine that gave the salesman a view of the inside of my foot. Suddenly, the boring exercise of shopping for my new fall shoes seemed intriguing and fun. I tried on a pair, stepped up on a little platform and put my feet in the bottom of a big box. There was a humming noise as the salesman started the machine and I was told to wiggle my toes vigorously. As I did so, we all had a look—Mother, Father, the salesman and I. I tried eight or ten pairs in the x-ray machine before our group reached consensus that the bones in my feet were nicely aligned in one particular shoe. I left the shop with a pair of those in black and a pair in brown—and probably enough radiation exposure to last me for a lifetime.

Beautiful Hair...*Me?*

In the 1950s, women's magazines like *Harper's Bazaar* and *Vogue* had full-page, color ads for Breck shampoo, with the slogan, "Beautiful Hair...Breck." The ads featured pastel portraits by Boston artist Ralph William Williams of idealized WASP beauties with radiant tresses. Prosperous families in Boston and the suburbs began to commission him for portraits of their offspring, to be hung over the mantel or on the wall ascending the staircase. Some of the families we knew were very large, with eight or ten children. Fortuitously, those big families tended to have large houses with long staircases. A Williams portrait was a status symbol of the day.

My parents were contemptuous of status symbols, and I'm surprised that they bought into the idea. Nevertheless, one Saturday morning when I was twelve, Ralph William Williams himself arrived on the doorstep of our South Street house with his easel and pastels. I was told to sit in a chair quietly and to "...look up a bit...that's good...now turn a little to the left...just a little..."—and so forth. This went on for a very long time. I would rather have been outside, running around.

"It's so camp!"

The finished portrait was unveiled on New Year's Day, when my parents hosted a buffet lunch. When I saw it, I was mortified. As a medium, pastel has an inherent, feminine softness, which is epitomized in Degas' many pastels of dancers. And Williams himself was almost exclusively an illustrator of women and girls. Hanging on the dining room wall above the sideboard, I looked like a chubby girl with fluttery eyelashes who had been shorn of her page boy locks and dressed up in a boy's jacket and tie instead of a Peter Pan collar and granny's pearls. In other words, it was a little too revealing.

One evening, after a few glasses of wine, I showed it to my friends Suzanne and Rachel. They loved it: "It's so camp!" I thought right away of Cocteau's notion that camp is the lie that reveals the truth. They took it home and hung it in their house for ten years. When they finally redecorated they gave it back. These days, it lives behind the bookcase in my office.

The Northfield

When I was in the seventh and eighth grades, my parents and I would go to a sprawling, creaky old hotel called the Northfield for my February school vacation. The place was about as far north as you could go in Massachusetts without winding up in Vermont. I'd ramble in the woods for hours on my Northland "bear paw" showshoes, discovering frozen streams with otter trails in the snow, woodpeckers, a pond with a beaver lodge and, once, an owl in a tree. It was an activity that fed my solitary nature. But I was also discovering girls. I took a liking to Bonnie, the daughter of a family that went on vacation with us. We'd share maple syrup on snow at the afternoon skating parties, ride down the big toboggan slide together and keep company at the Saturday night square dances, where a little trio in cowboy outfits played numbers like "Turkey in the Straw" and "Buffalo Gals" on accordion, vibraphone and steel guitar.

The sun porch at the hotel had a black-and-white TV with rabbit ears that pulled in a station from New Hampshire, if you wiggled them just right. A bunch of us gathered around to watch a team made up of American college kids take on the powerful Russians in the hockey semifinals of the 1960 Olympics. We had to get permission to watch, since there were strict rules that the TV was only to be turned on between eight and ten in the evening, so as not to disturb the daytime bridge and chess players. Or my father, for that matter, who liked to unwind in the afternoons with one of those diabolical jigsaw puzzles with 1001 pieces and an indistinct picture of fall foliage.

The Russians were heavy favorites, but some of the folks at the hotel wanted to watch anyway because they knew the families of U.S. players Bill and Bob Cleary from the Belmont Hill School and Harvard. The game turned out to be close, fast and exciting. The drowsy old hotel came to life with cheers as the U.S. tied the game in the second period. The crowd on the sun porch began to grow. By the time a kid from Minnesota named Bill Christian scored the winning goal, the porch was crowded with people clapping and shouting.

My dreams that night were filled with hockey. But when morning came, I was up early and off into the woods again on my snowshoes with a muffin and an apple in my pocket, looking for the owl.

Keeping Time

After Fa died, I inherited the gold watch that had been in his vest pocket for more than forty years. It's a lovely, thin sliver of gold from the old-line Newbury Street jewelers Shreve, Crump & Low. Governor Walsh had given it to Fa the day he appointed him a judge, in 1915. The back of the case is heavily engraved with Fa's monogram. Somehow, the chain had gotten lost by the time it came to me. On my eighteenth birthday, Father surprised me with a new chain. In the middle, where it secures to a vest buttonhole, hangs a little gold ornament of two cupids holding up the world. As a fob at the other end of the chain hangs the most beautiful of American coins, a Saint-Gaudens twenty-dollar gold piece. The obverse of the coin portrays Liberty as she strides forward with the torch of freedom in one hand and the olive branch of peace in the other. The coin has special significance to Bostonians, since Augustus Saint-Gaudens was the sculptor of the life-sized bronze re-lief across from the State House that portrays Colonel Shaw and the Massa-chusetts 54th, the African American regiment celebrated in the film *Glory*, as they marched down Beacon Street in May of 1863 to meet their destiny.

When he gave me this stunning gift, Father said, "The cupids will re-mind you that love makes the world go around. Keep the coin, and you'll never be broke."

Apocalypse

Father was not naturally inclined to mirth. But he was capable of a joke when the mood was on him. Once, when I farted loudly in the sunroom, he solemnly intoned, "Beware! The trumpets of doom! Run for your lives!"— and took his newspaper into the next room.

E-I-E-I-O...

When I was in the eighth grade, my parents took me prep school shopping. We went first to St. Mark's, where my uncle was the greenskeeper and golf instructor. It seemed very stiff and rather dreary. "Too Episcopalian," was

Father's judgment. Mount Hermon was pretty stodgy too, but I was captivated because it had a working farm. Every student did an hour of farm chores every day. It sounded like fun to spend that much time with animals and tractors.

We walked around the farm. Sheep were grazing. Chickens were scratching in a pen and laying eggs in their coop. Best of all, pigs were oinking and wallowing. I couldn't believe the size of the sows. One had a litter of piglets, and they were trotting around, squeaking and carrying on. Then came time to feed the pigs. When they saw the wheelbarrow coming, they went crazy. I was fascinated that the leavings from the dining hall and trimmings from the kitchen were their food. I thought it was hilarious that doughnuts were floating in the slop.

I never knew why my parents vetoed Mount Hermon, but it likely had to do with my enthusiasm for the farm. They weren't people who would spend a lot of money on my education only for me to become a farmer. All of their eggs (so to speak) were in one basket. And, as their only child, I was the basket.

November 22, 1963

I was a senior at St. Sebastian's, a private school on Nonantum Hill in Newton. I was in some class or other about 2 p.m. on a Friday afternoon, complacently daydreaming about the weekend to come, when the headmaster came into the room and turned on the TV. "President Kennedy has been shot," he said. We sat, stupefied, as Walter Cronkite told us that the president had been gravely wounded and had been taken to a hospital. Then, about a half hour later, Cronkite told us that Kennedy was dead.

Most of us in that classroom at St. Sebastian's had roots in the powerful Boston Irish Catholic political, business, educational and social culture. Kennedy had visited our school a few years earlier, when he was a senator. He was one of us. Still, I don't remember any rage or tears that afternoon. I don't remember that anyone said much of anything. A strange numbness had come over all of us. It was one of my first experiences of the inconceivable, suddenly and horribly, becoming real.

That Sunday morning, my parents went to church and stopped on their way home for fresh egg bagels at the Jewish bakery in Newton Center. It was our custom to spread out the Sunday papers in the sunroom and have bagels and coffee. On these mornings, we usually played classical music in the background as we discussed the editorial, sports and arts sections of the *Globe* and the *Times*. But on this Sunday, we had the TV on in the corner of the room and were half listening while we read about the calamity of Friday and its aftermath. Then someone on the TV said "Oswald." We looked up to see the assassin being led toward the camera by some tall officers. I noticed that one of them was wearing a cowboy hat. I was about to say something about that to my father, when someone rushed into the picture from the right. A shot. Oswald cringed and grabbed at his abdomen. Shouting and struggling. Chaos. The announcer was yelling "Oswald has been shot!" Father sprang to his feet. He was furious. He spat out, "Someone is orchestrating this! Some bastard is pulling the strings!"

The next day, we watched in silence as the riderless horse named Black Jack and the caisson with Kennedy's casket made their way through the streets of Washington and across our TV screen to the sound of muffled drums.

Fourteen Items or Less

My Aunt Betty was elegant, highly cultured and often acerbic. She had graduated from Brown in the 1940s with an English degree and continued her lifelong learning with courses at Wellesley College. She taught English in a suburban high school, where she stressed Shakespeare, the classics and effective writing. She did not suffer fools, dimwits and scoundrels gladly.

Betty stopped at the grocery store one day to pick up a few things on her way home from work. Carrying one of those swing-handled baskets, she headed toward the express lane: FOURTEEN ITEMS OR LESS. Ahead of her in line, a woman was unloading a mountain of groceries and household items from a shopping cart. As the pile grew higher, Betty addressed the woman with an icy "Pardon me."

The woman looked up and responded with a tentative "Yes?"

"I'm puzzled," Betty continued. "I can't decide whether you don't know how to read, or don't know how to count."

Professor Onion

Professor Zwiebel was my German teacher for two years in college. In English, *zwiebel* translates as "onion." Oops. Zwiebel, who allowed us to speak no English, would have insisted that I say, "Auf Englisch, Zwiebel bedeutet *onion*." Or would it be, "Zwiebel es wird mit *onion* ubersetzt"? You see the problem. Even after six years of German study in high school and college, I was still perplexed by this annoying, pedantic language.

But I liked Professor Onion, whose nickname on campus was Rings. He was a jolly little chap who wore a Tyrolean hat with a brush in the band and drove a Volkswagen. He had a positive, almost bubbly outlook on learning; his favorite word was *"Ausgezeichnet!"* ("Excellent!") We studied the obligatory Goethe, Schiller and Brecht. But we also listened to some

Wagner, Mahler and Kurt Weil, learned a bit about the Bauhaus, read *Der Spiegel* and discussed German cultural affairs, and watched a clip from *The Cabinet of Dr. Caligari* as an introduction to the aesthetics and psychology of Expressionism. Yet, somehow, the Third Reich escaped mention.

The highlight of the term was Professor Onion's party for his students at his home out in the country. He framed the event as an afternoon of cultural immersion; we students viewed it as a kind of mini-*Oktoberfest*. Oom-pah music blared in the background as the professor served up several kinds of *wurst*, homemade *kraut* from his garden and hot potato salad with smoked meat. Meanwhile, his buxom nieces circulated among us with glasses of German beer; they were fetching in their braids and dirndl outfits with the lace-up bodices. We were strictly limited to two beers apiece, but it was still a pretty *ausgezeichnetes* party. At least it was until Professor Onion began the slideshow of his recent trip to Bavaria and the Harz Mountains, with lengthy narration in difficult, idiomatic German. He loved his Leica camera, and he took lots of slides. Lots. As the slide talk droned on, I was tempted to ask, "Will there be a quiz on Tuesday?"

The Surfer

My college basketball teammate Wee liked to visit me at Scraggy Neck. He was from Long Island and thought of himself as a surfer—even though I don't think he had ever actually been surfing. But in any case, he had seen *The Endless Summer* four times, purchased a pair of surfer jams and had adopted a surfer's blasé attitude toward life. He also loved clamming. At low tide we'd spend a couple of hours in front of the house, feeling in the mud for quahogs with our feet. We'd pry them open, give them a dash of Tabasco from a bottle Wee kept in the pocket of his jams and down them on the spot.

During one visit, Wee took a liking to my neighbor Linda—a willowy blonde who spent lots of time in a tiny bikini on the beach next to ours. He daydreamed about sweeping her off to some sand dune in his new red Sunbeam Alpine sports car—just like the one James Bond drove in *Dr. No.* "You're wasting your time," I advised him, and pointed to a chubby, dopey-looking kid who was wading out to a Cape Cod Knockabout with a sail bag over his head. "Her true love. They go sailing together every afternoon." Wee couldn't believe it. "She's with *that guy*?" He resolved to win her affections by the end of the week, and he had a plan. "I'll work on my tan and lighten up my hair a bit in the sun. She won't be able to resist." Wee's sister had told him the secret. Just mix peroxide and lemon juice and let the sun do the rest, she instructed. Wee mixed up his potion and we went sailing that afternoon. It was a marvelous day for a sail and we rode the southwest breeze for hours. Every few minutes, he'd douse his head with the stuff.

We got back to the house about five. Mother met us at the door with a bag of charcoal in her hand. "If you get the grill going, I'll—*holy mother of God!* What the hell did you do to yourself?" She was looking at the top of Wee's head. I looked, too. His hair was the color of a carrot. As Wee stared at himself in the mirror in horror, I couldn't resist: "I sure hope Linda likes redheads."

The Secret to Success

From time to time during my high school and college years some associate of my father would give me this sage piece of Horatio Algeresque advice: "When the time comes that you are called upon to clean a toilet, make sure that you clean that toilet better than it has ever been cleaned before. That's the way to get ahead in this world." Of course, these nuggets of wisdom came from Harvard Law School graduates who had never cleaned a toilet in their lives, and who hired Irish immigrant maids to keep the numerous toilets in their Wellesley Hills homes and their Oyster Harbors summer getaways gleaming and ready for their distinguished posteriors.

Shame

I was walking on Newbury Street with a girl I'd met a few days earlier. The softness of an early summer night settled over Boston as we talked about books we'd read and films we'd seen. Her hand found mine as we walked toward the quaint ice cream shop on Clarendon Street. The shop was in a picturesque cottage with a tiled roof and three dormers—a charming, unlikely survivor of the old Back Bay. It had handmade ice cream and comfortable booths, a perfect place for two college kids who were getting to know each another.

As I reached for the doorknob, I caught a glimpse of a man standing at the counter, waiting to give his order. He was horribly disfigured. He may have been a burn victim. He may have been afflicted with the Elephant Man's disease. Whatever it was, I felt a shock of revulsion and dropped the doorknob. "There's a long line at the counter. I know another place," I said to my new friend. "Let's go there instead."

When I didn't go through that door, I turned my back on human suffering. A person, perhaps about my own age, was trying to do something that ordinary people do without a thought—knowing, I'm sure, that his extraordinary disfigurement would cause people like me to walk away. And that's exactly what I did, because I selfishly didn't want to spoil the mood of the evening. I think it's the most shameful thing I've ever done.

21
13,909

Every Boston Celtics fan from the 1950s and '60s knows the significance of this number, as it was intoned by the raspy voice of radio announcer Johnny Most: "Fans, this is Johnny Most speaking to you from high above court-side at Boston Garden, where thirteen thousand, nine hundred and nine fans have filled this place to the rafters to see the World Champion Boston Celtics do basketball battle with the Los Angeles Lakers." Or Philadelphia Warriors, Detroit Pistons, New York Knicks or any other reviled opponent. More often than not, Johnny's 13,909 was a fantasy. In spite of the several world championship banners hanging over the court, Boston was still a hockey town. The old barn was often half empty for basketball games.

When I was in high school, my parents would give me a season ticket to the Celtics as a Christmas gift. It sounds extravagant, but a season ticket twenty rows back from center court cost $165 for the entire season—less than the cost of a ticket for one game these days. My high school team-mates and I would take the MTA to North Station, and then make our way through the musty corridors that smelled of burnt popcorn, past circuses and long-forgotten rodeos. Inside the grimy arena, magic would happen. The supreme dynasty in the history of sports would take the floor: Bill Russell, the greatest winner in the history of team sports; Bob Cousy, who revolutionized basketball into a fast-paced thrill ride; Tom Heinsohn, the reckless scoring machine; Bill Sharman and Sam Jones, the slick outside shooters; "Satch" Sanders, the master of defense; Frank Ramsey, the "Kentucky Colonel" and prototypical "sixth man"; and "Jungle Jim" Loscutoff, the muscle-bound enforcer and Cousy's protector. Every Celtics game was a morality play. We, the faithful, devoted ourselves to the cause of the righteous as our champions contested the forces of darkness led by the likes of Wilt Chamberlain, Jerry West and Oscar Robertson. Ultimately, it seemed, good always managed to prevail.

In the meantime, there was some fantastic basketball. My father and my uncle Julie took me to my first Celtics game, the final game of the 1957 championship series against the St. Louis Hawks. We sat in the third balcony "nosebleed seats" and ate hot dogs, even though we'd had a huge dinner at Durgin Park right before the game. The game went to two overtimes. I have some vivid visual memories of that night. At some point near the end, Bill Russell chased down a Hawks player who had an easy breakaway and blocked the shot from behind, slamming it off the backboard to Cousy. The entire crowd stood and roared in hysteria. I jumped up and down and added my ten-year-old voice to the din. Soon after, Frank Ramsey hit a shot at the basket nearer to us and we all roared again. In the final seconds, there was a long pass to the Hawks' Bob Pettit, and the graceful and gifted six-foot-nine Cajun somehow missed the easy layup from the right side of the basket. Then it was over, and Russell bounded across the floor like a gazelle. We had won! It was the most fun I'd had in my young life. I became a Celtics fan.

My friends and I were making our way to our seats one night in 1962 when my high school teammate Danny asked if I had ever noticed the long fire escape that went up the outside of the building. I hadn't. Well, he had, and he had a scheme. "The Celtics practice on Saturday mornings. Let's climb the fire escape and sneak inside. Murph's up for it." I didn't hesitate to sign on, despite my morbid fear of heights.

Saturday morning came and Danny, Murph and I rode the train to North Station and went around the building to reconnoiter the fire escape. It looked *really* high from the ground. I started to get the jitters. But before I could talk my way out of the escapade, Murph had swung himself up a ladder to the first iron step. Danny followed and I took up the rear. Up we climbed to a kind of landing. Then up some more, easily a hundred feet in the air. I was afraid to look down. Or up. I fixed my gaze on the backs of Danny's sneakers and kept climbing. By the time we reached the top, a strong wind was whistling though the stairs. A large, blank door confronted us. Murph pulled at the handle. It opened. We rushed inside.

We were at the very top of the arena. It was in darkness, except for the bright lights directly over the court. A few of the Celtics were down there, shooting around. Their dribbling echoed through the cavernous building. Red Auerbach, the coach, was talking to them but we couldn't make out what he was saying. "We've got to get closer," Murph urged. "You've got a camera," Danny said to me. "If they give us any trouble, we'll just say we're from the school newspaper." You have to be a high school sophomore, as we were, not to recognize the idiocy of that suggestion. At any rate, I had brought my Kodak Hawkeye with the flash unit to record our adventure. In the panic of our climb, I had forgotten to take pictures.

Down we went, finding our way through lightless passageways and past empty banks of seats. Finally, we were actually on the floor. The Celtics—our warrior heroes—were right in front of us, talking casually and joking with one another. Suddenly, John Havlicek, the promising rookie from Ohio State, emerged from the passageway. Without thinking, I raised my camera and shot. *Poof* went the flashbulb. Havlicek grimaced and blinked a few times. But he wasn't angry; he just smiled at the gaggle of three dopey kids with a camera.

We tried to make ourselves scarce in the shadows as the Celtics started a scrimmage. They went up and down the floor a few times, and then Cousy threw one of his signature blind passes to Havlicek. It hit him square in the face. "Damn it, Havlicek!" Auerbach yelled. "You gotta be ready. Didn't you see that coming?"

His star rookie rubbed his nose, checking for blood. "Couldn't see it," he responded. "Those kids with the flashbulb…"

"Kids? What kids? *Flashbulb*?" Auerbach thundered. Someone pointed at us. "Those kids? What the…? Get them out of here!"

Danny and I wanted to bolt, but Murph held his ground. The jig was up, and he knew it. We were led away by two men in suits who took us into a little office and closed the door, ominously. One of the guys asked the questions. I tried to answer, but when I got to the bit about the school paper, the guy put up his hand. "Don't give me any bullshit, kid. I can get the cops here in three minutes. As a matter of fact, maybe I'll go get them now." With that he left the room.

I was already rehearsing the story for my parents. "You see, it was like this. We saw a fire escape and thought…" They just wouldn't get it. I was doomed. I waited for the interrogator to return with the cops. Off we would go in handcuffs. Probably to the dreaded "reform school."

Then, after quite a while, the other guy said, "I'd better find out what's keeping the cops." Then he smirked at us. "I might just forget to close this door. Understand? And don't try this kind of crap again."

He walked out and we sprinted like hell for the nearest EXIT sign. We hurled the door open and burst through into the sunshine, running and laughing.

22
Aunt Grace

My great-aunts Grace and Mary had been what used to be called "maiden ladies." They lived together in a nice apartment that overlooked the reservoir in Chestnut Hill. Sometime in the late '40s, a suitor appeared, in the person of Frank Elbery. Frank had been a celebrated football player at Boston College in the 1920s. His incongruous nickname in his playing days had been "Kewpie," because of his resemblance to the chubby-faced kewpie dolls that were offered as cheap prizes in arcade shooting galleries and Skee-Ball alleys. He owned a Ford dealership in Cambridge and had a trim Cape Cod cottage on First Cliff in Scituate.

Aunt Grace

Frank started "keeping company" with the ladies, taking them to dinner and the theater. After a while, he approached Fa, as patriarch of the family, to discuss the prospect of marriage. "They're both such lovely ladies," Frank began. "I just can't seem to decide which one to marry."

Fa cut him short: "Then you'd better stop acting like a horse's ass and go home and make up your mind."

Frank decided to marry Grace, who was the elder. Mary evidently took it well. The three of them went on a honeymoon to Ireland and settled in the nice apartment with the reservoir view. Together, they spent weekends and summers in Scituate. They always went to restaurants together. They went to Florida and to Europe together. My mother used to joke snidely about "Kewpie's harem."

After a few years, Frank decided that a yacht would suit a man of his means. The idea was that the boat would spend winters in Florida and summers in Scituate Harbor. He engaged John Alden, the famous yacht designer from Boston, to draw him a forty-eight-foot motor cruiser, which was built to order by the Quincy Adams yard. I still have the mahogany box that once

Yacht *Delia-Grace*

held the fractured bottle of Moët White Star with which the boat had been christened. The brass plaque on the box reads "Yacht *Delia-Grace*. September, 1957." It's a lovely sounding name for a boat—and it gave my mother occasion for great mirth. She knew that Delia had been the name of Frank's mother. "*Delia-Grace*, huh? The old gal got top billing after all," she chortled.

Frank traveled only once to Florida and back aboard *Delia-Grace* before he died. Afterward, Grace sold the boat and spent quite a bit of time gazing out at the water from the house on the cliff in Scituate. She would watch the boats and the birds through Frank's old tripod telescope. One day she saw a dog clinging to a rock a mile or so offshore. *Poor dog,* she thought. *He'll drown if he tries to swim to shore.* She took down the telephone directory and looked up the number of the Coast Guard. She explained the dog's predicament, and the officer of the day said he would send a boat to investigate. "Please hurry," she urged. "The poor thing must be frightened and exhausted. He's just lying there." In short order, a Coast Guard patrol boat appeared and approached the rock. Grace watched through the telescope. The drowsy seal did not appreciate having his nap in the sun interrupted by the boat's noisy engine and grudgingly slid into the water.

As I wrote this chapter, I recalled something about Grace I hadn't thought about since I was perhaps twelve years old. Grace always seemed a benevolent, grandmotherly figure, which I liked since I had never known either of my grandmothers. But at small family gatherings she used to call me "Thomasina"—always with a kind of chuckle and smirk. I found it intensely embarrassing. I don't recall much of a reaction from the other elders, but I'm sure I blushed deeply whenever she made her little joke. I was shamed by hearing the feminine version of my name. I was frightened that somehow she knew my secrets. I wanted my parents to intervene and make her stop, but I was too mortified to ask.

Those little family gatherings were quite frequent after Fa's death and Frank's demise. We spent most holidays with Grace and Mary. Easter is the most important holiday among Lithuanians, and my father used it as an occasion to celebrate his ethnic heritage. Grace and Mary were what was known in the clannish Boston hierarchy as "two toilet Irish"—a snobbish notch above "lace curtain," and two whole pegs above "shanty." When I was about ten years old, Grace admonished me, "Remember that on the Curry side of the family [her side] you're seventh generation." I had no idea what she was talking about. Grace and Mary were the kind of Irish American gentility who took a subscription to the *Illustrated London News*, evidently without a thought to "the troubles" and Easter Rising of 1916. They had their provisions delivered from the S. S. Pierce store in Coolidge Corner, a Yankee bastion. Securely smug, they were quite bemused by Father's Baltic heritage.

One year, he insisted on serving the traditional Lithuanian Easter meal of roast suckling pig. We went to a butcher shop on Hanover Street in the North End and selected the pig. Mother got out her copy of the *Gourmet Cookbook* and set to work—a lot of work, as it turned out. The preparations took all day. Finally, with Grace and Mary enthroned at our table, the pig was served forth on a bed of parsley, roasted to a nut brown and complete with an apple in its mouth and a necklace of cranberries around its neck. Father took a picture and Mother waited for the compliments from our guests. "Oh! My goodness," Aunt Mary exclaimed. "It looks like a little dog." There were plenty of leftovers.

23
Be Prepared!

Tom Lehrer was a satirical songwriter who was very popular in Cambridge in the early 1960s. One of his songs was a cheerful, lilting parody of the Boy Scout anthem:

> Be prepared! That's the Boy Scouts' marching song
> Be prepared! As through life you march along...
> And if you should meet a Girl Scout who is
> similarly inclined
> Don't be nervous, don't be flustered, don't be scared...
> Be prepared!

When I was a freshman in high school, my friends and I thought this sly reference to condoms was hilariously smutty. Many of my friends considered it a sign of worldliness to carry a condom in their wallets. The "rubber," as it was called those days, would be strategically placed in an outside compartment of the wallet so that, over time, a visible outline of a circle would be formed. This was a signal that the owner of the wallet was experienced in the ways of sex.

Of course, this was absurd. When I was fourteen, my chances of needing a condom were about the same as my chances of needing a spare airplane propeller. And I had no idea how to obtain either. Condoms were never on display; in Massachusetts they were sold only by druggists "for the prevention of disease." The notion that I would somehow stride up to the druggist's counter and announce, "I'd like a condom, please," made my scalp itch.

My schoolmate Henry, who seemed to know much more about girls than I, became my advisor in condom acquisition. "Nothing to it," Henry assured me. "There's a secret code. Just walk up to the counter, extend your arm and make a fist. Turn it so your thumb is on top. Now put your thumb inside the crook of your index finger. Then balance a quarter on your thumbnail." Henry demonstrated. "Make sure that George Washington is facing the druggist. That's very important. When the druggist looks at the quarter, you say, 'George was the father of our country because he didn't have one.' When he says, 'I've got what George needed,' put the quarter facedown on the counter. He'll put a rubber in a bag and slide the bag over the counter."

I practiced this hocus-pocus several times under Henry's supervision. "You got it," he finally announced. "No sweat."

In reality, there was plenty of sweat. *What if someone I know sees me buying a rubber? What if the druggist knows who I am and tells my parents?* For weeks, I was stymied by these fearful questions.

At last I gathered my fortitude and rode my bike to Hubbard's Rexall drugstore in Newton Corner to make my fateful purchase. I hadn't anticipated that the store would be so crowded on a Saturday afternoon. Suburban matrons and their husbands browsed the patent medicines for liniments, laxatives and headache remedies. Young mothers pushed strollers up and down the aisles. I had to wait until the coast was clear, so I sat at the soda fountain counter and ordered a Coke. Customers came and went without a break. I finished my Coke and ordered another. Some kids came in and picked through the baseball cards and the comic books for a while and then sat at the counter and ordered grilled cheese sandwiches. By the time they'd finished, I'd drained my Coke, so I ordered another. A lanky older gentleman went up to the prescription counter and had a long conversation with the druggist. I ordered another Coke and waited.

Then, finally, the store was empty. Now was my chance. After four Cokes, I urgently needed to pee, but I grabbed the quarter in my pocket and pressed on. The druggist met me at the counter.

I made a fist, as Henry had shown me. I turned it thumb up and tucked my thumb inside the crook of my index finger. I balanced the quarter on my thumbnail. I made sure George was facing the druggist. I was sweating, barely able to blurt out: "George Washington. You know, the father of our country. He didn't have one."

The druggist looked at me blankly.

"You know," I urged, shoving the quarter closer. "George. What he needed. The father of our country. You have it."

The druggist stared. His jaw went slack.

By now, I was on the verge of panic and about to pee my pants. I was aware of voices; a line was forming behind me. My words came out in a desperate, hoarse whisper: "George. He didn't have one. You know. *George Washington. The code. You have what…*"

The druggist interrupted, as I hopped from foot to foot: "Young man, whatever this is about, I don't have time for it. Please step aside so I can serve other customers."

I had been snookered.

24
Hootenanny '63

Inspired by our foray to see Flatt and Scruggs at Jordan Hall and by our endless listening to Bill Monroe, Osborne Brothers and Stanley Brothers records, my friend Neil and I decided to start our own bluegrass band. We got an additional jolt of inspiration from some Cambridge musicians, Bill Keith, Jim Rooney and the Charles River Valley Boys. I was fifteen and Neil was a year ahead of me in school.

We certainly weren't alone. Like others my age, my morbid adolescent imagination was gratified by bluegrass songs about natural disasters ("The Great Baltimore Fire"), sleazy romance ("The Great Philadelphia Lawyer"), untimely death ("The Little Girl and the Dreadful Snake"), faithless lovers throwing their pregnant sweethearts off bridges ("The Banks of the Ohio"), maudlin sentimentality ("Mother's Not Dead, She's Only Sleepin'") and deep existential alienation ("Rank Strangers"). Small wonder bluegrass music mania was sweeping Greater Boston and other young folks like Peter Rowan had started bands of their own. My

High school bluegrass picker, 1963

idea for a name for the band was the Bunker Hillbillies. Neil insisted that that name had already been taken by a bunch of little kids in cowboy hats who played ukuleles during the breaks on some bowling show on Saturday morning TV. I can't remember what we wound up calling ourselves.

Neil was our leader. In a world of preppies, he had a swept-back hairstyle and carried a comb in his pocket. He wore jackets with zippers, not buttons. He brought his guitar to school. He knew that Roy Orbison was cool. He was a natural musician and could pick the hell out of a banjo. So, we built our act around Neil. I pretty much stayed out of the way, playing an upright bass and telling a few cornball jokes. The other guys sang harmonies and filled out the arrangements. I never expected we would actually play anywhere but the big living room of Neil's parents' house in Hingham.

Somehow, we got hired as the opening act for some shows called Hootenanny '63. These were traveling road shows put together to capitalize on the folk music craze. The regulars on these programs were Tom Rush, the Jug Band, the Charles River Valley Boys and Bonnie Dobson. The promoter was explicit about our role. "Go out there, play three fast bluegrass songs to get the audience going, and then get lost." He figured young kids, fast songs, how can you lose? For this, we would split fifty bucks four ways.

Neil had a hand-me-down '58 Pontiac station wagon from his parents. We loaded it with instruments and cowboy hats, strapped my bass to the luggage rack, and set off for our first gig. We'd never played in public. Not for one minute.

We arrived at Fitchburg State College with no idea what to expect. We asked directions to the gym, parked and loaded our stuff inside. The place seemed huge, with a big stage and seats for several thousand. I started to get really nervous. We went backstage and were suddenly face-to-face with some of our heroes from the Club 47 and the Newport Folk Festival. Tom Rush and Geoff Muldaur were in the corner, talking with Eric von Schmidt. Joe Val and Bob Siggins were eating sandwiches and drinking beer. Fritz Richmond was thumping away on his washtub bass. I just stood there, sweating, trying to avoid notice.

We unpacked our instruments as unobtrusively as possible and started to tune up. None of the real pros paid us any notice. In those days, a sound check was unheard of. The promoter said, "Five minutes." I could barely believe what was happening. I looked at Neil. His hands were shaking. If he couldn't carry it off, we were doomed. I prepared for a complete meltdown. I put my cowboy hat on my head and closed my eyes.

Suddenly, somehow, we were on stage. Three or four thousand people were looking at us, waiting for something to happen. Our first song was the instrumental "Cripple Creek," featuring Neil's hot banjo playing. I looked at him. His hands were still shaking. Badly. Then he kicked it off—at twice the speed we had practiced it. Fueled by abject panic, he just ripped through it. The rest of us could barely keep up. By the end of the song, my right hand was numb. My cowboy hat fell off. *Oh God*, I thought, *this is a nightmare.* Then the song ended. The last note hung in the air for longer than it should have. Then the entire place went crazy, stomping and hooting. The promoter had been right. Young kids, fast songs. How can you lose?

25
Mother and the Jetty Jockey

As I write this, I'm looking at two photographs of my mother. The first shows an anxious girl of sixteen in a party dress. She is the ungainly center of attention at her own coming-out party at the Lenox Hotel in Boston in 1934. The second is of a woman in her mid-forties, with a broad, confident smile. She's holding a nice-sized bluefish she had caught a few hours before. It's difficult to fathom that it's the same person in both pictures.

Mother with her parents, 1934

The same might be said of her own mother, who in an oil portrait that hangs in our living room is a vivacious, beautiful girl of about sixteen who seems ready to embrace life joyfully. By the time the photograph of Mother's debut into polite society had been taken, she had become a dour, gnome-like creature who looks like she could single-handedly spoil any party. It was she who named my mother Isabel.

I've been told that Isabel is currently a very fashionable name for baby girls. In 1917 it was not. Mother always seemed ambivalent about her name. She hated the nicknames "Iz" and "Izzy," but she enjoyed carrying a name that connected her to the Portuguese heritage on her mother's side of the family. Family lore has it that an Irish girl from New Bedford married an Azorean whaler in the 1820s or '30s. One result of that union was the deep brown eyes and almost black hair

Grandmother at sixteen

that my mother shared with her cousin, Rufina—who also had a Portuguese first name. Another, less tangible legacy was the seafaring spirit. Like me, Mother loved the water and loved boats. And eventually she learned to like fishing pretty well, too.

Father would get the latest fishing lowdown when he went for the mail at the Falmouth Heights post office. The postmistress' husband fished every day and night, and she was authorized to pass top-secret intelligence along to The Judge's son-in-law. Father came home one morning with the mail, the paper and the doughnuts and told us that we had to catch the outgoing tide that night at "the trunk," a pebbly beach just east of Nobska Light. Nice stripers, he had been told, had been hanging around the outlet of the herring run and would fall for a swimming plug.

We made the mistake of taking John XXIV with us. As usual, he played the trickster, standing in the middle of the flow in the herring run and barking and snapping frantically at the herring as they swam between his legs on their spawning run. For a few minutes, it was funny. Then it got very annoying. I plunged in to haul him back to the car. John resisted, and we were having quite a tug-of-war when a guy with a surf rod walked past us and commented, "Nice dog. Lots of spirit." I told him that John XXIV had a wild streak and ran off to places like New Hampshire. "Like I said," he replied, "lots of spirit." He shook my hand and introduced himself as Cappy.

As the night wore on, Father and I watched in a state of wonder as Cappy caught fish. It seemed as though he would reel in a good-sized striper every ten or twenty minutes. Meanwhile, we thrashed the water into a froth, with no success. The age-old fisherman's question is, *What's that guy doing that I'm not?* After a couple of hours, my father was bold enough to ask him.

"Well, first off, the kid's got a swivel ahead of his plug. Never want to fish a plug with a swivel. Plug's supposed to wobble, not roll. Second, crank in real slow—just as slow as you can stand it. Water's cold. These bass ain't in no chasin' mood."

Mother with a bluefish

I took the swivel off, fished for another half hour, and right at the end of the night caught my first big striper. As we put the fish into the back of the station wagon, Cappy came over for a look. "You're lucky to get 'im," he remarked. "Tide's over. Run's over for tonight." We thanked him profusely and said we hoped to bump into him again and get some more pointers. "I fish every night. Meet you tomorrow night if you like. Menauhant. Eight thirty. Bring a little somethin' to ward off the chill, willya? And bring that dog. I like 'im. Lots of spirit."

The next night, we were waiting by the Menauhant road at eight. We were bundled up for what promised to be a frosty early May night. We had a thermos of coffee and, as instructed, John XXIV and a fifth of Bonded Old Fitzgerald, a premium bourbon of the day. At eight thirty on the dot, Cappy pulled in behind us in what seemed an unlikely vehicle, a Chevy "business coupe," vintage 1950 or so. Later that night, we would learn the virtues of that car. He greeted us cordially and asked if we had any painting that needed to be done around the house; he was a house painter when the fishing slowed down in midwinter and for a couple of months midsummer. Father said he would think about it. Then Cappy said to Mother, "Sure is chilly, Missus. Get chillier later, I 'spect." As if on cue, she pulled the fifth of Old Fitz out of our picnic bag. "Oh, jeez, Missus! That's some Christmas whiskey you got there. Too rich to be drinkin' out on the jetty. I'll just take it off your hands for safekeepin' and go back to the car for a little nip that's better suited for jetty drinkin'." He came back with a half-depleted bottle of Four Roses, a cheap rye.

We set off across the sand. Cappy slapped his thigh, called "C'mere pup" and the ordinarily unruly John XXIV trotted along obediently at his heels. After fifteen minutes or so, we got to the jetty at Green Pond. "Tide's wrong," Cappy announced. "Not runnin' right yet. Gotta wait it out." That was the cue to break out the Four Roses. Mother announced that we had roast pork sandwiches, and we'd made an extra for him. "That's lovely of ya, Missus. Don't mind if I do."

So we sat on the rocks of the jetty and ate our sandwiches. We didn't have any cups, so the bottle of Four Roses went hand to hand. I was only sixteen and not that used to alcohol and by the time the bottle had made its third circuit, I was half way to La-La Land. I looked over at Cappy. John XXIV was curled up on the sand and sleeping at his feet.

"Smell that?" Cappy suddenly asked, and jumped to his feet. I had no idea what he was talking about. "Smell it! Like watermelon. Stripers feedin' right here! 'Scuse me while I go piss in the water. Oops, sorry Missus. Forgot there was a lady present. Anyway, if I do what I just said I was gonna do, it'll call 'em in."

I began to think Cappy was mad and this whole escapade was a scam to get a bottle of booze and a house painting job from us. Then he yelled from the end of the jetty. "Water's movin' good in the cut now! There's some breakin' fish! Git fishin'!" By the time we negotiated the rocks and got into casting position, Cappy had already landed a hefty striper. While we were getting ready to cast, he hooked another. Over the next hour or so, Cappy beached fish after fish. Father and I each managed one. We were thrilled. Cappy seemed to take the whole thing in stride.

Without warning, he announced, "That's it. It's over. Pretty good night. Gotta get these fish back to the car before the rats get at 'em. There's rats in all these jetties."

Mother, who was sitting on a rock in the jetty at that moment, jumped up and screamed, "Rats?"

"Jeez, Missus. Take it easy. They're after the fish, not us."

Cappy grabbed his gear and walked back briskly toward the car. John XXIV followed at his heels. Twenty minutes later, he returned with the dog and a canvas tarp. "Best to drag 'em on this," he explained. "That way they don't get full of sand." We loaded thirteen stripers onto the tarp. We hauled the tarp down to the water's edge where the tide had just gone out and left the sand wet and firm. With three of us pulling, we got the fish back to Cappy's car in pretty short order. Cappy opened his trunk. The coupe had no back seat and there was an enormous luggage space between the driver's seat and the rear bumper. He laid down another tarp and we stacked the fish.

"What do you do with all these fish?" Mother asked.

"Sell 'em, Missus. They're goin' to Cahoon's in Woods Hole tonight. The kids gotta eat. And it seems like it's gettin' a little chilly now, don't it?" The bottle reappeared.

For the next few years we'd run into Cappy from time to time. "How's your pup?" he'd always ask. We learned that for most of the year Cappy provided for his family of five children by fishing all night with a rod and reel, and clamming all day. He was what is known in some parts of the coast as a jetty jockey and in others as a pinhooker or waterman. Whatever you call it, he was a master at what he did.

When I recalled that night for my mother years later, she had a big laugh. "God, that Four Roses was wretched. My father would have been so proud of his darling daughter, sitting on a jetty in Menauhant in the middle of the night, passing a jug of rye. But that Cappy was a nice fellow, wasn't he?"

26
Eateries and Dives I

Casa Barbi, Brighton, Massachusetts

When I was a youngster, my parents had a favorite neighborhood Italian place, Casa Barbi. For me, a trip to Casa Barbi was an exotic adventure. The entrance was down a few steps from the sidewalk. I always went first so I could push aside the beaded curtain that separated the entryway from the dining room. The room was dark, lit for the most part by candles that burned in old Chianti bottles. The wax from the candles dripped down the glass and straw bottles and onto the gleaming white tablecloths. There was a wedge of cheese, some fruit and a knife in a bowl on every table. The waiters had mustaches and spoke with heavy accents. A violinist circulated among the tables.

Casa Barbi had a huge menu. My parents usually ordered several courses: soup, followed by fish and then some kind of scallopini. They seemed to like dishes with mushrooms and parsley. They always shared a bowl of something that looked like spinach. *Ugh.* All this perplexed my young mind. We came to Casa Barbi for Italian food. As children do, I always ordered the same thing: spaghetti and meatballs, covered with a mountain of grated cheese. Spaghetti and meatballs. That was Italian food. Didn't my parents know that?

Maria's, Boston's North End

Maria's was upstairs from one of those meat markets on Hanover Street in the North End that had whole rabbits and sheep's heads hanging from hooks in the window. I'm not sure that Maria's was actually a restaurant, in any common understanding of the word.

A steep staircase led to Maria's door on a second-floor landing. You knocked and Maria herself came to the door and let you in—to her apartment. The room on the left had her sofa (with her cat snoozing among the cushions and pillows), her TV (with a copy of *TV Guide* beside the rabbit ears), a statue of the Blessed Virgin, a huge aquarium and two tables, each set for four. Across the hall in another room there was a table for four and two tables for two. Straight ahead, in an alcove, was her kitchen.

Everyone went into the kitchen, first thing. Maria would stir a big kettle on her four-burner electric range. "You smell this," she would insist. "You like some of this? Delicious, yes?" Then on to another big pot. "Marinara. I start at six this morning, chopping, cooking. You like some of this, yes?"

Then she'd open the oven and pull out a roasting pan. "I make nice pork on the bone with rosemary tonight. Right from the downstairs market. You like some?" There was no menu. Everyone ate whatever Maria was cooking that night. As I recall, dinner was ten dollars in the mid '60s, which was quite steep. But for your ten spot, you got a really good home-cooked meal and—at least for a few hours—the doting Italian *nonna* you somehow always wished you'd had.

Miss Worcester, Worcester, Massachusetts

I nearly lived in this place for my four years of college. I pulled all-nighters studying for exams, and even hauled my Remington portable into a booth a few times to work on papers. After all, the library on campus closed at midnight—and it didn't serve food or coffee. Besides, in the wee hours Miss Worcester had its own soundtrack that pleased me: the Vic Damone and Patti Page records on the jukebox, the satisfying *clack* of the heavy Syracuse China plates and bowls as they were stacked behind the counter and the rasping, mechanical bell that sounded whenever the old National cash register rang up a sale.

Miss Worcester is still there, at the foot of the hill occupied by Holy Cross. It's a classic Worcester Dining Car Company diner, built in 1948. It's on the National Register of Historic Places and it's been voted the #1 diner in the country several times. These days it's open for breakfast and lunch, with a trendy menu that features things like apple pie-stuffed French toast and something called a "travel the world gypsy omelette."

Back in the '60s, "Miss Woo" was open twenty-four hours and served up the apotheosis of the cheeseburger. One of the three brothers who ran the place was the cheeseburger king—he mixed raw onion and spices into the meat in a large bowl, formed the patties by hand and fried them on a blistering grill. The very hot grill made a kind of amalgam of the cheese and the meat. The edges of the burger were crispy, while the inside was pink and succulent.

Meanwhile, his brother Russ would be working on the home fries. Russ was jug-eared and buck-toothed, an adult incarnation of the *Little Rascals* character Alfalfa. When he talked, he sounded like someone who had been in a few special-needs classes. Nonetheless, Russ was the maestro of the home fries. He had his own grill and his tools—a big spatula, an oilcan with a spout, a big shaker of paprika and a big shaker of salt. He had a pile of parboiled potatoes in the corner of the grill that was just warm; the hot side was waiting for a splash of oil, a spatula full of potatoes and two shakes each of paprika and salt. Russ worked the sizzling potatoes with his spatula, coaxing and massaging them to a lovely burnt umber color. This might have been Russ' only skill, but with spatula in hand he was in complete command. Russ became a kind of cult figure at Holy Cross. We'd bring him a pair of gloves, a scarf or some other small gift at Christmas, and his picture wound up in the college yearbook.

Joyce Chen's, Cambridge, Massachusetts

One of our neighbors on Scraggy Neck in the 1960s and '70s was Helen Chin. Helen's lover and frequent "house guest" was George, a former priest. This scandalized the more conservative residents of the Neck. They called her "Dragon Lady" behind her back and gossiped about her liaison as they swilled gin-and-tonics with Rose's lime juice on the beach at the clubhouse of the Buzzards, a WASPy, down-at-heels, Madras-shorts, old-money sailing club on Wings Neck. To their everlasting credit, my parents didn't have much truck with that crowd. They liked Helen because she was literate, witty and didn't give a tinker's damn what anyone thought. They liked George, too. They would have them over for cookouts on the beach, and they were delighted with invitations to Helen's beautifully staged and crafted wintertime dinner parties. Helen took an interest in my graduate studies at Penn and could ask me questions about the psychology of a poem by Robert Lowell that were as provocative as those of my professors. As it turned out, her family had been members of the Boston Athenaeum for generations. In a gesture for which I am still grateful, she enrolled me as a guest member at the Athenaeum when I completed my doctorate.

At one of Helen's dinner parties, the conversation turned to the Cantonese and Mandarin dishes Helen had included in her menu. I had recently bought the *Joyce Chen Cookbook* and was eager to find out as much as I could about Chinese cooking.

"Joyce is my friend," Helen told me. "We'll go there."

I assumed it was one of those idle comments that people make at dinner parties. But Helen was serious.

At the time, before the cuisines of Hunan and Szechuan stole the thunder from Mandarin cooking, Joyce Chen's in Cambridge was the ultimate destination for Chinese food. She had a television show and her cookbook was a best seller. She was the Asian Julia Child. She even has her own U.S. postage stamp.

One winter evening, Helen, George and I trundled off to Joyce's restaurant. Joyce greeted Helen like a sister and showed us to a particularly nice table. We never saw a menu; the food just started coming—rich soups, dumplings, a whole fish, platters of steamed vegetables with sesame and garlic. This was a completely different Chinese food than what I was used to in suburban restaurants like China Sails and Kowloon. Helen told me that Joyce's heritage was from northern China, and the food was very satisfying on a blustery night. After a while, Joyce came to our table. "You are liking?" she asked. I was most definitely liking.

Agnes' Lunch, Worcester, Massachusetts

Aggie's had been a speakeasy in the 1920s. It had the look of a classic luncheonette, with a green-and-cream-colored enamel sign over the door that advertised Coca-Cola in florid lettering on big red enamel discs. I suspect very few people actually went there for lunch.

My basketball teammate Horace was a regular, and he walked me through the protocol: If Aggie knew you, she gestured toward the back of the place, where a staircase led downstairs. There were booths along the walls and a small dance floor in the middle of the room. Under the edge of the table in each booth was a little shelf. You ordered a "ginger ale" and put a buck on the table. A waitress brought a bottle of Polar ginger ale and one of those little quilted paper cups that dentists used to use for mouthwash. In the cup was a stiff shot of some kind of cheap rye. You put the rye on the little shelf. All this was in case of a raid—oh, and if that happened, you could down the booze and eat the cup. Well, Aggie's hadn't been raided for decades—but noble traditions die hard.

The main attraction for me was the jukebox. It played an amazing selection of blues and R&B 45s: Junior Parker's "Mystery Train," "Finger Poppin' Time" by Hank Ballard and the Midnighters, Louis Jordan's "Ain't Nobody Here but Us Chickens" and Little Walter's "My Babe" and "Juke." If it was a slow night, the girls who worked upstairs on the third floor (and provided Aggie with her main source of income) would come down to talk and dance with the college boys. They were an amazing sight on a dismal March weeknight in Worcester —all dolled up like the Supremes and soaked in drugstore perfume. I imagine they knew we were safe, and just naive enough to buy them a five-dollar bottle of "champagne."

Aggie's is long gone now—bulldozed along with the Golden Nugget showbar and the entire Black neighborhood that surrounded them, with its community churches, neighborhood markets and rib joints. In a grotesque irony, the new highway that traverses the vanished Black enclave is named Martin Luther King Jr. Boulevard. In any case, it's remarkable that Aggie's lasted as long as it did—a speakeasy more than three decades after the repeal of Prohibition. I once mentioned Aggie's to my father when I was a senior in college. "That place? That's still there? Hell, we used to go there in 1937!"

George's Coney Island Lunch, Worcester, Massachusetts

This place has been a Worcester landmark since 1918. My grandfather used to eat lunch here. Foodies be damned; "the Coney" is known for one thing—hot dogs topped with a secret chili meat sauce. It was a favorite stop for my college friends and me when the midnight munchies came over us. Our standard order was three each, with "the works." In those bad old days, the chili meat sauce sometimes had an odd, reddish, fluorescent glow. This might have been due to the weird lighting in the place or perhaps to the

lingering effects of the resinous Michoacan buds we'd been smoking. I've never been certain. In any case, the sauce sure looked risky, sitting in a pot in the steam table for some indeterminate period of time. But the effect of the dog, roll, sauce, onions, ketchup, relish and yellow mustard was sublime. At least it was at a certain time of night. Side orders? A huge dill pickle on a plate. Thirsty? 'Gansett long necks. Want dessert? They sold those individual Table Talk pies in their own little boxes.

I checked in not long ago, and the interior hasn't changed much. Just a bunch of booths, including some cozy ones for two. My father probably sat in these same booths with his college sweetheart. The exterior of the place is dominated by one of the great illuminated signs in America, featuring an eight-foot-long hot dog gripped by a giant hand and dripping neon mustard toward the sidewalk. Yum.

A Little Portuguese Place in Provincetown

I'm sure I knew the name of this joint forty-five years ago, but I can't remember it now. Even my friend Mike, whose Italian family ran a restaurant in Provincetown for years, can't recall the place. It was in the West End, a little neighborhood spot with superb *caldo verde*—the traditional Portuguese kale soup.

I liked staying at the Scraggy Neck house in the off season. Sometimes I had a concert to play in Connecticut or Massachusetts. Other times I just went to read, burn up some firewood and walk the beach at Sandy Neck. There was a year-round restaurant in Falmouth that I liked, a comfortable, fuddy-duddy spot called the Town House. It was the kind of place my parents would go to in the '50s for a whiskey sour, some chicken à la king or Welsh rarebit with bacon and a hot apple pandowdy. It was pretty good, but hardly exciting. But by November, there weren't a lot of choices; just about everything else in town was shuttered tight.

Once or twice a year on a cold, bleak night I'd forsake the Town House and make the trek to the little neighborhood café in Provincetown for kale soup. I'd often eat at the bar and watch the Bruins game with the owners. In those days, any conversation in New England about Bruins' star Bobby Orr was an icebreaker, and soon the woman was telling me how to make linguiça and unveiling the secrets of her soup. Make your own rich broth from a whole chicken, she told me—but no chicken meat in the soup. Mince the chicken liver and add it to the onions and garlic as you brown them in some fatty skimming from the broth. Blend the boiled potato in with the broth—it will absorb fat from the chicken and make it rich. And use real Portuguese kale.

"Where do I get that?" I asked.

"You can't. Well, maybe Fall River. We grow it for ourselves."

I've since learned that the authentic *caldo verde* is made with *tronchuda,* a broad-leaf cabbage. I grow it now, but my soup still lacks the magic.

One night, with a nor'easter brewing, I headed up Route 6 for soup. "Bruins on tonight?" I asked as I pulled up a barstool.

"We got something new," my friend replied. "VCR. Movies on tape. Okay with you to watch a movie?"

I said sure and as she went in the back to get my order a few of her friends came in and staked out seats at the bar. They had brought the tape for movie night. I wondered what the film choice would be in a Portuguese restaurant in P'town.

As I started my soup, the opening sequence came on. A beautiful young woman runs along a sand dune, disrobing as she goes. She plunges into the water for a twilight swim... *Jaws.* Of course!

27
Rufina

Rufina was the family bohemian. She'd been born in 1904, had graduated from Radcliffe in middle of the Roaring Twenties, and never lost the glint of flapperish mischief in her eye. Her candid shot in the 1924 Radcliffe yearbook displays her renegade spirit. Other graduates of her era pictured themselves nicely dressed, carefully coiffed and posing with their grandmother's Staffordshire tea set, a nicely bound volume of Ovid, a cello or a tennis racquet. Rufina chose a fuzzy snapshot of herself on a nondescript beach, wearing an unbecoming, sack-like bathing costume and a knit cap. An indolent Labrador retriever lies behind her, its back to the camera. A mysterious cloud of smoke rises from the cockeyed horizon. I suspect the picture was her way of flipping the bird to the old-money, WASP oligarchy, of which Radcliffe was a bastion.

In my memory, Rufina didn't dress at all like other women of the 1950s. She wore long, colorful skirts, even more colorful shawls and a beret. She was the daughter of the Irish American poet Denis McCarthy. He was regarded by some in his time as a kind of American Yeats, and he seems to have made a good living publishing books of poems and lecturing at Catholic colleges and to Hibernian cultural organizations, of which there were many at that time. His papers are in the special collections of the Boston College library—an indicator that he was taken seriously as a writer. I have two of his books of poems. With some regret, I have to say that a catalog of what distinguishes Yeats' poetry from

Rufina (left) with her father (right) in Carrick, Ireland, 1925

Uncle Denis' could take up a lot of this chapter. Simply put, Yeats was a visionary; Uncle Denis was a sentimentalist. So in deference to Rufina, who was very devoted to her father, I'll leave the topic.

One thing she did inherit from him was a real love of literature and writing. She followed one of the few career paths open to women at the time and became an English teacher at Arlington High School. If passion for the subject is the foundation of good teaching, I suspect she was a very good teacher.

During a 1934 stay at Willey House, a seaside hotel in Swampscott on the North Shore of Boston that seems to have catered to unattached ladies and gentlemen, she met Louise Bogan, who would come to be recognized as one of the major American poets of the century. They established a fast friendship right away and had a very active correspondence until Louise's death, thirty-six years later. Based on her reading of that correspondence, Bogan's biographer concluded that, in her friendship with Rufina, the poet had found "an educated, tough-minded and witty companion."[4] I've spent a few afternoons myself in the special collections at the Amherst College library, where Bogan's papers are housed, reading the originals of their hundred or more surviving letters and postcards. There is an easy familiarity in their correspondence that suggests a deep trust between them. And Bogan was not a woman who trusted easily.

Dear Label:

   I'm not forgot!
Last year I promised, did I not?
That when your day came around next-time
I'd write for you a little rhyme.
Well, here's your Birthday Eve once more,
Today you've reached the age of four,
Today you're more mature, you see,
Than when you were just only three.
So here's my very bestest thought,
May life be sweet as life it ought,
And may your blessings be a score
On this sweet day when you are four!

       Uncle Denis

Feb. 26, 1921.

Rufina's father, Denis McCarthy wrote, illustrated and hand lettered this poem for Mother's fourth birthday.

For most of their friendship, Bogan ruled American poetry. As the poetry editor of the *New Yorker*, her review could establish a writer as a major presence in the American literary landscape—or not. She traveled in very heady circles in New York with the likes of Edmund Wilson, Theodore Roethke and Rolfe Humphries. Rufina, meanwhile, was teaching her students and tending her tidy Dutch Colonial house in Arlington Heights. That house became a refuge for Louise when she needed to escape New York.

Rufina the renegade

In her last year, my mother told me that there were postcards from Rufina somewhere in a box in the basement: "Radio City Music Hall kind of picture postcards from when she was in New York with Louise. You know, 'Bill Faulkner is drinking heavily again. Hollywood no good for him.'—that sort of gossipy stuff." I never found them.

Nor have I ever uncovered a trace of the novel Rufina had written, and to which Bogan pointedly refers in a letter of 1944: "You have produced a book. Now you must stand outside it, tear it apart, and put it together again." She encourages Rufina to work "as a conscious artist works," and continues on in a later, unpublished paragraph of the same letter, "I say these things to you because I know you have gifts, and intelligence and wit."[5]

My most loving memories of Rufina are of our trips to Harvard Square when I was of grammar school age. Around the time of my birthday, she would take me to lunch at the Window Shop, a restaurant and gift shop on Brattle Street that was run by refugees from Hitler's conquest of Eastern Europe. She would indulge me shamelessly. We would have goulash or paprikash with noodles and some kind of sticky honey dessert. Then we'd go into the shop and she would tell me I could have any one thing I wanted for a gift. I still have three of those gifts. One is a small Perfex pepper mill from France. I was too young to know much about cooking, but I was enthralled because it had a handle on the top that you cranked and a door in the side into which you put the peppercorns. I think I liked the fact that you started a mechanism, did something, and got something in the end for your efforts. Another is a book about a mischievous squirrel, with wonderful watercolor illustrations. It's called *Winkie*, and I am looking at it as I write this. The third is a toy of a little bull on a pedestal. Press your

Resilience!

thumb under the base and he collapses; take your thumb away and he pops back to life. That little bull has been my personal symbol of resilience for sixty-five years.

Rufina's last extended visit to our house on Scraggy Neck was my chance to get to know her more fully as an adult. We had conversations over iced tea and Fig Newtons about whether the arts have a social responsibility. At the time, artists were often judged by the intensity of their commitment to the peace movement and racial and gender equality. We were of the shared mind that art is fundamentally autotelic and the responsibility of artists is simply to do their art. If the world gets changed for the better in the process, that's a bonus. We talked about poetry, and about Louise. Louise had a book coming out, she told me. Would I like to come to New York and visit with Louise for an hour or so the next time Rufina was there? I agreed that I would, very much.

After lunch, Rufina would set out on her walk, which was an essential event of her day. She would lace up her new blue Adidas shoes, pull her big tennis hat down over her ears and set off. The loop around Scraggy Neck was about a mile and a half. Rufina, who was in her seventies, would do the loop twice, at a brisk pace. One day she seemed to have been gone for a long time, and Mother asked me to go looking. When I found Rufina, she was cruising along. "It's such a lovely day," she said. "I just had to go around the loop one more time. After all, we only have so many days like this to enjoy." At dinner that night, she unexpectedly told me I was to have her Portuguese great-grandfather's sea chest after she died.

A few months after her visit, I got an inscribed copy of Bogan's *Blue Estuaries* in the mail, with a note from Rufina. She was sorry, it read, but when she had seen Louise in New York in October she had been ill and in no mood to receive visitors. Louise had decided to retire from her position at the *New Yorker*. "At least I won't need to write anymore about lousy poetry," she had joked to Rufina.

Blue Estuaries contains "After the Persian" and other poems in which death is a conscious presence. Remarkably, the copy Rufina sent me has a correction in Louise's own hand to a line in "Song for the Last Act"—the word "voice" is crossed out. She had written in its place: "fear."

28
Rory

Rory had been my mother's boyfriend in college. Evidently, he'd been a hell-raiser at Harvard, had sobered up for Harvard Medical School and his residencies, and was a well-regarded orthopedic surgeon in Boston. But the hell-raiser still wasn't very far under the surface. Rory sped around in a blue Triumph TR3 with the top down, a tweed sports car cap on his head, kidskin driving gloves and a cashmere muffler around his neck. Among his other interests, he had ten children and a weakness for playing the ponies.

One Saturday morning, Rory pulled into the circular drive at the South Street house and announced to my father that the two of them were going to Suffolk Downs, the seedy thoroughbred track near Boston. Rory, it seems, had been doing a little surgery on lame racehorses in his spare time and had saved a couple from having to be put down; they were happily standing at stud on some farm in Connecticut. To show their gratitude, the owners had given him tips on three races that afternoon. "Sure things!" he called over his shoulder as they roared around the drive.

That night I was in bed, not quite asleep, when I heard the guttural rumble of the TR3 pulling into the drive. I looked out the window and saw my father and Rory cavorting on the front lawn, singing "The Whiffen-poof Song":

> We are poor little lambs who have lost our way
> Baa, baa, baa.

It was the only time I ever saw my father do anything resembling cavorting, and the only time I ever heard him sing. They were as drunk as lords. Mother rushed out the front door and hustled them through the house and into the kitchen. As I came into the room, Rory put a brown paper grocery bag on the kitchen table. *Ta-da!* It was full of money.

As it turns out, the owners of the horses had been very grateful indeed. The races were, in fact, in the bag. Mother told me later that Rory had started with $1,000 on the nose and let his winnings ride for the next two races. He hit a 3/1, a 5/1 and a 2/1. There was $30,000 in the bag. This was in 1957 or '58 dollars. Father was considerably more conservative. He had started with $10, had taken his winnings off the table after each race, and wound up with $180. But, knowing my father, who was no gambler, I'm sure he didn't think he'd wound up $29,820 short. He seemed genetically incapable of envy. He likely was happy with a wallet that was a bit plumper than it had been that morning.

When I was a senior at Holy Cross, Father had a stroke. I have learned since that his own mother and father had died when *he* was a senior at Holy Cross. Father was gravely ill in the hospital for thirteen weeks before he died. He never spoke, but there were times when he seemed to understand what was said to him, and he would make gestures with his eyes and one of his hands in response. Those times were very important to me, since most of the time he was unresponsive, staring vacantly, rubbing with his finger a smooth seashell I had given him. I wanted to be with him whenever the cloud lifted, even a little bit. After a couple of weeks, I got into a routine. I would go to classes and the library during the day, eat dinner early at college and drive to the hospital in Wellesley. Some nights, I'd stay until midnight and try to do some reading if he was asleep. Other nights, I might catch a few good moments with him and find myself waking up in the chair in his room at four or five in the morning. When the whole thing got overwhelming, I'd visit a girl named Chris I knew at Wellesley College. We'd go into the village for coffee and just talk. One night, we sat in my car in the driveway of Beebe Hall for a long time. She held my hand while I cried, hard.

Early one morning, I was waking up in the chair in Father's room when Rory came through the door. He was on staff at the same hospital. "Just checking to see how he's doing," he said. I nodded. I couldn't seem to find words. "How are you doing? Have you been here all night?" I nodded again. He frowned, and then brightened up with an idea: "Hey, you could help me with something," he said. "Got an hour?" I nodded again. "Good. Afterwards, we'll go for some breakfast."

I got up and followed him. As we were going down stairs into the lower levels of the hospital, Rory explained. "I have to set a guy's arm. It's simple, but I need someone to hold his wrist up in the air—really steady—while I set the bones. Easy stuff, since you're tall and strong. And you sure as hell need a distraction right now."

We went into a sort of locker room with sinks, and Rory explained that I would have to scrub, and that one of the nurses would help me. It was amusing to do the hand washing thing like Dr. Ben Casey on TV, and to put on the gown and cap and mask. The nurse was a real jokester, and I was feeling lighthearted for the first time in weeks when we went into the operating room.

Then I saw the patient. He was a man of enormous girth, with more body hair than I had ever imagined it would be possible for a human being to have. He was lying on his back, breathing heavily and making soft, agonized noises. There was something very ugly about his left arm. I tried not to look too closely. Rory introduced me to the other people in the room as "the distinguished Dr. Akstens" and everyone had a good laugh as the anesthesiologist put the guy under. Then one of the nurses tilted the patient's head back and put a tube down his throat and a mask over his face. I felt faint for the first time in my life. Rory was watching me closely. His eyes were very serious over the edge of his mask. "Easy now, hang in there," Rory said. "Here's where I need you." He maneuvered the guy's arm so that his wrist was in the air. "Just hold this for a minute or two. Just like that. Still."

I took the patient's wrist and held it as Rory had instructed. I tried to focus my attention on the second hand as it moved around the clock on the wall. But I could feel the patient's pulse against my little finger. And I could feel it when Rory moved the bones in his arm. At one point I could actually hear something move. I felt really wobbly. "Just twenty seconds more, doing great," Rory urged. Moments later, he reached over and took the wrist from me. "All done. Go splash some cold water on your face. You'll feel better. I have to get some plaster on this guy."

When Rory came into the locker room, one of the nurses had my head between my knees and was rubbing the back of my neck. I still felt queasy. "Look," he said, and his voice got husky. "I'm sorry about your dad."

"I know," I said. "I told him I got fellowship offers from Penn, Princeton and Vanderbilt. I told him he didn't need to worry, that I would be alright. I think he heard me, but I'm not sure."

"He heard you," Rory assured me. "People in his condition hear things, but they just can't respond." Then he cleared his throat. We looked at each other for a long moment. A joke seemed like the best way out of the situation. Rory quipped, "Anyway, it's a damned good thing you weren't pre-med."

In the seventh grade, I wanted to be a goalie. That lasted two days. The pucks flew past me as I fumbled with the big gloves and the oversized stick. The hockey coach sat me down for some advice: "You're a head taller than anyone else. My advice is to try basketball." In other words: *Kid, you stink at hockey*.

So I became a basketball player. As the coaches say, "You can't teach height," and height was what I had—if not an abundance of talent. Nevertheless, by the time I was a high school junior, I could rebound pretty well, play some gritty defense and hit a few shots. I began to think I might have a chance to play college basketball. The problem was, I didn't play that much in high school. Our team, St. Sebastian's, was a powerhouse. We won the New England Prep School Championship. In one game we held the defending Boston public school champions to fourteen points. For their entire team. For the entire game.

I was the understudy for my friend Grady, a dominating rebounder who went on to play for the Atlanta Hawks in the NBA. Our first team would methodically dismantle our opponents, and then I would lead the shock troops off the bench in the second half and score six or eight meaningless points. We often won by thirty; in reality, our second team could have beaten most of our opponents handily. We were also a pretty brainy bunch: four Ph.D.s, four law degrees and an MBA or two.

My only basketball trophy. One point saved me from total obscurity.

I thought the way to get some game experience was to go to a summer basketball camp. Bob Cousy's camp had a reputation as the most competitive, so I went for a week. We scrimmaged the first day, and then the coaches posted their rosters. There was an elite A league, with a lot of players who had been invited to camp to be scouted by college coaches; my name was on a team in the B league. But I was determined to test myself against the best competition.

I walked across the grass from the bulletin board to the counselor's cabin where Cousy had his office. He was seated at his desk, looking at the same sheet of rosters. I knocked politely on the screen door and walked in. "Excuse me, Mr. Cousy. If you have a moment, I'd like to talk with you about my roster assignment."

I felt a bit like Oliver Twist asking for another bowl of porridge. Cousy was clearly amazed that one of the campers would have the temerity to knock on his door and question the judgment of the coaching staff. But he was patient enough. He explained that he had watched me, and that I had potential but didn't have enough quickness and didn't seem to get into the flow of the game. He said I could develop more by playing against the B league competition.

"Excuse me, Mr. Cousy, but I hope to play college basketball and I want to play against the best."

By now he was less patient. He asked where I intended to play. I told him Holy Cross, where he himself had been a Hall of Fame player. "Look," he explained, "I have to tell you that you won't play basketball at Holy Cross. Maybe at Middlebury or someplace. But not for a nationally ranked team. But, if you want, let's put you in the A league anyway and see how you do."

As it turned out, I did pretty well. One of the star players at the camp was Bob Whitmore, a six-foot-seven forward from DeMatha, the high school team that broke the seventy-one-game winning streak of Lew Alcindor's Power Memorial team. Whitmore was graceful, fluid, talented—but not very aggressive. I had noticed that the referees in the camp were forgiving; I suppose they wanted to give high school players a taste of the much more physical college game. In two games against Whitmore, I grappled and hacked my way to something approaching a standoff. My strategy attracted the favorable attention of "Jungle Jim" Loscutoff, the Celtics' enforcer, who was scouting prospects at the camp for some college coaches. He took me aside and told me I was playing his kind of basketball.

That same summer, five of us would pile into my teammate Danny's father's silver Buick Riviera and find pickup games in Roxbury and Jamaica Plain. The winning five got to hold the court and keep playing; the losers went to the end of the line. The competition was fierce, but fair. Some nights we were the only White kids on the court, but that didn't seem to matter to anyone. The only thing that mattered was holding the court, which we managed to do from time to time. One night, Danny came over to us between games with a huge grin on his face. One of the local pimps wanted to buy his father's car.

Those experiences, and another year of battling Grady in practice, made me more confident about making a college team. I was still set on Holy Cross, but Harvard had also come into the picture. I discussed the options with my parents and explained to them that I would go to Holy Cross, because everyone knew that Harvard had a "rinky-dink" basketball team.

In those days, college freshmen weren't eligible for the varsity, so I gained another year of valuable game experience on the freshman squad. We also scrimmaged the varsity regularly and I got to face big, strong, skilled players in a game that seemed to move at twice the speed of high school. My roommate, Obie, had been an All-State guard in high school. He was a great passer—a master of the pick-and-roll play. In one game against the University of Connecticut, everything suddenly fell into place. UConn's star center, Bill Corley, seemed bewildered. I would set a pick for Obie, Corley would switch off to cover him and Obie would hit me with a nifty pass as I cut to the basket. We ran the play over and over; Corley got frustrated and started to foul. The UConn coach sat him down for a stern talking-to. We won, and I scored in double figures for the first time in a college game. Corley and I faced off again the following season at the Worcester Auditorium, during an epic brawl that cleared both benches. Our personal donnybrook was limited to some shoving and cussing, but it was clear he hadn't forgotten.

A few nights later, we played Providence. Obie and I ran our play again and again. At one point, Obie fed me as I popped out to the corner and I hit a turnaround jump shot. It felt sweet. I was finally "in the flow of the game" as Cousy had said, and my confidence was brimming.

Our next game was at Boston College. Bob Cousy himself was their new coach. He had used his status as "Mister Basketball" to recruit what sportswriters said was the greatest freshman squad of all time. Anticipation was high, and the stands were full. I knew some of Cousy's players from my second stay at his basketball camp, in particular Jimmy Kissane, a smooth six-foot-eight scorer from Chaminade High School in New York. Like Whitmore, he was athletic and skilled. But he was also hard-nosed and strong. When I faced Kissane at camp, he had given my clock a thorough cleaning. I entered the game about midway through the first half and, inexplicably, everything bounced my way. I worked the pick and roll with Obie twice before Kissane caught on. I got a cheap basket on a BC turnover. I filled the lane on a fast break and tipped in a missed shot. I felt like I was flying. Kissane went up for a rebound and I went over his back and took it away. The BC crowd screamed for a foul but the whistle never came. I kicked it out quickly on the right side to my teammate Keith, who banked home a short jumper. Halftime. Somehow, we were ahead. The crowd that had turned out to see Cousy's wonder team crush us like bugs had developed an affinity for the underdogs. They cheered us enthusiastically as we headed for the locker room. Waiting at the tunnel, I found myself standing next to Cousy. I couldn't resist. "Hello, Mr. Cousy," I said. "Do you remember me?" He just stared.

Our coach, Bob Curran, had been a teammate of Cousy's and a starter on the 1947 Holy Cross team that won the NCAA basketball championship in one of the more remarkable upsets in college basketball history. He was a former marine with combat experience in the South Pacific. He'd been around the track, and he commanded respect. He let us have a minute or two in the locker room to congratulate ourselves. We were munching on orange quarters when he made his entrance. "You don't get any oranges," he snapped as he grabbed the orange from my hand and threw it in the trash. "You don't deserve any oranges. What the hell are you doing, standing around out there while Kissane reads you his press clippings?" *Huh?* I had just played the best ten minutes of my life (and the best I would ever play, as things turned out). But Curran knew the score at halftime didn't mean much. "I'd rather you were behind." He said. "You're too satisfied with yourselves. You're complacent. They're not. Now they've got something to prove. Be ready." BC came out blazing. They won handily.

At the end of freshman year, I tore my ACL. In those days, there was no surgery to repair the injury. I was in a cast for eight weeks. I rehabbed for two months. I played with a heavy brace, iced my knee daily and had it drained several times during my sophomore season. I had lost at least six inches off my vertical leap and half a dozen strides down the floor. I was

---

TOM AKSTENS

Center—Sophomore   19   6'7"   218 lbs.   Newton, Mass.

Akstens has the height that the Crusaders lack, but he is hampered by a lack of experience as the season opens. He played well on the freshman team last Winter, with particularly commendable performances against the Providence and the University of Connecticut Freshmen. He will be slated for reserve duty, with the hope that he'll be able to help the team more as the season progresses.

The lanky sophomore played basketball for three years at St. Sebastian's and also was a member of the golf team. He is majoring in English and hopes for a career in law.

Question: Whatever happened to that career in law? Answer: I read *King Lear*.

---

lucky to even make the varsity. Then I lost three weeks to pneumonia. I was hanging by a thread, but at least I had a purple uniform with number 40 on it when the season started.

Our first home game was against Harvard, the team I had derided as "rinky-dink" when I was a high school senior. We were heavily favored. The Worcester Auditorium was jammed to the rafters for our first game of the season. The band played the rousing Holy Cross fight song. We threw down thunderdunks in warmups. The home crowd roared, egged on by the cheerleaders. Then the rinky-dinks from Harvard methodically kicked our ass. I watched the proceedings from the bench. After the game, my father wrote me a letter, telling me how proud he was just to see me a member of the team:

My teammate Wee, mixing it up against Harvard

> Dear Tom: Many years ago when I put on my rented tuxedo and prepared to go up the hill to Holy Cross to my first varsity debate, I came out of the bedroom and asked my old, ailing father how I looked. He was quite speechless, but through a tearful and admiring eye he simply nodded and wished me good luck. I never knew how the old man felt until Saturday night, when you bounced out onto the court with the rest of the varsity. Then the full impact of that moment came home to me. It was a feeling that has to be experienced to be appreciated. All my love and good wishes, Dad

He was not a man who expressed affection easily, and the letter touched me to the heart.

Very early in the season, I had brief stints against Mike Silliman from Army and Dave "Shorty" Newmark from Columbia, both NBA prospects. In the Columbia game, I got caught in the open court on defense against Jim McMillan, an offensive dynamo who would go on to star with the Los Angeles Lakers; he blew by me on his way to the hoop as if my sneakers had been glued to the court. Still, I was pleased that Silliman and Newmark hadn't completely mopped the floor with me. At one point, I even faked the seven-foot Newmark up in the air and hit a little hook shot.

But it was clear that my knee was hampering me, and I couldn't really keep up with the pace of the game anymore. I managed a decent showing against Boston University, when our bench had been thinned out by a flu bug, but the rest of my appearances were in the last few minutes of games that had already been decided. During one of these forays, it only took me a minute or so to lose my man on defense, throw an errant pass and commit a stupid foul that gave our opponent a chance to get back into the game. I was unceremoniously yanked. As I made the long walk from the far end of the floor to our bench, a loud, boozy voice rang out from the balcony: "Hey, number forty! YOU STINK!!!" My parents were sitting a few rows up from our bench. When she heard the heckler, my mother burst into tears.

Gradually, I disappeared to the end of the bench, next to the stack of towels and the water cooler. But I still enjoyed the run. The soundtrack for the season seemed to be a record my teammate Monk played to get us up for games: Jimmy Reed's "I'm Goin' to New York."

Fordham had a live ram for a mascot. The ram was housed in a little cart. During timeouts, the cheerleaders would roll the ram around the perimeter of the arena, the band would strike up and the home crowd would sing some sort of Fordham fight song. I couldn't figure out why the cart was parked next to the end of our bench—which meant next to me. At some point in the second half, it became clear. The ram expressed his opinion of our team, in the form a very large bowel movement. The crowd had evidently been anticipating this event for the entire game and went completely insane.

We traveled sometimes by train in a Pullman car. We each had a tiny little room with a fold-down bed and little stainless-steel sink. On other trips, we flew in DC-7 propeller planes. We took long bus rides in the middle of the night. We slept in featherbeds in the Hanover Inn at Dartmouth, where we had breakfast with white linen and fresh flowers on the table (I kept my appreciation of those lovely details to myself). We stayed in hotels in New York and ordered room service. We played in Madison Square Garden (the old one, at 49th and Eighth, with the *very* forgiving rims). We beat St. John's on their home court in New York when they were ranked sixth nationally, and a thousand people and the marching band met our bus back at Holy Cross for a spontaneous rally and epic snowball fight at three in the morning. For a second-string prep school player, it was an adventure.

My roommate on the road was "Big Don," an amiable six-foot-nine Swede. When we checked into a hotel, Don would immediately put a framed picture of his girlfriend back home in Minnesota on his nightstand. He would gaze at her picture as he wrote her a very long love letter. Every night. In my sardonic young imagination, my secret code name for her was "Brunhilde." In my mind, he was code-named "Siegfried." Perhaps the next time they embraced in Mankato or wherever, Don would give her the Ring of the Nibelungs for their engagement. Don wasn't much of a player, but he was a great roommate. He was so absorbed in his amorous correspondence that he required no attention and barely ever said a word. He would just fixate on the image of his beloved and "scribble, scribble, scribble," as the Duke of Gloucester said of Edward Gibbon.

This left me free to step out on the town with a few of the other stalwarts from the end of the bench. Our ringleader was Horace, an excellent player whose insubordinate streak caused his periodic exile to the vicinity of the water cooler and towels. When we were in New York, he'd take us to Greenwich Village bars where the tapsters greeted him by name. When we played a tournament in Buffalo, he and Monk led us across the square from our morning shoot-around at the Civic Center to the early matinee at the Palace, one of the last of the classic burlesque houses. The Palace had a real pit band, and they were pretty good—a few jazz types earning some extra bucks playing a day gig. The headliner of the show was "Chantelle Capri, the Frisco Earthquake." Her act was only mildly risqué, but Chantelle herself was strikingly tall and rangy—a dynamo, strutting and gliding around the stage like a very good athlete in sequins, feathers and impossibly high heels.

When her act was done I was eager to get back to the hotel, concerned that I would be called upon to explain my whereabouts for the past two hours. I had already drawn suspicion from an assistant coach for my transgressions, such as wearing a pink button-down shirt with a bow tie on the team bus and spending time in bookstores on road trips. But Monk was unfazed. "I'm going backstage to make the acquaintance of Miss Capri and invite her to the game," he announced. *Invite her to the game?* This was madness. We waited to see what would happen. Finally, Monk emerged, ushering Miss Capri herself toward our group. She held out a gloved hand as he introduced us one by one. She expressed her regrets that she would not be able to attend our game that night, since she had three shows to do. She wished us the best of luck. She bent forward on her towering heels and gave Obie a little smooch on the forehead.

When we had a Saturday night home game, we'd have a light practice on Sunday afternoon and be free for the evening. Keith and I took to having Sunday dinner at a local Italian joint in Worcester called the Black Orchid. The owner seemed to really like us. The arm around the shoulder, the big smile. "Steak pizzaiola for everyone, guys? And a nice bottle of Chianti? Everything on the house for my favorite basketball team!" While we ate, he'd ask us questions about the game the night before: "And by the way, Keith, how's that ankle feeling? Gonna be a hunnert percent for Wednesday night?" *This guy's a real fan,* I thought.

Then one Saturday, Keith, who was our dominant player, missed four free throws toward the end of a game against some weak team like Dartmouth. It didn't seem to matter—we won by a few points anyway. When we went to the Orchid the next night, we got a very different reception than the one to which we had become accustomed. "Hey, you bums. No more free ride, yunnerstand? Can't even make a fuckin' free throw. Can't even make the fuckin' spread!" Like a bolt from the blue, it dawned on me: *Wait a minute, these guys aren't our friends! They're gamblers!* A lawyer friend of my father with strong Worcester connections told me later that the Black Orchid was a Mafia bank for central New England: "Ever notice all those locks on the freezers when you look past the bar into the kitchen? Those aren't to safeguard the lamb chops. On any given night, there's a million bucks in those freezers. What they call cold cash. Very cold."

The season ended badly—and my basketball career with it. Before one of our last practices, one of my teammates and a friend of his came into the locker room and stuffed several of last year's warm-up jackets into a duffel. The other guy dashed out the door with the duffel. My teammate said, "You didn't see that." The next day, the other guy was caught with the loot in his car. I knew that my teammate had a serious problem with theft. On one of our New York trips, he and I had gone into Brooks Brothers. He came back to the hotel wearing two pairs of pants and two sport coats under a trench coat that still had the price tag on the sleeve. The irony was that he was from a private school in one of the wealthiest suburbs of Chicago and always had plenty of cash to toss around in restaurants and bars. He did it for the thrill. I had chosen to look the other way then, and I did so again. That was wrong, and I knew it. At the time, Holy Cross professed the same honor code as West Point; if you were aware of cheating or stealing and didn't report it, you were complicit.

Two days later, I was called into the coach's office. Without any histrionics, he asked me to explain my actions. I simply said, "I have no excuse. I didn't do what was my responsibility to do. I regret that." He told me that he hoped I would understand that he would have to suspend me for the last game of the season, a contest against Boston College in Boston Garden. He also said that he had been disappointed in my performance during the season, and that I needed to be aware that two high school All-Americans from the freshman team, Ron Teixeira and Ed Siudut, would be in the front court for the varsity the next season. That didn't leave room for me. I simply told him that I understood. I went to the pay phone in the hallway and had a very difficult conversation with my parents. I told them how ashamed I was and that I knew I had let them down. It would be years before I could read that letter my father had written about how proud he had been to see me in my uniform.

My parents and I listened to that last game on the radio. It was close for a while, but BC pulled away in the last few minutes. I was stung by the thought that the disruption I had caused the team might have made victory that much more difficult. Although he didn't see any action, my teammate, who had orchestrated the theft, was suited up and on the bench for the game. That really hurt.

I had been hoping for some sort of redemption from the whole fiasco. One evening that spring, my parents and I went to the Landfall, their favorite dinner spot in Woods Hole. The place had a nice water view and a savory fisherman's stew that was served with superb Portuguese bread from Jean's Bakery in Teaticket. We were working on blueberry cobbler when I heard a young voice from the table next to ours: "Hey, Dad! That guy plays for the Cross!" *Not anymore*, I thought to myself. Then I heard the boy's father explain that yes, he could go up and ask me for an autograph, but that he would have to wait until we had finished our dessert.

When I was about twelve, my father and I had been having dinner at the Union Oyster House before a Celtics game when I saw Bob Cousy and Tom Heinsohn at a table across the room. I had asked the same autograph question that the kid next to us just had, and my father had also told me that I would have to be polite and wait. I wondered if he remembered, too. I looked at him and he just smiled. Then the boy came over with a menu. Father handed me a pen to sign it and as I did, he reached over and rested his hand on my shoulder.

30
A Whiter Shade of Pale

It was snowing hard as I walked back toward the dorm from the Dinand library at Holy Cross. I turned my collar up and pulled my watch cap lower. Three girls in a burgundy Mustang convertible with Connecticut plates pulled up beside me. The driver rolled down the window and explained that she was looking for her boyfriend. She mentioned a name. Did I know him?

"Sorry, I don't." I said. "Can't help."

"We were supposed to meet him. But he's not here. We drove from Cambridge in the snow. My asshole boyfriend." She was pissed. The other two other girls in the car were laughing, teasing: "You mean your asshole ex-boyfriend."

"Look, if you're going back to Cambridge tonight, I could use a ride," I ventured. "There's a friend I'd like to visit."

A voice from the back seat called out, with some sarcasm: "An adventure!"

I hustled back to the dorm, threw some things in a bag and grabbed a half-empty pint of Drambuie. When I got back to the car, one of the other girls was behind the wheel. I gave her a piece of paper with the address of my friend's apartment. She knew where it was. I opened the door and the girl in the passenger's seat said, "Hop in back." Squeezing my six-foot-six self into the back seat of a Mustang convertible was a trick that caused quite a bit of mirth.

When I finally got my head inside, the girl who had been looking for her boyfriend was waiting. She smiled at me. "Hi. I'm Claire. But you can call me Claire." I thought that was pretty funny, and I told her so.

Now, a Mustang convertible is not my vehicle of choice in a snow-storm. We skidded down College Hill and slipped and slid our way toward the Mass Pike. The heater was blasting, the little back seat was chummy, the Drambuie was making the rounds, and the radio was playing Creedence and the Kinks. Things were pretty cozy.

When one of the greatest slow-dance songs, "A Whiter Shade of Pale," came over the radio, Claire looked at me intensely. Her eyes were dark and luminous. "I love this song," she whispered. We smiled and started to do the kinds of things young people have been doing in the back seat of Mustang convertibles since the first Pony Car rolled out of Detroit.

Suddenly, the song was over, and the mood shifted.

Claire tensed. "My boyfriend wouldn't like this," she declared.

For once in my life, I didn't miss a beat: "I guess that's why I'm here with you instead of him."

31
Rugby

My friend from the rugby club pulled up in his VW as I was coming out of the Campus Center. "I've been looking for you. We need a tall guy to be our jumper," he said. "Can you come up to the pitch at four today to try out?"

"Jumper? Pitch?" I told him I didn't know anything about rugby except that you drank beer and sang rude songs after the games.

"Not 'games.' Matches," he corrected. "On line-outs, you jump up and make sure we have possession of the ball. Hence 'jumper.' It's like an out-of-bounds play in basketball. Then we'll show you where to be in the scrum. Rucking and mauling can come later."

"Rucking? Mauling?"

"See you at four at the pitch!" He didn't give me a chance to answer before he cranked up his window and sped down the drive.

So I showed up as directed and became a poor facsimile of a rugby player. Before we got started, I reminded him that I had a torn ACL, wore a cumbersome knee brace and wasn't much of a "jumper" anymore. In fact, I really shouldn't be playing rugby at all.

"No worries about that," he declared. "You're tall, and there's a guy on either side of you to kind of boost you up. Besides, everyone plays hurt in rugby. It's part of the ethos."

I didn't like the idea of winding up a cripple, but I was warming up to the notion of playing a sport that actually had an ethos.

At practice, my new teammates gave me the lowdown on the line-out play and the scrum. Finally, I asked the obvious question: "So why do you need me in such a hurry?"

"The last jumper got hurt. He's out for the rest of the year."

"What happened?"

"Torn ACL."

I don't remember much about the first two matches, one of which was against a rugby club from Boston that had some huge guys who had played college football and grimly beat the hell out of our A team. Fortunately, I was hidden away on the B team, matched against competition of more human dimensions.

I was a lousy player and knew there wasn't much chance that I would make the A team, unless the A team jumper got injured (say, with a torn ACL?). But I also knew that our Holy Cross A team went to Bermuda every spring to play in a rugby tournament against Notre Dame, Dartmouth,

Navy and the like. As remote as it might be, the prospect of a week in Bermuda was incentive to stick with this violent and most remorselessly macho of sports.

Then came the match at Wesleyan. The pitch was a morass of barely frozen mud, covered with a thin crust of ice. A squally wind ripped across the field. The sullen clouds looked as if they'd floated out of a painting by Constable. They spat sleet at us as we tried to warm up for the contest, but the very idea of "warming up" on such a day was ridiculous. The sleet intensified as the match started. Every step I took broke through a crust of ice into two or three inches of muddy slush. I was pounded into the mud over and over as I tried to "maul." I was the one getting mauled—and soaked with frozen mud. While all this was going on, a crazed Britisher in a Beatles mop-top haircut and a Harry Potter sort of scarf was slogging up and down the sideline yelling "Go Wes! Go Wes!" a thousand times.

That afternoon was the coldest I have ever been in my life. I lost all sensation in my hands and feet. My face was burning from the sleet. At the end of it all, our Wesleyan hosts told us they were very sorry but there were no hot showers. When it came time to drink beer and sing rude songs, I was shivering too violently to do either. All I wanted to do was curl up in a blanket and get into a car with a cranking heater.

Still deluded by visions of Bermuda in springtime, I stuck with rugby for another week. Our next match was against a club team from the Harvard Business School. The weather had turned unseasonably lovely and we went to Cambridge in high spirits. During warmups, I noticed that several players for Harvard seemed highly skilled and very athletic. "What's the deal with those guys?" I asked my friend.

His mood had darkened. "We're screwed," he replied. "Those guys are Kiwis. University and club players from New Zealand. The best anywhere."

There were no New Zealanders in the B game, but I got pummeled, regardless. At one point I reverted to my high school football days and tried a low tackle on a Harvard player who was rambling down the sideline. I missed him, but he tromped on my forearm anyway as he headed for the goal line.

The A game was frightening. The New Zealanders played with harrowing ferocity. They roared up and down the pitch, scoring try after try. They rucked and mauled with a vengeance and generally drubbed our guys into submission. Near the end of the lopsided match, one of the Kiwis scored a drop kick of about thirty yards while running in full stride. I think he was just showing off.

After the match, we all limped off to some basement room with stackable plastic chairs to drink beer and sing rude songs. But my heart wasn't in it. My visions of lollygagging on the white sand beaches of Bermuda between tournament matches dissolved, and I said my goodbyes to the hairy manliness and forced camaraderie of rugby. As I made my way down the corridor toward my car, one of the stupid songs droned on, a ditty that asked the musical question, "Do your balls hang low?" I just couldn't relate.

32
Concerts I

Bobby Darin (1958)

When I was eleven, my favorite record was "Splish Splash" by Bobby Darin. The song was bouncy, funny and had a life-is-a party message that appealed to me, a kid who was just beginning to wonder what life was about, anyway. I had the 45, and I played it relentlessly.

My parents attended a lot of charity functions. In 1958, one of these was at Blinstrub's Village, a large nightclub in South Boston. Looking now on the internet at old advertising, I find that Blinstrub's billed itself as "the most magnificent place of rendezvous in New England" and "a proper place for nice, congenial people." It all sounds a little seedy now, but I guess most people in those days thought it was pretty swanky. The headliner for this particular function was my favorite, Bobby Darin. It was an adult event, but my parents always treated me like a small adult anyway and they asked me if I would like to go with them.

As a well-trained small adult, I would have said yes in any case, but the idea that Bobby Darin would actually be there and would actually sing "Splish Splash" sent me into a tizzy. It would help the story if I said I couldn't eat or sleep. But, as I always did, I actually slept like a log and ate like a horse. Still, I was excited and played the record over and over to the point of mania.

The big night came and off we went. On the way, we stopped to pick up a Filipino client of my father's and his wife and daughter. Wikki, as he was known, was Ferdinand Marcos' physician. Marcos was not yet president of the Philippines, but for all I know, Wikki may have been a kleptocrat like his notorious patient, since my father defended him in law-suits concerning his business interests in America. Father must have been successful, since Wikki often picked up the tab at ritzy Boston restaurants like Joseph's and Locke-Ober. He also sent my father weird gifts, like a wooden effigy of a water buffalo with the word "attorney" carved into its flank, and a nutcracker in the shape of a lady who cracked the nut between her thighs. Mother was not amused by the latter.

When we got to Blinstrub's, I was dismayed to realize that I had been paired off with Wikki's daughter, Amor ("Lovey"), a pretty sylph who was half my size. I was in the "Girls are creepy" stage—read "Girls scare me to death." I was supposed to dance with her, which I did, grudgingly. Some-where there may still be a photo taken by the nightclub photographer—me shuffling around with a Filipino girl who came up to my solar plexus. Then there was a big, fancy dinner, and French champagne in a silver bucket— which seemed to liven up the proceedings for the adults. Lovey and I were each allowed a sip.

Then the lights went down, a band started to play, and there he actually was: Bobby Darin, dancing around in a spotlight, gesturing, singing. He did sing "Splish Splash" and "Queen of the Hop." I don't remember the rest of it. At the end, everyone stood up and clapped and cheered. And then it was over and we went home. In bed that night, I wondered if it all had really happened.

Flatt and Scruggs (1962)

When I was a sophomore in high school I went completely buggy over bluegrass. In his characteristically methodical way, my friend Neil made a list of ten records I ought to buy. Number one: *Flatt and Scruggs at Carnegie Hall*. Number two: *The Stanley Brothers and the Clinch Mountain Boys*. Number three: *Bill Monroe Bluegrass Ramble*, and so forth. I made a pilgrimage to Briggs & Briggs in Harvard Square and bought the first three on the list. Over the next year, I played those records until they turned gray. The Flatt and Scruggs record was my favorite. It was more than a bunch of songs. It captured the excitement and fun of the event, and the band's laconic interaction with the audience.

When Neil and I found out that Flatt and Scruggs would be playing at Jordan Hall in Boston, we resolved to go. The show was everything I had hoped it would be. Lester crooned some of my favorite songs, like "Footprints in the Snow" and "Jimmy Brown the Newsboy." Earl brought the house down with "Foggy Mountain Breakdown," trading breaks with "Fiddlin' Chubby" Wise. There was plenty of cornball humor, including the theme song from their old radio show, a jingle celebrating the virtues of Martha White Self-Risin' Flour. I was fascinated by "Uncle Josh" Graves, who played the "hound dog" dobro guitar and cracked dopey jokes with Lester. But there was an extra person on the stage. Like the rest of the band, he had a cowboy hat and one of those Kentucky Colonel–style bow ties. He stood slightly off to the side and played along on the guitar. *Who was this guy?*

Neil, who seemed to know everything about bluegrass and country music, had the answer. He was Johnny Johnson, the bus driver for the band. *You mean he actually gets to be on stage with Flatt and Scruggs and play along?* Evidently, Neil assured me, and added that the fellow was a pretty competent guitar player. I think he even sang the chorus on the gospel song with which they closed the show.

Every encounter with adults when I was in high school seemed to end with the same question: Do you want to be a doctor or a lawyer? The question annoyed me no end. The concert at Jordan Hall gave me a novel answer. I'd say, "Actually, I'd like to be Flatt and Scruggs' bus driver."

Martha and the Vandellas (1966)

The Supremes played Holy Cross the fall of my freshman year. It was a big social weekend, and everyone I knew and their dates were carried away with the glamour and velvety purring of Diana Ross, the captivating choreography and the lush orchestrations that accompanied the group. To me, their performance was great show biz, but not very interesting music. I mean, *where was the groove?*

I kept telling everyone that I wished the concert had been Martha and the Vandellas, instead. The reaction to this idea was hardly cordial: *Martha and the whats?* How could a group have a lead singer named Martha? Somebody scoffingly said they had a great-aunt in Rutland named Martha.

So I retreated into my world of blues and funk with my musical ally, Barry. Barry had a splendid old Gibson J-200 guitar and a stack of albums that he'd hauled with him from Saint Louis. We'd get together to play guitars and listen to *James Brown Live at the Apollo* and some wonderful Reverend Gary Davis records. We were freaking out over Brown's "Cold Sweat" and Gary Davis' "If I Had My Way," a song about Samson and Delilah ("So the bees made honey in that lion's head"). No wonder we were pretty blasé about a bit of fluff like the Supremes' "Baby Love."

As it turned out, Martha and the Vandellas were booked at the college the next year. Their show was everything that the swoony, polished Supremes hadn't been. The band locked into the backbeat of every song until it popped. Martha sang with raw, gritty power. The Vandellas added wailing harmonies and attempted choreography that sometimes devolved with a laugh into dance steps like the Swim and the Frug. Martha careened through her hits, including "Quicksand," "Heat Wave" and "Nowhere to Run," with its merciless groove and its challenging lyrics, sung from the point of view of a woman trapped in erotic obsession:

> I know you're no good for me,
> But free from you, I'll never be

Of course, she ended with a long rendition of "Dancin' in the Streets," the ultimate party anthem—and along with Little Eva's "The Locomotion," Fontella Bass' "Rescue Me" and Aretha's "Chain of Fools" among the most danceable of the Motown classics. These ladies laid down some serious soul. If you could stand in front of that stage for ten seconds and not move your ass, something was seriously wrong with you.

The Doors (1967)

In the 1960s, Harvard Square was still a brainy, creative mecca for the individual spirit. Before the corporate tentacles of the Gap and Starbucks moved in and strangled the place, the Square was alive with bookstores, coffeehouses, sandal shops, bike shops, camera shops, ethnic eateries and wandering eccentrics. My girlfriend at the time and I loved to roam the Square. We'd rummage through the poetry books at the Grolier, order a roast beef special with double Russian dressing from Elsie's and eat it on a bench by the river, then grab a schooner of beer at Cronin's. One August afternoon we were in a booth at Cronin's, looking through *Boston After Dark* for something to do. *Maybe there was a Bogey film at the Brattle Theater? Who was playing at the 47?* Then I saw a small ad: "The Doors. One Night Only. Hampton Beach Casino." The show was that night.

I had seen the first Doors album in the window of Briggs & Briggs that January. I was intrigued by the dramatic cover and bought the record on impulse. I thought—and still do—that "Break on Through" was the greatest opening cut I had ever heard on any album. The weird guitar and organ sounds and deep echo on the album mesmerized me as one insistent, insinuating song followed another: "Soul Kitchen." "Light My Fire." "The End." Nothing in rock had excited me so much since I had first heard "Satisfaction," driving my VW at midnight on the Mid-Cape Highway with my sunroof open to the full moon.

The Hampton Beach Casino was a dump. In the '40s it had been a dance hall on the big band circuit. Now it was a sorry derelict on the boardwalk, marooned among the threadbare arcades, T-shirt shops and hot dog stands. One side of the room was set up with a stage, with the kind of cheesy lighting you'd expect to see at a high school dance. In the style of the day, the show was a "dance concert"—just an open floor. No seats. There might have been five hundred people in a hall that could have easily held a thousand.

The Doors—without Jim Morrison—took the stage and started to play the restless, tribal riff that begins "Back Door Man." They played it for a long time. People were looking at one another, looking around, waiting for something to happen. The riff went on. Some wiseass yelled, "Vamp until ready, guys!"

Suddenly, there was a disturbance behind us. I turned. Someone was pushing through the crowd. A voice called out, "Hey! Fuck you, man!" The pushing intensified. More angry voices. Anxious laughter. The riff went on.

Then the person who had been pushing and shoving broke free of the crowd. He catapulted himself onto the stage. It was Morrison. The crowd was stunned. The riff went on. Morrison started to pull violently at the zippers of his motorcycle jacket. His torso was naked. He ripped the jacket off and started to beat the stage with it in time with the riff. I could sense a coming explosion. He grabbed the microphone and let out a guttural howl.

I have never heard anything like it in a concert, before or since. The audience went off like a bomb—one percussive roar. Morrison responded with another howl. Then the song began.

I wish I did, but I don't remember much about the rest of the concert. I do remember standing on the darkened boardwalk, looking out at the midnight ocean and knowing I had been present for something extraordinary.

Janis Joplin (1968)

I've read endless jabber about Dylan "going electric" at Newport in 1965. People have written all sorts of nonsense, including a story that Pete Seeger grabbed an axe and tried to cut the sound cables. There are two flaws to that story. Why would there be a handy axe backstage at Newport? Why didn't Pete succeed? If you were determined to cut some XLR cables with an axe, it would take maybe nine seconds. Either the axe was dull or Pete hadn't had his Wheaties that morning. Or it didn't happen.

I was there. I got my seat early because the Paul Butterfield Blues Band was scheduled to open that concert. The sound system was horrible, and it got even worse later, when Dylan came on. Even before Dylan had played a note, some jerk a few rows away was standing on his chair, screaming "Judas!" People were yelling at him to shut the fuck up. My only real interest in the proceedings was to see Mike Bloomfield, the guitarist from Butterfield's band, who was sitting in. Dylan's set went on for about a half hour before he sent the band packing and came back with his acoustic guitar after a lot of fussing. No more Bloomfield. I got bored. I never had much interest in Dylan in the first place. Only a crank would deny that "Blowin' in the Wind," "A Hard Rain's a-Gonna Fall" and "Like a Rolling Stone" are songs of vision and power. But, in the end, Dylan's sanctimony turned me off. If his appearance at Newport with a Stratocaster in his hands was the death of folk music, it died with a whimper.

I think it was Janis who drove the real stake into the heart of folk music, three years later, at the same festival. And she did it gleefully. Her get-up for her evening concert was a calculated affront to every hippie girl at Newport. She pranced the stage wearing a ton of jewelry, a decolleté black cocktail dress and black lace stockings and heels. She shook her maracas, she shook her hair and she shook her ass. She was trying to emulate her heroes, the great blues shouters of the twenties like Ma Rainey, but to update the idiom. In reality, most of the folkies in 1968 could barely cope with the original Ma Rainey. After all, Ma had recorded with Louis Armstrong, and he had played the *trumpet,* that most un-folk-like of instruments.

The problem with Janis was her absurdly self-indulgent band, Big Brother and the Holding Company. I think the fatal blow to folk music was Big Brother's Newport rendition of "The Coo Coo," originally a poignant lament recorded in a modal banjo tuning by Clarence Ashley in the 1920s. On her recorded version of the song, Janis sings the lead. The whole thing is frantic and misguided, but at least Janis sings honestly, from the gut. At the festival Sam Andrew, the guitar player, took the lead vocal for the first half of the song. It may be the most irritating music I have ever heard in my life. At the very least, he took a lovely piece of Americana and defiled it. What had been folk music had finally become an unlistenable bunch of noise. It was over.

33
Orthodoxy

My former teammate Keith and I had spent the afternoon at the RISD Museum in Providence and were having dinner at Siena, a very good restaurant on Federal Hill. We hadn't seen each other for several years and we had a lot of catching up to do. We had a great table for conversation and were making the most of it.

He told me all about clamming and beekeeping on the Cape, and I told him about exploring the coves and backwaters of Narragansett Bay. We joked that while he might have thrown in forty points against Syracuse, I put up a "pretty respectable" four against BU. Hey, we can't all be scorers. We joked that while I generally seemed to get an A in Shakespeare or Chaucer, he would sometimes settle for a "pretty respectable" B. What, were there only so many A grades in the world? "They also serve who only stand and wait," as Milton wrote.

I suggested we compare notes about what we had learned from sports. That turned out to be easy. We both had the same answer: How to lose, how to learn from losing and how to go on.

Keith had a more engaging question: "So is there one particular moment that you remember from college that changed you, that challenged your way of thinking?"

I had my answer in an instant. I asked him if he had a moment in mind when he asked the question. He did. "I asked the question. You go first," he insisted.

I told him I had been profoundly affected by something one of my philosophy professors had said in a class on the Hegelian dialectic: "It is the responsibility of every thinking person to challenge orthodoxy. *Start with your own.*" The brazen intellectual and moral courage of that statement inspired me at that moment and it still does, even to this day. I lost my ideological complacency that afternoon and I have been grateful ever since. I looked at Keith, waiting for his answer. He just smiled and nodded. "I was thinking of the same thing," he finally said.

I had forgotten that Keith had been in the same class. "Two varsity basketball players taking a philosophy elective in Hegel, Nietzsche and Feuerbach. That might not happen very often these days," I suggested.

The professor was John Walsh, a learned Jesuit for whom I had unbounded respect. He was a fervent believer in Socrates' dictum "The unexamined life is not worth living." I didn't have many Jesuit professors at Holy

Cross, but I had enough to know that Walsh's teaching was a credit to the Jesuit tradition of rigorous, informed, independent inquiry. I haven't been a churchgoer since I became one of those insufferable teenaged apostates when I was seventeen. And, like everyone else with a brain and a heart, I've been revolted by the sex abuse scandals. Still, it troubles me that it's so fashionable now to make a punching bag of all things Catholic. That, of course, is part of a new, secular orthodoxy. As Walsh said, orthodoxies need to be challenged. We could all do ourselves a favor by starting with our own.

John Walsh, S.J., philosopher

34
Stay in School

During summers in college, I would pick up a job from the end of the spring term until the beginning of August, when I would join my parents at Scraggy Neck. Freshman and sophomore years, I worked for a landscaper. When work was slow, he would order me to drive the tractor with a fertilizer spreader aimlessly back and forth on the field hockey and soccer fields at Babson College and Wellesley College so that he could run up the tab. "Just drive real slow," he told me. "Make it last." I was a young idealist and had a crisis of conscience about the scam, at least until Father told me I'd better get wise to the realities of the workaday world.

One of the places we manicured was an estate in Weston. I had dated the elder daughter of the family once or twice, and we had a number of mutual friends. She was one of those preppy girls who were known in those days by cutesy nicknames like "Cricket" or "Muffin." Our job was to cut the lawns, weed and edge the perennial border and trim the shrubs. One day, I was sent to the pool area to do some cleanup and trimming. The girl I knew was by the pool, on a chaise lounge. She was wearing a big hat and applying suntan lotion. Her transistor radio was playing Lovin' Spoonful and Young Rascals kind of stuff. I paused and said "Hi" as I walked by with a rake in my hand.

She looked at me vacantly. "I'm sorry, but do I *know* you?" she asked, archly.

I tipped my sunglasses and Red Sox hat back and reminded her who I was.

"Not really. What happened? Did you drop out of school or something?"

I told her no, I just had a summer job.

"You mean—cutting lawns?" she asked.

I actually liked my jobs. I got to meet some interesting characters, the most interesting of whom was Timmy, my foreman when I worked on the fish pier in Boston the summer after my junior year. Timmy was a stringy little Irishman from Mission Hill, full of what Fa would have called "piss and vinegar." He had the look of a Sinn Fein fighter in a movie about the Irish Rebellion—steely gray eyes, a three-day stubble and a jaunty tweed cap. He was clever and passionate about doing the job right. He was demanding, but fair. He played no favorites.

We started work at 6 a.m., unloading haddock, cod, hake, whiting and pollock from trawlers. On good days, I got to drive the forklift—which gave me a chance to recover from the hashish and retsina of the night before. I worked with three other college kids: a classics major from Harvard, a broken-down pitcher from Ohio State and a poet who was an Oberlin dropout. Our lunch break was at ten. The college kids and the regular workers would all go together to a place called the Fisherman's Grotto. Most of the regulars would preface their lunches with a shot of Seagram's and a bottle of Narragansett or Carling Black Label. Timmy usually had a couple of 7&7s. I stuck with ginger ale. We all ate fried clams, fried haddock, fried scallops, fried onion rings, French fries—just about anything that could be fried—with a paper container of coleslaw the diameter of a silver dollar on the side.

Every day, Jimmy would take me aside on the way back to the pier. "Stay in school," he'd urge me. "Don't wind up like me. Forty years on the docks and nothing to show for it. A bum." I would tell him that I didn't think he was a bum, that he put in an honest day's work and handled a lot of responsibility. I'd remind him that he had a daughter studying business administration at Northeastern. This became our daily ritual.

One day Timmy didn't come to work. The regulars told us he hadn't missed a day, ever. They were worried. The next day our employer gathered us together and told us that Timmy had died.

I hoped that Timmy didn't really believe the things he said to me about being a bum, with nothing to show for his hard work. I hoped it was just some self-pity, fueled by a few drinks. I hoped his daughter respected him and was grateful. He was an honest, hardworking man.

Where Real Music Was Played I

Club 47, Cambridge, Massachusetts

Neil came to school one Monday morning with breathless stories of a place he had been in Cambridge, a coffeehouse where Joan Baez sang. It was called Club 47. A few weeks later, we walked down the hill from school on a Friday afternoon and took the MTA to Harvard Square. We stood in line, paid a dollar for our "membership" and entered a world that was vastly different from the suburbs and prep school. This was a place where music and conversation were the things that mattered; it wasn't a place for "noogies" and other adolescent goofing around. I had just turned fifteen, and it's one of the first times I really felt like an adult. Neil and I were at a table, drinking coffee and listening to someone named Tom Rush play songs about railroads and gamblers that came from somewhere called the Mississippi Delta. Between songs, he told stories and cracked jokes. It was all completely new to me, and I loved every minute of it. A month later, I got my first guitar.

Over the next several years, Neil and I went to the 47 dozens of times. We'd get there as early as possible and try to be the first in line at the bottom of the stairs, so we could get a table right in front of the stage. We'd actually draw little diagrams of chord positions and jot down lyrics as the band played. Bob Siggins of the Charles River Valley Boys eventually came to call us "the finger watchers."

Siggins and the rest of the CRVB quickly became our favorites. I loved his zany renditions of Uncle Dave Macon songs from the 1920s and '30s. He captured all the zest of the "Dixie Dewdrop," one of the first stars of the Grand Ole Opry. Uncle Dave was the Babe Ruth of country music, a ribald scoundrel. Or was Babe Ruth the Uncle Dave of baseball? In any case, fifty years later, Neil and I still regularly included "Johnny Grey" in our own concerts, one of the Uncle Dave songs we learned at Siggins' knee. John Cooke, a suave crooner from Harvard who later became Janis Joplin's road manager, sang most of the leads, and the enigmatic Fritz Richmond thumped out time on his washtub bass. Joe Val rounded out the band on mandolin and sang high tenor. Joe stood out as a working-class hero in a world populated by renegade Ivy Leaguers—Siggins, for example, was working for a Ph.D. in molecular biology and Jim Rooney was a Fulbright Scholar in ancient Greek. Joe was a typewriter repairman during the day and took quite a bit of grief from his wife for gallivanting around Cambridge with his mandolin at all hours of the night. Joe will always live in my memory for his rendition, in his irrepressible Boston accent, of the Jim and Jesse classic "Hahd Hahted Hahtbreakah."

Besides Rush and the CRVB, the regulars at the 47 included Keith and Rooney, Jim Kweskin's Jug Band, Eric von Schmidt, Mimi and Richard Farina and Taj Mahal. Sometime in 1965, Rooney took over as manager of the club and turned the focus to more well-known, national acts. The list of performers I saw at the 47 still makes me blink in disbelief: Tim Hardin, Mississippi John Hurt, the country blues trio Koerner, Ray and Glover, the Kentucky Colonels with the incomparable Clarence White, Jesse Colin Young, the Chambers Brothers, Skip James, the Paul Butterfield Blues Band, Mose Allison, Sleepy John Estes, Bill Monroe, Doc Watson, Judy Roderick, the New Lost City Ramblers, Tim Buckley, Roscoe Holcomb, Hazel Dickens, Hobart Smith and the Young Tradition.

Club 47 Summer '67 calendar. Bill Monroe, Howlin' Wolf, Doc Watson, Mose Allison, the Chambers Brothers, Tim Buckley, Junior Wells, Merle Travis, the Young Tradition, the Jug Band...simply amazing!

The two best shows I ever saw at the 47 were Howlin' Wolf and Muddy Waters. Wolf's show was the only time I ever had misgivings about being in my front-row seat. Wolf introduced himself as "three hundred pounds of joy." From four or five feet away, he was an overwhelming presence. He heaved his huge torso and sweated freely as he roared and snarled the words to "I'm Evil," "Ain't Superstitious" and "Smokestack Lightnin'."

He seemed to be pulling the band—even the great guitarist Hubert Sumlin—along through every song by sheer force of will. Muddy, on the other hand, was a cool character. Perched on the edge of a stool with his battered Telecaster, he let his band do the heavy lifting while he coasted over the surface of the music, teasing the audience with his insinuating lyrics and bravado persona. As I recall, Muddy played an unprecedented five nights in a row; I went for three of those and sat so close to Muddy's great piano player Otis Spann that I could smell the Chivas Regal Scotch whiskey in his coffee mug. Spann had the greatest right hand in Chicago, and the way his piano answered Muddy's vocal lines was pure magic.

There were girls around the 47, too, like Debbie Green and Ann Tansey, girls who played guitar and sang, went barefoot, wore black leotards and had long, ironed hair. As a matter of fact, all of the girls seemed (à la Baez) to play guitar, go barefoot, wear black leotards and have long, ironed hair. That certainly didn't make them any less attractive. On my sixteenth birthday, my parents gave me a wonderful old Washburn banjo. I had no idea how to play it. After a Sunday afternoon "hoot" at the 47, one of the barefoot, long-haired girls walked with me to the Cambridge Common. We sat on my jacket on the ground and she showed me how to put the banjo in the archaic sawmill tuning and play "Shady Grove" in the old-timey frailing style. As the buses and cars rumbled past on Massachusetts Avenue, we created our own little world in that song.

The 1960s folk scene has attracted a lot of historical interest recently in books and documentary films. Much of the attention has been focused on the Newport Folk Festivals. I went to Newport several times from 1963 to '69, and I can attest that they really were as glorious as people now claim. But I felt a connection with the performers and the music in that little room at 47 Palmer Street that I never felt at Newport. There was no single place more important in my young life than Club 47. It gave me the confidence to be an independent-minded adult who values creativity and self-expression. And it affirmed for me that it was a good thing to be my own person, even at the risk of seeming off-kilter to everyone in the suburban mainstream.

The Hillbilly Ranch, Boston

"You went *where*?" Father demanded.

I had told him that the night before, Neil and I had gone to a place called the Hillbilly Ranch to see the Lilly Brothers and Don Stover. "Tex Logan played the fiddle. It was fantastic!"

He was not pleased. "Do you know what goes on in that place? Sailors and prostitutes. Probably drugs, too. Someone got stabbed there last year."

I tried to explain that Tex Logan surely wasn't a gangster. He taught engineering at MIT.

"I don't care who does what where. I don't want you anywhere near the Hillbilly Ranch." He was very serious.

So as was usually the case in my teenage years, I had to fly under the radar to seek my pleasures.

Except for the brilliant music that filled the place night after night, my father pretty much had the place pegged. The Hillbilly Ranch was a sticky-floor kind of dive that smelled of stale Schlitz. It was next to the Trailways bus station in the Park Square section of Boston, not far from the notorious Combat Zone. The area around Park Square has now been swallowed up by upscale hotels, restaurants and condos; in those days it was a pretty sketchy part of town.

The décor and the theme of the place ignored the fact that so-called hillbillies live in the mountains and don't have ranches. Wagon wheels and a corral fence surrounded the cramped dance floor where (as Father had said) sailors shambled around with ladies of the evening, to the unlikely strains of "Are You Tired of Me, Darlin'?" and "Bring Back My Blue-Eyed Boy to Me." The sailors were mostly young guys from the South who found themselves at the Charlestown Navy Yard while their ships were being refitted. They paid much more attention to their companions than to the music.

Neil and I were there strictly for the music. I suppose other bands played at the Hillbilly Ranch, but I only ever saw the Lilly Brothers. Everett Lilly played the mandolin and his brother Bea Lilly the guitar—which, according to Everett, he had carved out of a tree stump with a jackknife, or some such thing. Everett considered himself a showman and handled the corny patter between songs; Bea was shy and never had much to say. But when they sang together, their voices blended in that magical way that only brothers or sisters seem to accomplish. They had started on radio in West Virginia in the early '40s and had somehow landed in Boston. The Ranch was their rent gig. They played fifty minutes every hour, from eight o'clock until one, five or six nights a week. Somehow, it always sounded fresh. Two reasons for that were Don Stover, the banjo player in the band, and Tex Logan, who often sat in on fiddle. Stover played with tremendous rhythmic drive, which was matched by Logan's propulsive shuffling. They seemed to simply love playing together. As a group, the four of them were one of the greatest of the traditional bluegrass bands. It's a shame those sailors didn't pay more attention.

World Control Studios, Germantown, Pennsylvania

World Control Studios was a little piece of hippie paradise in a run-down brownstone in Germantown, an old suburb of Philadelphia. I lived about a mile away, near the Queen Lane train station, and would walk down Germantown Avenue on balmy evenings to see what was going on at WCS, as it was known. Sometimes it was just a jam scene, with fifteen people playing out-of-tune guitars and singing Crosby, Stills and Nash songs. That made for a short night. On the good nights, there was a real concert. Everyone sat on the floor on cushions and pillows, very close to the performers. Big bowls of popcorn laced with Spike made the rounds. I saw Bonnie Raitt with Freebo. I saw David Bromberg with his rotund bass player Steve Burgh, who Bromberg billed as "The Fabulous Torpedoes" and who went on to play with everyone from Billy Joel to Willie Nelson.

The "vibe" (as we used to say) at WCS was so "laid back" (as we also used to say) that it almost defied the imagination. In some ways it was the ultimate house concert—before there really was such a thing. People just came to "hang out" (we used to say that, too) and enjoy the music and each other, without any "hangups" (you dig?). Evidently the FBI didn't think the place was quite so "groovy" and launched an investigation, instigated, one might assume, by the name. I don't really know what caused the demise of WCS, but one night I walked down to see what was going on and the place had been abandoned and the windows were covered with plywood.

Caffè Lena, Saratoga Springs, New York

Caffè Lena is the Fenway Park of folk music. Like Fenway, it's a monument to itself. And, like Fenway, it's timeless. Walk up the steps from Phila Street and you don't just enter a room, you enter a world where people listen to one another, and where three-chord songs are the barometer of truth and human emotion. If you haven't been there, you need to go.

A musician on the road, 1978

Like everyone else who has played Lena's, I have my own trove of memories.

I first played there in 1976, in the days when performers were booked for the entire weekend, including Sunday. I recall I got $175 for the three nights. The Turf and Spa Motel was $16.95 a night, so with meals, gas and a few rounds of drinks at the "Exec," I might have broken even. But I made friends and had wonderful audiences. Lena herself always sat in the back during the shows, drinking triple-strength espresso and playing Scrabble with her friend Dorothea. Every once in a while, you'd hear one of them: "I know how badly you want to use that Q again, but that is *not* how you spell 'questionnaire!' You need *two* Ns, my dear." The stage was a postage stamp and the sound and lights were minimal. But the desserts were great, and after every set, people would come up and ask about a particular song, or even a particular line in a song. These were folks who listened.

On my second or third booking at Lena's, Joe Venuti played a surprise Sunday afternoon show. I knew he had done some landmark jazz recordings in the 1920s with guitarist Eddie Lang, but I'd never heard them. I didn't realize that he had also played with Bix Beiderbecke, the Dorseys, Paul Whiteman and Benny Goodman. It turns out he was an old friend of Lena's and she arranged the Sunday afternoon show for him, guitarist Bucky Pizzarelli and a bass player (whose name I wish I could recall) on their way back to New York from Montreal. I had planned a pike-fishing outing for the afternoon on Lake Lonely in a rented rowboat, but a friend of mine talked me out of it. I'm very glad she did.

Venuti was about eighty years old, portly, wore a business suit with a skinny tie and had cataract glasses that must have been a quarter-inch thick. He might not have looked the part, but he swung his ass off. I sat on the bench that was reserved for musicians and friends of the Caffè and simply couldn't absorb everything I was hearing. The old man had a command of his instrument and his early jazz idiom that I'd heard in recordings by Django, Bix and Armstrong—but had never witnessed in person.

He kicked off with "Lady, Be Good" and played a blues called "That's a Plenty." I don't remember what other songs he played, but I know his performance changed my outlook toward music forever. He was authentic, and he played with absolute confidence. Every phrase he played said, *Get as good as you possibly can at what you really want to play and forget the rest of it. Express yourself!*

Onstage at Caffé Lena, 2010—thirty-five years after the first of my many shows at the Fenway Park of folk music.

I've found a video clip from the Paul Whiteman movie *The King of Jazz* that shows a young, impossibly suave Venuti in a white dinner jacket and slicked-down hair, trading licks with Lang. It's from fifty years earlier, but the player I saw still had the gift. He was funny, too—in a quirky way. He told a story about trying to decide on a Christmas gift for the one-armed trumpeter "Wingy" Manone. He finally sent Wingy one cufflink, nicely gift wrapped.

36
Out of Tune

Skip James was one of the rediscoveries of the 1960s folk revival. Everyone assumed that the country blues legends Son House, Bukka White, Sleepy John Estes, Mississippi John Hurt and Skip, who had made immortal country blues records in 1931, must be dead. The great Tommy Johnson, Charlie Patton and Robert Johnson were certainly dead. But it turned out that some of the others were just living their lives day to day, until some young blues aficionado with a road map, a telephone directory and a couple of treasured 78s unexpectedly knocked on their door. In Skip's case, the acolyte knocking on his door was John Fahey.

When these artists were rediscovered, the impact was monumental.

Mississippi John, Skip and the rest came out of history and were suddenly right in front of us. I went to Newport in '63, '64 and '65, and there they were, playing in workshops and concerts. All I knew about them were the few cuts on Harry Smith's wonderfully screwball *Anthology of American Folk Music*. I had few preconceptions. I took them and their music as it revealed itself to me in the moment. Many thousands of others did, too. Soon, everyone I knew seemed to be playing "My Creole Belle" about four hours a day.

Mississippi John's easygoing personal charm, as much as his accessible music, won over people of my generation immediately. Jim Rooney told me that, back at the hotel after one of the Newport evening concerts, the party was getting rolling and so were the joints. He and Geoff Muldaur thought they ought to explain things to Mississippi John: "You see, Mister Hurt, some of the younger folks here are just going to unwind a bit with some marijuana. We hope you won't mind."

"Oh, my word. Not at all. That Miss Mary Jane just grows wild all over the field behind my house in Avalon. It does have a nice smell, doesn't it?"

"My Creole Belle" was easy to play, and Mississippi John was a delightful man. On the other hand, there wasn't much about Skip that could be called delightful. He sang in a high, keening voice that was nothing like Mississippi John's comforting whisper. His relentlessly dark songs were off-putting for most of the folk crowd. Burdened by poverty and cancer, he seemed sullen, resentful and more concerned with putting some money in his pocket than being chummy with anyone. Hurt was genial and deferential; James was neither.

There was a rush to record these people, partly to capitalize on the folk boom and partly to archive the performances of these incomparable musical originals. Vanguard did a lot of the recording and released most of the albums. One night, backstage at the Towne Crier, Chris Smither told me he had been a fly on the wall for the sessions that produced the Vanguard album *Skip James Today!*

Like country blues guitar wizard Paul Geremia, Smither was a Boston folkie who absorbed the blues from the Delta and the Piedmont like oxygen. I first met them in the '60s, when they were playing for five or ten bucks at the Sword in the Stone and the Turk's Head, part of the coffeehouse scene on Charles Street that thrived in the shadows of the more famous Club 47 and Unicorn.

Smither told me that the session started, and Skip began to play some of his classic songs, like "Cypress Grove," "Hard Time Killin' Floor" and "Crow Jane." The performances were a revelation. But Skip's guitar was woefully out of tune. The producer said over the talkback, "Skip, your B string sounds really flat."

Skip was a creative genius, but he was no musicologist. "Which one is that?" he asked.

"The second one. No. That's the A. The second one from the bottom. The plain one. No winding."

Skip started turning the knobs, hoping for the best. The guitar wound up even more out of tune. Finally, Skip announced that he had to go to the bathroom. The producer seized the opportunity. "Get in there and tune his guitar," he told Smither. A minute or two later, the guitar was in perfect tune.

Skip returned from the toilet, zipping up his pants. He sat down and picked up his guitar. "This is 'I'm So Glad'," he said into the mic, and launched into the song that would be made famous by Cream, and would give him some $15,000 in royalties that made his last couple of years more comfortable. The notes rang true. Smither and the producer smiled at each other in satisfaction. Then, after a few seconds Skip abruptly stopped playing and leaned into the microphone with a scowl: "Who's been fuckin' wit' my gittah?"

37
The Summer of '69

The main event of my first year at Penn was the Ph.D. qualifying exam, late in the summer of 1969. It was a grueling, make-or-break affair. For three days, there were morning and afternoon sessions of three hours each. The examiners could ask anything at all about your three chosen fields of concentration. You wrote four long essays each day in response. Pass, and you continued with the fellowship program and were on track to your doctorate. Fail, and they sent you a master's degree in the mail as a consolation prize and showed you the door. No do-overs.

There really was no way to prepare for the exam, but I tried anyway. I pored over my notebooks and literary histories. I reread some critical books of essential importance. I made notes. Then I made notes about my notes. The questions from the three prior years were posted, so I studied them and tried to anticipate what the examiners might ask this time around. But my time was limited. I was fending off the draft board, taking four courses, teaching a section of Shakespeare and beginning a dissertation topic proposal on Alexander Pope's poetry and eighteenth-century historiography. Meanwhile, there were some serious distractions. Ted Kennedy drove off the bridge at Chappaquiddick, astronauts landed on the moon, a half million people of my generation rolled around in the mud at Woodstock and the Manson cult went on their murderous rampage. By the time the exam came, I simply wanted it to be over. My plan was to drive the seven hours to the Scraggy Neck house immediately after the last exam and recuperate for a few days.

My Volkswagen was packed and ready to roll after the last exam on Friday. I hit some traffic around New York and stopped at a HoJo's in Connecticut for a quick dinner. It was well past midnight when I drove into the driveway. I didn't even unpack the car. I just threw my overnight bag on one bed, threw myself on the other, and fell into a profound sleep.

The birds sung me awake. It was dawn. For some reason I felt restless and groggy just lying there, listening to the sounds of the morning. I decided to get up and go to the doughnut shop at the Otis Circle. The proprietor made perfect doughnuts, dark brown and crisp on the outside, but flaky and light on the inside. He opened at six and on a Saturday morning he would be sold out and closed by eight. I stumbled my way to the car. I was, as the saying goes, totally out of it.

I got my bag of doughnuts. I don't think I've ever written the word "scrumptious" before, but they really did smell scrumptious. On my way past the counter, I grabbed a copy of the *Globe* and hurried home to make coffee. Coffee, doughnuts and the paper on the patio, watching the morning rise over the bay. It sounded like a good way to start my little vacation. When the coffee was ready, I settled myself in a chair facing the water, had a bite of a doughnut, a sip of coffee and reached for the paper. I was surprised to realize that it was two inches thick. For a moment, I was puzzled. I looked again: the *Boston Sunday Globe*. Sunday? I had arrived Friday night. *What happened to Saturday?*

38
Kingfish

My first advisor in graduate school was a rough-and-ready Louisianan named Arthur Scouten. He was a world-renowned scholar of the Restoration theater, but an unlikely presence in a tweedy Ivy League English department. He dressed like a pool shark, not a professor. He told roguish, salty jokes. He laughed loudly and often, with a mouth like Joe E. Brown's that showed all his teeth when he did so, in a magnificent and somewhat scary display. When I told him that a famous Shakespeare scholar in the department was giving me a hard time about a topic proposal, his advice was, "Don't take any shit from that guy."

One day, Scouten told me how he had come to be an academic. He had graduated from high school with no money and no sense of direction. He'd gone to work for a landscape gardener in Baton Rouge. One of their jobs was to take care of the grounds of the governor's mansion. He was trimming hedges one day when he heard a cry for help. He rushed to the pool area and saw a young boy foundering in the deep end. He dropped his shears, jumped in and pulled the child to safety. After a few minutes the boy seemed fine, and Scouten went back to work. As it turned out, the boy was Huey Long's son.

Next day, his employer told Scouten that the governor would like to see him. Someone came to fetch him and he went, hat in hand, to the governor's office. The Kingfish himself came forward to greet him and shook his hand warmly. "I can see you're a fine young fella, Arthur, a fine fella indeed," Long said. "You saved my boy, and I owe you a *pro-found* debt of gratitude. How would you like to go to the Louisiana State University?" Scouten said that he would surely like that, but that he didn't have any money. "Now, don't you worry about money, son. You just leave that to your governor."

Long picked up the phone and told someone to get the chancellor of the university on the line, "and make it quick." After a few minutes, the phone rang back and Long told the chancellor, "I got a fine young fella here named Arthur—spell your last name for me, son—S-C-O-U-T-E-N. You got that? Now, he's gonna be attendin' your fine university for the next four years. And he's not gonna be payin' for anythin'. You set that up, now, y'hear?" The Kingfish hung up the phone without waiting for an answer.

When he finished his story, Scouten laughed like Falstaff at his own whimsical tale. I did the same.

War

The Vietnam War frightened everyone I knew. My friends worried about the draft, the disruption of their lives, and the threat of death or horrible injury in some jungle swamp. The young women I knew worried about burying their husband, boyfriend or brother in a casket with a flag on it. Everyone worried that their dreams would be derailed. But what could we do? I protested with my friends on the grand steps of the Dinand Library after Philip Berrigan spoke at Holy Cross. I marched in Philadelphia when Noam Chomsky spoke at Penn. I went to Washington with a half-million others for the Moratorium where Pete Seeger sang. In retrospect, we were right that the war was a boondoggle. But, to be honest with myself, I didn't do these things solely out of conviction that the war was morally indefensible. I did them to try to save my ass.

A few months before our graduation, I gathered with twenty or so friends in the TV lounge of our dormitory to hear President Johnson talk to the nation about Vietnam. Without warning, he announced that he was stopping the bombing of North Vietnam and that he wouldn't run for reelection. We all jumped to our feet, yelling and clapping. We were exhilarated by the false hope that the war would soon end and we could escape the draft. Johnson's announcement was on March 31, 1968. The last Americans killed in Vietnam died in a rocket attack on April 29, 1975. Seven years later.

The same knee injury that ended my basketball career kept me out of the war. I had passed my first draft physical and hired a lawyer. "If you can breathe and you can walk, you pass the first round," he told me. "Don't worry, we'll appeal." A few weeks went by. My wife Susie and I talked a lot about moving to Canada. We looked at maps and travel guides. We tried to be optimistic. *Newfoundland looks pretty nice...*But the consequences couldn't be ignored. I would lose my fellowship. She would have to give up her job. We had a thousand bucks in our bank account. Would we be able to work there? Would we ever be able to come back? There wasn't much discussion about the moral objections Berrigan and Chomsky had raised about the war. It had come down to self-preservation.

Finally, I got a letter instructing me to report for another physical at 7 a.m. on a certain day at the end of August, 1969. The location was 601 Broad Street, a forbidding, souless building that is shown in the opening credits of the film *Philadelphia*. The letter informed me that my knee would be examined by an army orthopedic surgeon. It also informed me that there would be no further appeal. I arrived on time and was shown into a tiny examining cubicle. There was nothing in the room but a chair and a blood pressure cuff hanging on a hook. I was told to strip to my underpants and socks, put the rest of my clothes in a paper bag and write my name on the outside. Someone came in, took the bag away and said, "The doctor will be a while."

It was chilly in the room. I sat on the straight-backed chair and waited. I could hear muffled voices over the walls of the cubicle. The hours passed. I had nothing to read, nothing to divert my thoughts from what was certain to be the loss of my career. I got angrier and more frightened as the day wore on. I hadn't eaten or had anything to drink all day. I felt cold. I lost my perspective of time. I sat, staring at my clenched fists. There was nothing else to look at. Then I heard a voice over the wall: "See you tomorrow." Lights started to go out. People were going home, it seemed. *Had they forgotten me?* I called out, "I'm here. Hello, I'm still here. Do you know I'm here?" No response. Still more time passed.

Without warning, the door of the cubicle opened and a doctor entered with a clipboard. "Left knee?" he asked. I nodded. "Straighten your leg." As I did so, he grabbed my kneecap on both sides and squeezed. I jumped and yelled in pain. "Osteochondritis. 1-Y." I would be spared. I thanked him. He looked at me contemptuously. "I don't want your thanks," he snarled, and shut the door. The whole thing had taken less than a minute.

Someone brought the bag with my clothes. "What time is it?" I asked. "A little after six," he replied. Later I was to wonder how many men of my age had been killed and wounded in Vietnam during the eleven hours I sat shivering in that cubicle at 601 Broad Street.

Respectfully dedicated to my college classmate Lt. Mike Quinn, USMC. Killed in combat, August 29, 1969.

40
Drum Solo

In the 1970s, quite a few musicians spent unplanned stays in North African jails on drug raps. Among the by-products of this miserable situation were unexpected vacancies in rock and blues bands. My friend Jeff, a trombone player with a creative imagination and solid jazz chops, told me about one such opening in his own band, Streamline. I was a pretty limited electric player, but I thought I'd give the audition a shot for the experience. I put my gold-top Gibson Les Paul and my vintage Explorer amp into the '63 Olds and drove to the rehearsal, which was in a trailer very well hidden in the woods outside Rosendale, New York. The drums in the trailer were so loud that I couldn't hear much of anything, but the band did mostly twelve-bar shuffles in E and A. We played "Willie and the Hand Jive" for what seemed like an hour. I stumbled along as best I could and mustered up a pentatonic solo whenever anyone nodded in my direction. I realized right away that the class of the outfit was Robbie, who sang and played wonderful blues harmonica. After a break for some beers, Jeff told me that everyone in the band except me was tripping and that they had decided I had a predominantly yellow aura, so I was hired. The first show would be at the Homestead in New Paltz that Sunday night.

I arrived early and set up. Some sound guys came and then the band filtered in. It was soon obvious that nobody except Jeff remembered who I was or what I was doing there. I heard him saying to Robbie: "Remember? The cat with the yellow aura?" Robbie looked at him blankly. Jeff came over and said, "Okay, just sit in the first set. Keep your head down and we'll sort it out later. No hassles, man." He spoke too soon. A blond guy with a Telecaster came in and started to set up. I have no idea what color his aura was, but he didn't take kindly to my presence. "Who the fuck is *that*?" he asked no one in particular and everyone in general. There was a confab while I sat on a barstool. Then Jeff came over and said, "Sorry, man. It's turning into a hassle." I packed up and left. That was my career with Streamline.

My next shot was with a band called Blues Power. Streamline had been a very good R&B combo; Blues Power was a dreadful psychedelic blues band. We did long, rambling versions of Delta blues songs at ponderous tempos. At times, the effect was that of a brontosaurus moving sullenly through some Jurassic bog. In other words, we were an unconscious parody of Cream. I could play ambling, pointless solos with the best of them, so I got the gig right away. One of our first shows involved a road trip. We were booked for a weeknight at Grendel's Lair, a club in Philadelphia. I had played there a few times before with a folk group. I packed my purple velour bell-bottoms, my Afghani shirt with the mirrors sewn into the embroidered front and plenty of turquoise rings and love beads. I was ready to plod. Oops, I meant to say, ready to *rock*. Actually, my Les Paul sounded pretty darned cosmic through the old Explorer amp with everything turned up to ten—a kind of gritty, howling tone, with lots of sustain. I liked it—the more sustain, the less I actually had to play.

The week before the show, we added a new member to the band. Andrew was an electric blues fiddler in the style of Sugarcane Harris. We welcomed Andrew to the band because he had a large apartment in which we could rehearse. Well, it wasn't *actually* an apartment. It was really two big spaces on the third floor of some loft or warehouse building near Dobbs Ferry. The two sides of the space were joined by a sheet of plywood that served as a bridge. You could look down the foot-wide gap to the first floor. Andrew was a pretty interesting player, but he suffered from chronic nosebleeds. Before we rehearsed or played a show he would cut one of those cotton cylinders dentists use in half and stuff one end in each nostril so he wouldn't bleed all over his fancy cowboy shirt or his fiddle.

Grendel's was a nice club and drew a pretty good crowd for just about anything. There was a convention in those days that bands would unplug at some point in the show and leave the drummer alone on stage to play an extended solo. Everyone did it, so we did it, too. In the middle of "Stop Breakin' Down" we left the stage and the drummer launched into one of those mind-numbing solos that made the '70s we remember into the '70s we would like to forget.

The rest of us went up the stairs to the green room, where we indulged in the herbal pleasures of the day. A big bowl of popcorn laced with Spike, the zesty seasoning, was on the table. A bottle of bourbon was making the rounds. Everyone was feeling pretty loose and we lost track of time. I was talking with one of the guys from Sweet Stavin Chain when our harmonica player suddenly jumped up and cried "The drummer! The drummer! Oh, God!" We scrambled down the stairs and there he was, still going at it, his eyes wild, his shirt drenched and his tongue drooping. We jumped on stage and hit the downbeat. Fortunately, we all remembered which song we had been playing. The crowd responded wildly—perhaps with relief that they had been rescued from the tedium of one of the longest drum solos ever. After all, there were limits, even in the '70s.

41
Detroit Iron

1965 Ford Fairlane Squire Wagon

My second year at Penn, my treasured red VW bug with the sunroof was stolen off the street in the middle of the night. The police officer who came to investigate later the next day told me, "Forget it. You'll never get it back. Bugs are a chop-shop favorite. It's in pieces already." I was screwed without a car, and I was living on a stipend of $3,800 a year. My mother came to the rescue. She said she was bored with her 1965 Ford Fairlane Squire Wagon with the fake wood on the sides and had been planning to buy a new car soon. She didn't need a wagon, anyway. I could have the Squire.

I took a Trailways back to Boston. I stayed at the house for a couple of days and looked the car over. Good tires, no rust. I fired it up. It seemed to run okay, but it was really low on gas, so I took it down to the Texaco in Newton Center. The guy filled it up and asked if he should check the oil. "Good idea," I said. "It might need a change." A minute later, the guy appeared at the window with the dipstick cradled in a red rag in his hand. "I checked the oil," he said. "There is no oil."

"What do you mean, 'no oil'?"

"No oil on the dipstick. How'd you drive this thing? We better drain whatever's in there and get some fresh oil in it quick."

So he did. There was less than a quart in the crankcase. Run it for a hundred miles, the guy said, and do another oil change. Maybe you'll get lucky. I followed his advice and drove it back to Philadelphia without incident.

A couple of months later, some friends invited me to Southwest Harbor and Acadia National Park in Maine. There were five of us and a bunch of luggage, so I volunteered the Squire for the trip. We were having a jolly time, roaring up the Maine Turnpike at ninety, when there was a god-awful noise under the hood. Oily steam and dense blue smoke shot out of somewhere and coated the windshield. The wipers couldn't keep up with it. I was driving blind, lucky to get the Squire to the side of the road. The engine had exploded. Shrapnel had shot through the radiator.

Later, I said something to Mother about preventive maintenance on her new car. Her icy response was, "Just because your car blew up, you don't have to lecture me."

1963 Oldsmobile Dynamic 88

After my divorce in 1977, I had no car, less than $1,000 in the bank and was living miles from nowhere down a country road. I needed a cheap car, fast. One of my friends came to commiserate and told me he had seen a car just up the road with a sign on the windshield: *$200 Firm. Runs good.* We rode down to take a look. It was a white 1963 Oldsmobile Dynamic 88. The car looked clean and, like the sign said, it "ran good." Best of all it had a "Wonderbar" radio; you could change stations with your foot. The downside was that the car had gone 175,000 miles. The owner was a retired minister who swore (not on a stack of Bibles, I noticed) that he had bought it new and babied it since day one. I made a deal for $175, registered it the next day, and ran it for almost three years. I drove it to Virginia, Ohio, Rhode Island and Ontario to play gigs. I drove it to the Cape and to Montreal on vacations. When I sold the car, it had 235,000 miles on it. Another musician paid me $175 and seemed delighted to get it. "No guarantees," I warned him. "Lots of miles." He just smiled and drove off.

About three years later, I pulled into the Mobil station in New Paltz in my cheapo Toyota on my way to Manhattan. There she was, my old Dynamic 88, at the next pump. She'd lost her hubcaps somewhere, but she still looked pretty good. The guy I had sold it to was filling her up. "She's runnin' great!" he said, anticipating my question. "Just got back from Madison and Ann Arbor. She turned 300,000 a month ago!"

And to think. You could even change the radio station with your foot.

42
The Hotel Rio

In the 1970s, the cheapest way to get to Europe was on Icelandic Airways. The route was New York to Reykjavik, then on to Luxembourg and then four hours by train to Paris.

I took the trip a few times and grew to like its quirkiness. The train ride on SNCF passed through Belgian and French villages where the small vegetable plots were planted to take advantage of every available inch. Those glimpses out the window as the train rushed past still influence the way I plant my own garden forty years later—close planting and vertical trellises for extra space. The experience of popping up from the Métro into the sunlight and bustle of Place de L'Opéra after the long flight and long train ride is still one of the great thrills of my life.

As an inducement, the airline used to offer layovers in Reykjavik, with a free hotel room and free dinner and breakfast. From the small balcony of one of these rooms, I could look across the bay toward a grandly imposing range of mountains. The town was trim and appealing, the people beautiful and the *brennivin* very cold. If I had been fond of pickled herring and fermented shark meat, it would have seemed an earthly paradise.

But travel being travel, the dark side showed itself soon enough. Leaving Paris on a late train homeward bound, I got to Ville de Luxembourg close to midnight. The lovely hotel at which I had stayed before on Place de la Gare was full, so I started to wander in search of a room. As I walked, it began to rain heavily. I walked and walked and couldn't find a room. Finally, I turned the corner of an alleyway and saw a frosted globe glowing over a doorway. On the globe in an Art Nouveau script were the words HOTEL RIO. It looked extremely seedy—but on that dark alleyway in the rain it also looked like a set from *The Third Man*. A spirit of adventure and my wet shoes overtook my better judgment, and I went in. The atmospherics of the place seemed perfect: the scrollwork cage where the night clerk sat, the oak clock ticking loudly, the old-fashioned keys on hooks, the massive ledger book. I almost expected Inspector Maigret to walk out of one of his novels and into this shabby lobby. The room was twenty francs—about five bucks.

Soon it was more than the atmospherics that overwhelmed me. As I climbed the stairs, I started to smell an acrid, ammonia-laced odor—like a cat box that ought to have been cleaned yesterday. My room was at the end of a long corridor. *I'll just open the window,* I thought. That helped quite a bit, so I settled my bag and went down the hall in search of the WC. It was locked—a sign on the door read PAS EN SERVICE. *Oh hell, out of order.* I went up another flight, and then to the top floor. Same sign, same trouble. Suddenly, it struck me that the bucket of sand in the corner of my room might not be in case of fire, after all.

At this point, the odor in the place was making me want to puke. I wanted to bolt, but I had no place to go, and it was raining harder. I opened the window further. The rain started to blow in. *Fuck it,* I thought. I checked below for innocent bystanders and pissed out the window into the alley below.

Maybe if I just don't touch anything, I said to myself. I spread a towel that didn't look so very dirty on the chair, spread my jacket on the towel, stuffed a rolled-up sweater under my head and tried to sleep.

Paris, about 1976

In my dreams, I heard yelling in Italian, then a shuddering bang and more yelling. I struggled to awaken but the yelling and banging went on. Why couldn't it be just a dream? I peered through the keyhole—young hooligans in green soccer shirts running around, hollering. Then *bang*! Cheers. Finally, I figured it out. An Italian soccer team had come back to the hotel, very drunk, and was having an impromptu match in the hallway. My door was the goal. More yelling. *Bang*! Cheers. I calculated: What were my odds against a team of drunk Italian soccer players? I pulled the sweater over my head and endured.

At some point, I woke up to find that the ruckus had stopped. It was still raining hard. My watch had stopped. My flight was at 8:15. I had to get the shuttle to the airport. *What the hell time was it*? I grabbed my bag, ran down the hallway, down the stairs and out into the street. It was still dark. *Wait a minute,* it occurred to me suddenly, *I can check the clock in the lobby, the loud one.* No—the door had locked behind me. I started to run through the rain with my jacket over my head. I bolted into the train station and looked at the clock: 5:40.

At least there's a bathroom, I thought, in anticipation of a monumental pee and a good washup. I saw the WC in the corner of the waiting room and made a beeline. The door was locked. The sign on the door read PAS EN SERVICE!

43
Tuxedo Cats

There's just something different about black-and-white cats. I've read that they were prized by Phoenician sailors as surefooted, rat-killing shipmates on voyages across the Mediterranean. Could they somehow be aware of their heritage of screwball cartoon cats? I've had four, and they've all been in touch with their inner Sylvester, Felix and Krazy Kat.

Rodeo Fritz

My first tuxedo cat was Rodeo Fritz, a whimsical little alley cat who lived with us through graduate school. As it is with cats, Fritz knew that our only purpose on earth was to keep him fed and entertained. Our third-floor apartment in Germantown was a shotgun affair with a long, narrow hallway. Fritz nightly took exception to the closing of the bedroom door, which was at one end of the corridor. He would launch himself from the back of the couch at the far end of the living room, gallop the length of the hall and hurl himself against the door. He'd repeat this as many times as he needed to until the door opened, whereupon he'd saunter in and claim his spot on the corner of the bed. I needn't mention that this was not conducive to romance.

He also loved Ravi Shankar records. (Yes, we did actually play Ravi Shankar records in the early '70s.) As the long ragas droned on, Fritz would climb to the highest point in the apartment, the top of our china cabinet. He'd stand on this Himalaya on his hind legs, with his forepaws pressed against the wall. Just stand there, motionless, until the music ended.

One day I returned from campus and couldn't find Fritz. I looked under the furniture and in every cabinet and closet. No Fritz. *How could he have escaped?* The windows were all locked, the door was bolted. We scoured the apartment for the next three days. We hung lost cat posters on lampposts. On the third night, there was a knock on the door. It was our landlady from the first floor. "You're looking for a black-and-white cat?"

"Have you seen him?"

"Yes. I heard him crying after dinner. He's in the basement."

The basement? Down we went—and there he was! About as dirty and bedraggled as a cat could be, but seemingly well. The first thing Fritz did when we brought him upstairs was to show us his escape route. He sniffed under the bathroom radiator, and there it was, an old construction hole about five inches wide that was well hidden by the radiator cover. Presumably, he had heard a mouse in the walls and gone after it, down the hole. He somehow found his way through the walls and came out next to the furnace flue, four floors below. Fritz had a can of tuna for his dinner that night. And we left the bedroom door open.

Eddie

Eddie was a barn kitten from Fort Edward, New York. He was the last of his litter to find a home, perhaps because of the odd white squiggle on his black nose. Funny looking or not, he was a very smart cat. He'd watch me open a door or a cabinet and then give it a try himself, grabbing at the knob with both forepaws and twisting. A friend of mine once said, "If that cat had little monkey hands, we'd all be in a lot of trouble."

Eddie and I had a ritual on blizzardy Adirondack nights. I liked Ray Smith's public radio program *Jazz Decades*, three hours of bands like McKinney's Cotton Pickers, the Casa Loma Orchestra and the Wolverines—great music from the 1920s and '30s. I'd go to bed at nine with a pile of blankets and a pot of gunpowder tea and listen to the entire program. When Eddie saw that I was getting ready, he would perch on the bottom step, watching me with anticipation. When I moved toward the stairs, he'd bound to the top step and wait again. When I reached the first step, he'd dash into the bedroom and onto the bed to reserve his favorite spot. When I got into bed, he'd squirm until he was comfortable, curl himself up just so and give a deep sigh of contentment.

Eddie had been a friendly little chap until my friend Billy decided to teach him to roll over. Why anyone would want a cat to roll over on command escapes me. It escaped Eddie, too—and escape he did, upstairs, under the bed. From that time on, whenever a car came up the drive, Eddie would scoot under the bed and hide, even for days. The first time Susanne visited, I coaxed him out from under the bed. He ventured, she petted him gently, and they seemed to hit it off. When she visited again the following weekend, Eddie heard her car come up the drive and dashed for his hiding place.

"Where's my Eddie?" she asked, even before setting down her bag.

"Under the bed."

"Not my pal Eddie," she declared. She sat at the bottom of the stairs and called in a gentle, singsong voice "Eddie. Eddie." In a moment a squiggle nose appeared around the corner of the doorway. Eddie peered at her to make sure she was actually his new friend. Then he trotted down the stairs and

Eddie with his new friend

---

hopped into her lap. Susanne has always contended that Eddie chose her; I had no choice but to follow his lead and marry her.

Eddie had a favorite rock in the garden behind the great room. In the afternoon it was washed with sunlight. It was a perfect spot to watch for a wayward mouse or chipmunk. The afternoon before Eddie died was one of those special gifts in the Adirondacks, a dazzlingly clear October day. The air was cool, but the sun was warm. I carried him very gently to his rock and sat with him on my lap for a long time, listening to him purr. Together we watched the dragonflies in the field until the sun reached the edge of the mountain across the valley.

Tippy

We rescued Tippy's mother from a local barn. She was undernourished and very pregnant. So we fed her heartily and set up a place on our porch for her to give birth. And then we waited. One morning I came down to check on her, and there they were—four kittens. Three of them were ginger. One was black and white, and when I saw him, I said, "That one's mine!" The mother couldn't feed her little ones, so we fed them with cat formula through an eyedropper. The other three kittens didn't make it. We cried and buried them in the garden. But Tippy thrived. He had been the strongest to begin with, and he grew quickly. Every night I would feed him a concoction of mushy chicken cat food and kitten formula, warmed just so. He grew even more quickly. Soon he was jumping on tables and counters—the places, of course, where you don't want your cat to be. But, as our vet had warned us, the hand feeding and coddling had created an undisciplined adolescent cat that assumed he was the master of the universe.

When Tippy was three months old, Susanne and I took him to Ontario with us on vacation. We went each year to Lake on the Mountain, a small, family-run resort on a pristine limestone lake in Prince Edward County. We always loaded the Honda Element to the roof with our gear and supplies for our stay: canoe stuff, fishing tackle, guitars, sauté pans, pepper grinders, tea infusers, down pillows and lots of books and CDs. We had a kitty passport from the vet, his dish, his food, his kennel and his toys. We saved a prime spot for Tippy's carrier, right between our heads, facing forward. We hoped we could keep him calm if we talked to him and he could see us.

We needn't have been concerned. Tippy just rode along, as composed and quiet as could be, looking around and enjoying the world as it passed by him. Toward the end of the six-hour trip we got to the ferry at Glenora. I got out to stretch my legs and Susanne joined me on deck. There was a lot of clanging and banging and chugging of the ferry's diesel engine. We went back to the car to check on Tippy. He was out like a feline light.

Tippy spent most of his vacation romping on the deck of our house-keeping cottage. His energy and exuberance for playing with his new toys seemed boundless—at least until he crashed. Then up again after a nap, a quick stop at his food dish and off on another romp. Susanne took him in the canoe, an event that turned Tippy into a celebrity. Everyone at the waterside grabbed their video cameras and cell phones: "Hey! Look at the kitten in the canoe!" *Click*!

The woman who ran the lodge had two young nieces who came to visit during our stay. Tippy soon became their favorite. They would come to the door and very politely ask, "Can Tippy please come out and play?" Then we'd hear them frolicking on the lawn with the kitten, laughing and calling "Tippy! Tippy! Tippy!" One day their cousin came to visit with her pet rabbit, a young French lop. The rabbit was contentedly grazing on the lawn when Tippy decided to investigate. He trotted over and gave the rabbit's tail a sniff. The lop spun around, saw the cat and sprung a foot in the air. Tippy zipped off as fast as his little legs could travel.

During this trip, Tippy became fixated on an orange plush toy that was a goofy representation of a happy-go-lucky rodent. He started to carry it with him wherever he went. He would strangle it and then bring it to us, chirping a strange tune, and drop it at our feet. When he was a little guy, I think he killed Orange Toy about twenty times a day. As he got older, the delivery of Orange Toy became a ritual. If he saw me carrying a suitcase to the back hall to leave on a trip, he'd run to get Orange Toy, warble his little tune, and drop it at my feet. I guess it was a charm to prevent me from leaving. When I came home from the trip, he'd deliver Orange Toy, this time as a greeting. If we had guests, like Susanne's mother, Joan, who kept him out of the guest room while they slept, they'd awaken to find Orange Toy at the door in the morning. If Tippy's food dish was nearly empty, Orange Toy would be sprawled next to it. Orange Toy's magic never seemed terribly effective to us, but Tippy is still a true believer.

Poppy

Poppy came to the back door in a blizzard. Some stray cats yowl their heads off to get attention. Not Poppy. He just sat stoically on the edge of the porch, waiting for something to happen, the snow accumulating, like fate, on the back of his neck.

It won't surprise you that I fed him a large bowl of cat food that night. As I put it down, he swiped at me as if he was ready to fight me for it. I went into the kitchen and ran an egg under hot water for a few minutes. When I got back outside, the cat food was already gone. I cracked the egg into the bowl. It disappeared in ten seconds. I got a cardboard box and padded it with the remnants of an old down jacket and put it in a protected spot near the woodpile. Poppy climbed right in and curled up. In the morning he was gone. His trail led through a foot of snow a mile and a half up the road and disappeared under a squalid trailer where a nasty-looking dog was chained up. No wonder he had swiped at me. This cat had fought for everything.

Poppy became a regular visitor that winter. He developed a fondness for warm eggs and stayed close to his supply. The cardboard box was re-

placed by a small doghouse. The ratty down jacket gave way to a felt blanket augmented by a heating pad. Being no fool, Poppy decided all this was a much better deal than scrounging at the trailer. He had gone upscale. We decided to name him Poppy because he looked as if might have been Tippy's father.

Tippy inside, Poppy scheming to get in

One afternoon, as I was sitting on the back steps cleaning leeks, he unexpectedly jumped into my lap and started to purr. I thought of the exchange about being "tamed" between the fox and the boy in Antoine de Saint-Exupéry's *The Little Prince*. I realized that Poppy and I had been taming each other. Still, he loved to ramble. Sometimes in the late afternoons, I'd catch sight of him hunting intensely for voles in the foundation of the old silo, or along a swale at the edge of the cemetery field, a quarter mile away. I saw him there one evening and called "Hey, Pop! Hey, Pop!" My call broke his concentration. He looked up, turned in my direction, flicked his tail a few times, and came bounding across the field toward me. Every move he made conveyed grace, power and confidence. He was a magnificent animal.

The second year he was with us, a family of foxes moved into a den up the hill behind the house. I started to see the vixen in broad daylight, sometimes twenty feet from the back porch. She was likely distempered and wouldn't be scared off, but, thinking of *The Little Prince*, I certainly didn't want to shoot her. We decided to let Poppy into the house. He established dominance over our other cats in about two minutes. For the most part, they kept their distance and coexisted peacefully. But as insurance against nocturnal squabbles, I would take Poppy down to the studio building, where he would spend the night in a canoe that hung from the rafters of the heated garage. Somewhere I had read a theory that cats navigate, in part, by noting the position of the stars. On cold, clear winter nights when the majestic Adirondack sky was filled with thousands of stars and the Andromeda galaxy was a glowing fuzzball in the cosmos, Poppy would look overhead as he rode on my shoulder down the driveway. "Look at the sky, Poppy. Is that how you found us? Is that how you find your way home?" I would ask. One night, as I said that last word, the theme of Poppy's story suddenly struck me as he was stargazing. It was simple: Poppy, the wanderer, had found his home.

Years earlier, some contemptible lowlife left four little kittens on my back porch in the middle of the night. I didn't discover them until the next afternoon, when I went outside for firewood and heard them faintly crying. They were all huddled in a corner, hungry and terrified. One had what looked like a broken leg. I put them in a box with some towels and drove an hour through a sleet storm to get them to the vet who took in strays for the county. I kept trying to comfort them, petting them and saying, "I'll help you. I'll help you." But they just kept crying. I got there just after closing but pounded on the door like a lunatic until the vet himself came to investigate. "You have to help these kittens," I yelled through the glass, pointing into the box. He opened the door, took them out of the box and lifted them gently onto his examining table. He told me that he would feed them, get them hydrated, keep them warm and give them medical treatment for the next week. "It's always tight, but then I'll try to get them into the shelter," he told me. "They might have a chance. The little ginger guy with the bad leg? I don't know. He might have a better shot if I take the leg off. He's so young, he'll just adapt. Someone will probably feel sorry for him and take him in."

I tried to thank him, but I could barely speak through my fury. "How can anyone do this?" I finally growled. I recognize now that I was asking the existential question that King Lear asks in the depths of his madness: "Is there any cause in nature that makes these hard hearts?"[6]

The vet looked at me with great intensity. "Sometimes people are cruel. Sometimes they're appallingly stupid. Sometimes they just don't care. Either way, they cause suffering," he said.

Afterwards, I talked about this episode with Joe Roberts, a very wise counselor I was seeing. I asked him why I was so devastated when I heard the cry of those abandoned kittens and why I felt such anguish about their suffering. I knew it was something deeper than simple compassion. "You already know," he replied. "It's because somewhere inside of you, they are you and you are them. Frightened. Helpless. Abandoned. Just like most of us." It took me a long time to work through that realization. And I understand now why Poppy's story affected me so deeply. Poppy had found his home. And I have longed, as much as anything else in my life, to find mine.

The Beatles (1969)

The Penn campus in September of 1969 was buzzing with counterculture energy. In the slipstream of the Woodstock festival, the tentative explorations of the Summer of Love had been replaced by a kind of impatient tribalism. Jim Morrison's howl from the Doors' *Strange Days* was the new password: "We want the world and we want it NOW!"

I was starting my second term in the fellowship program, carrying a full course load, teaching two sections of Shakespeare and drumming up a dissertation proposal. I had even less time than I had money. One of the diversions I allowed myself was the English department "sherry party," an anachronistic affair held monthly in the garret of gothic Bennett Hall. It was a chance to drink some free Harvey's Shooting Sherry, eat some Carr's water biscuits with snappy cheese and listen to my cohorts talk a bunch of rubbish about *Mrs. Dalloway* or *The Merry Wives of Windsor* as lute music purred softly in the background. Tweedy jackets, Fair Isle sweaters and tweedy skirts were the uniform of the day. It was all amazingly out of touch with the antiestablishment social, political and cultural wave that was gathering force outside the window.

On a lovely fall day, I left the library to attend one of these functions. I stopped when I noticed a stage set up at one end of College Green. A band? No, it didn't look like a setup for a band. No mics, no amps, no drums. Just two JBL PA speakers and a big tape recorder in the middle of the stage. I saw Michael Tearson, who had a free-form rock show on WXPN, sitting to one side, taking a few furtive hits on a joint.

"What's up?" I asked him.

"Just don't go anywhere," he replied with surprising urgency. "Just sit down and get ready. Your mind is about to be blown. No shit."

That sounded a lot more interesting than sherry, cheese and academic playacting. I sat on the ground and waited. Gradually the Green started to fill. The crowd got festive—a few pinwheels, balloons, a Frisbee sailing overhead. Word had gotten out that something was about to happen. But what?

At four o'clock, Michael walked over to the tape recorder and, with a swooping gesture, hit PLAY.

A bass line. Shimmering cymbals. Then a pulsating groove:

> Here come old flattop / He come groovin' up slowly.
> He got ju-ju eyeballs… / Come together! / Right now

People looked at each other, puzzled, smiling, laughing at the political and sexual wordplay of the refrain.

"The Beatles!" somebody yelled. It was. Michael was standing with his arms crossed, grinning like a jack-o'-lantern. The Penn radio station had somehow scored an advance copy of *Abbey Road*.

As the tape played, I tried to make sense of what I was hearing. *Maxwell's silver hammer came down on her head? I'd like to be under the sea in an octopus's garden? She came in through the bathroom window?* The English professor in me was working overtime—and getting nowhere. Ultimately, the only thing to do was to surrender to the sublime, inspired lunacy of the thing. As Susan Sontag had recently argued in *Against Interpretation* and David Byrne would urge more than twenty years later, there comes a time to *stop making sense*. Perhaps the world was becoming just too crazy. Don't think. Don't analyze. Just listen.

By the time the tape had played through a second time, my entire awareness was on the way one track flowed into or rubbed against the one that came before it and the one that followed. Try as I might, I couldn't keep my inner academic at bay. I began to realize that this record was about *montage*, Russian silent film director Sergei Eisenstein's theory that when two things are juxtaposed, something very different from and more powerful than either of those two things may extraordinarily emerge. What that was, I didn't have a clue—and I'm not sure I have one now, for that matter. But I do know that one of the greatest challenges facing anyone who has made a record is to sequence the album. It's often been said that the B side of *Abbey Road* is George Martin's sublime achievement, pieced together from fragments and outtakes while "the lads" were off for the weekend. True or not, *Abbey Road* stands with its predecessor, *Sgt. Pepper's Lonely Hearts Club Band*, as two albums that redefined the concept of recorded music.

There is one thing I know for certain. The time has long passed when a thousand people would gather together on a lawn to listen to a tape recorder.

Glenn Gould (1970)

No, I didn't see this performance in person. Unless you were in the orchestra yourself or part of the CBC production crew, you didn't either. On a Thursday afternoon, Glenn Gould got a call from Karel Ancerl, the conductor of the Toronto Symphony, asking if he could fill in the next morning for a videotaping of Beethoven's Emperor concerto. The scheduled pianist was indisposed. Gould cordially agreed and spent a couple of hours that evening going over the score.

Gould had not been playing the orchestral repertoire much since he retired from the concert stage, six years earlier. He had recorded the Emperor in 1966 with Leopold Stokowski and likely had not touched it since. His time had been spent in the recording studio, immersed in his meditations on Bach and Schoenberg.

Although I wasn't present for this, I've watched it many times online, and it is one of the most imposing performances in my experience of classical music. The taping was done without rehearsal, and without editing. Initially, Gould seems almost detached, even a bit impatient with the conductor. Within minutes, he is carrying the performance on his back, pushing tempo, insisting on a broader dynamic range than this rather pedestrian orchestra seems capable of. In the adagio second movement, Gould is in a virtual trance, exploring the emotional landscape of this surpassingly beautiful nocturne. His rendering of the ascending theme is heart-wrenching and defies any sniping critique that he was an "algebraic" pianist. In the third movement, which is sometimes considered anticlimactic, Gould plays the mazurka-like beginning as if he's possessed. If the orchestra can't keep up, he'll take the risk of leaving it behind. Still, he conducts with his left hand, urging them on. The ending is stunning—the arpeggios are fluid and expressive, not mechanical as they have seemed to be in many other performances I've seen. Every note is articulated and given meaning.

Gould's monumental performance, which would be his last with an orchestra, is all more the impressive, given his professed boredom with the Emperor. Gould reportedly said that, "Nowhere north of the Grand Old Opry can we encounter more stark II-V-I chord progressions."

The Allman Brothers (1971)

If I could travel in time to revisit one concert, this would be it. The show took place a few months after the Allman Brothers recorded *Live at Fillmore East*, which is often mentioned as the greatest rock concert live album ever made. Dick Waterman, whom I had known slightly in the heady Cambridge days of 1962–65, promoted the show at the Civic Center, near the Penn campus. At the time, he was managing blues acts and put several of them on the bill.

Dick's protégé Bonnie Raitt opened the show, with her bass player, Freebo. Her bluesy posturings left the crowd restless; people started to grumble that it was going to be a long night. But Mississippi Fred McDowell charmed the audience when he opened his set by declaring, "I do not play no rock and roll!" Then he took us on an excursion through the music of juke joints and rural churches in the Mississippi Delta of the 1930s. His hypnotic "Woke Up This Morning with My Mind on Jesus" is still one of the most compelling blues and gospel performances I have ever seen.

The audience grew restless again as the roadies worked the stage changeover for Buddy Guy and Junior Wells. I was twitching with anticipation to see them; my copy of their old Delmark album *Hoodoo Man Blues* had been played until there were as many scratches, pops and skips as there was music. But the thin applause when Waterman announced them made me realize that most of the audience had no idea who these guys were. By the end of the first song, people were captivated. Junior approached each song like a psychodrama, toying with the balance between tenderness and aggression. He implored and raged his way through the lyrics. He strutted the stage like a bantam rooster that had taken a lesson or two from James Brown. He blew searing blues harp. Buddy played with a strange, dry tone through a Leslie tremolo device. He answered every shift of mood with guitar lines that toyed with the irony in Junior's voice and harp. They just destroyed the place.

Now the audience was finally ready.

I was about twenty feet from the stage. Greg Allman's organ was directly in front of me. He sat down and chugged a can of Pabst Blue Ribbon. His brother Duane plugged in his Les Paul and counted off. The band kicked into "Statesboro Blues." With the exceptions of some Brazilian and African music, I have never heard such a relentless, compelling groove before or since—and I likely never will. Driven by the two drummers, Jaimo and Butch Trucks, the entire band pulsed as a single organism. The guitar lines floated on cresting waves of drums, organ and bass. Duane and Dickie Betts set down thematic riffs with a vengeance and then launched into exotic excursions that somehow resolved and came together as if by instinct. These weren't just "jams." They were musically coherent and propelled by the same drive to build and resolve tension that makes Bach's Brandenburg Concerto no. 4 so immensely satisfying. The drummers played with, off and against one another, mixing time signatures. The bass player, Berry Oakley, broke all the rules. He didn't play with the kick drums; he inhabited his own syncopated world and added melodic counterpoint. Greg Allman's organ was the sweet syrup that saturated the whole thing and made it *flow*. When they hit the groove after the long introduction to "One Way Out" it was almost too intense, like pleasure on the edge of pain. It was simply the greatest musical performance I have ever seen.

B.B. King (c. 1971)

Randy was in the same fellowship program as I in graduate school. A Phi Beta Kappa from Stanford, he had run the 5K and 10K in college and had a framed photograph of himself running shoulder to shoulder with track immortal Steve Prefontaine in the Pac-10 championships. "His strategy was to run everyone else into the ground. I went out fast, way too fast. But I wanted a picture of me with Prefontaine. I hung with him around the first turn. A friend of mine was waiting with a camera and got the shot. Then I just about collapsed. The coach had me pegged for a top five finish if I had paced myself, and he was furious."

Randy was a scholar of the Victorian writer Thomas Babington Macaulay. When passing the hash pipe, he would sometimes quote Macaulay: "Perhaps no person can be a poet, or can even enjoy poetry, without a certain unsoundness of mind." But like me, Randy was also a blues freak. We swapped obscure albums by Johnny Young, Victoria Spivey and Otis Rush and books by Paul Oliver and Tony Russell. Randy called me one afternoon and told me B.B. King was playing that night someplace in North Philadelphia. Get ready. We were going. I put on my usual go-to-a-rock-concert outfit. Frye boots, bell-bottom Levi's, a splashy cowboy shirt with fake pearl buttons from Rodeo Ben's and a vest from some old worsted suit. On the way to the concert, we got high and laughed ourselves sick as we went through a car wash.

I have never felt as alien and out of place as I did that night. The venue was a fancy dinner theater, not some bar or nightclub. We were the only White people in the room. Everyone else was dressed in their best finery for a memorable evening out. The men had on sharp suits, snazzy ties and shined shoes. The ladies wore dazzling dresses in jewel tones with big hats, high heels, gloves and purses to match. I felt like a slob, an intruder.

The show opened with "Sonny Freeman and his Fabulous Upsetters Orchestra, direct from Brooklyn, New York." They were, as billed, fabulous. Led by Sonny himself on drums, the rhythm section swung like crazy. The horns were smooth and tight. They played a few instrumentals like "Night Train." I settled in and started to feel more relaxed. Then B.B. skipped onto the stage with his black Gibson guitar, Lucille. He just took the place over. Every gesture, every wry smirk, every histrionic vocal line was met with a volley of delighted shouts. The show became a blues revival meeting. He was testifying, and his audience was testifying back.

B.B. went through the litany of his classics. The crowd loved each song more than the last. By the time he got to "How Blue Can You Get?" they were responding to every phrase. He sang the punch line that's the climax of the song:

> I gave you seven children
> Now you want to give them back!

Immediately, a woman directly in front of me sprung to her feet, threw her arms in the air, shook her hands and hollered at the top of her lungs, *"Preach, niggah! Preeeach!"*

A wave of terror swept over me. I don't know whether I feared people would think I had said it, or whether my feeling of abject embarrassment at hearing that word shouted in public was simply too huge to contain. Sweat started pouring down from my armpits. Then I realized that B.B. had stopped playing and was bent over, laughing and pointing in her direction. The band and the audience were laughing, too. Voices were yelling, "That's right!" and "Amen, Sister!" I just froze.

The rest of the show was a blur. Randy and I sat quietly for quite a while after the concert was over, to be as inconspicuous as possible and out of deference to B. B.'s real audience. As we made our way to the door, an older gentleman smiled at us and extended his hand to shake ours. "Nice to see you young folks here. You know, we love B. B. as much as you do. Thank you kindly for coming."

George Jones and Tammy Wynette (c. 1975)

My friend Evan got wind that George Jones and Tammy Wynette would appear on a Sunday afternoon at a high school auditorium in Middletown, New York. Evan played fiddle and viola on my first album and was a member of David Bromberg's touring band. We filled a couple of cars with other counterculture folkies, bluegrass players and country music fans and off we went.

The Silver Eagle touring bus parked outside the auditorium had THE GEORGE JONES AND TAMMY WYNETTE SHOW painted on the side in foot-high letters. The driver was leaning against the bus, talking to some guy. The show was totally sold out, he was saying. They could have added another show, but they were playing in Harrisburg that night. Got to keep rollin'.

The high school auditorium was much larger than I expected—at least a thousand seats. By show time, every seat was filled with local people. These were people who had come out of blue-collar neighborhoods, from rural villages and off the local dairy farms to see their idols. They came dressed for a special occasion—the ladies coiffed, made up and wearing that treasured pin or strand of beads that didn't make it off the dresser very often. The men wore jackets, many with a kind of western flair, and a bolo tie and shined boots. I felt like a fool in my long hair and denim.

The show started pretty much as you'd expect. The band played a couple of numbers and then "the king of country music, George Jones" was announced. These were the dark days of addiction and mental illness for George, but there he was, singing songs like "She Thinks I Still Care" with forthright emotion. Then he whipped the crowd up with "White Lightning." Everyone sang along. Then the announcement: "Ladies and gentlemen, the one and only queen of country music…Miss Tammy Wynette!"

She drifted onto the stage in a cloud of powder-blue chiffon. The lady next to me cooed, "Oh, my!" Tammy was taller than I would have imagined. Her posture and bearing were, as the announcer had promised, nothing short of regal. Just by walking to center stage, she completely stole the show. George took her by the hand and they sang a duet—"We're Gonna Hold On," as I recall. Then she was alone. I thought "Stand by Your Man" would close the show, but she sang it first. The narrative of these three songs was clear: his song about booze, their song about enduring as a couple, her song about staying with him. Their audience got it. They knew the backstory. They thundered their approval.

Standing alone at the microphone, Tammy looked vulnerable. She sang "I Don't Wanna Play House," a narrative sung by a woman who has lost her husband because of her own infidelity. The chorus is in the voice of the woman's little daughter. When she got to the line "and then the teardrops made my eyes grow dim," Tammy let all the horses out of the barn at once. Her voice soared effortlessly to a shattering crescendo. She owned the song, and she owned her audience. Completely.

As we left the auditorium, the Silver Eagle was already pulling away. Acrid diesel fumes filled the driveway. The king and queen of country music were on their way to Harrisburg and another show.

De Dannan (1978)

They say rock is all about attitude. I saw the Stones a few times in the 1960s and '70s, and they surely had plenty of attitude. But ultimately, the attitude seemed fabricated and commodified, as if they turned it on for the audience in those moments when the music wasn't at its best—as in the "Uncle Sam" tour. Remember Mick's "Oops, I lost a button on me trousers. You don't want me to lose any more buttons on me trousers, do ye?" *Actually not, Mick, but it's amusing that you're enough of a narcissistic scoundrel to ask the question night after night.*

By contrast, the Irish band De Dannan reeked of unalloyed attitude. They were cocky and surly, and their attitude rang true with every note they played. Their marvelous fiddler, Frankie Gavin, tried to maintain some degree of rapport with the audience between songs. The rest of the band—Charlie Piggott, Ringo McDonagh, Alec Finn and the button accordion genius Jackie Daly—weren't concerned with ingratiating themselves with anyone. They just sat there, impatiently waiting for the next song to start.

And when it did, they played with stunning, virtuosic authority. Many Irish bands, even some very good ones, seem to get captivated by the lyricism of the music and wind up sounding as if they are picking their way through the melody from one phrase to the next. Even in their quieter numbers, De Dannan always seemed to be looking for the rhythmic heart of the music. And when they kicked into a reel, their effortless drive was electrifying.

De Dannan played the Great Hudson River Revival in 1979. Their performance was the outstanding moment of the festival. As one of the directors of the event, I was at the back of the stage, with a headset and a clipboard, watching the audience as the band played. At the start of the set, the crowd looked like a few thousand sunburned folkies and environmentalists who were probably hungry and needed to use the porta potty. After a song or two, the audience was a sea of grins. We had all been transported to some taproom or dancehall of the imagination, where sentimental songs provoked a tear and jigs and reels were the call to get up and move.

I produced the festival album. I spent weeks the next winter listening through hundreds of hours of tape to select the thirteen cuts for the record. I listened to De Dannan's remarkable set many times before I chose their medley of "The Black Thorn" and "P. J. Conlan's" for the record, two reels that captured their drive and spontaneity, which in Irish slang would be called *fierce*.

Unknown Guitarists, Isla Mujeres, Mexico, 1988

About two days into my trip to Mexico, I realized I was in the wrong place with the wrong person. We were in Cancún. I hated Cancún. She liked Cancún. It was going to be a very long two weeks. I suggested we rent one of those stinky-exhaust Mexican Volkswagen Beetles and head south. After a day of wrangling, we did. I was captivated by the Mayan observatory at Tulum; she was bored. I liked walking the graceful crescent of beach at Akumal to the little palm-covered beach bar at the end; she didn't. I wanted to keep going to Belize; she wouldn't. One thing we did agree about is that it might be enjoyable to take the ferry to Isla Mujeres for a couple of days. Our first night on the island we went to dinner at a place recommended by a German couple we met on the ferry. Good food and good music, they assured us.

I don't remember anything about the food, but the music was a revelation. Two brothers went from table to table playing guitars. One of the brothers was a blind albino. At first they played unusually tasteful versions of "Guantanamera" and other predictable tourist fare. The albino fellow played lead and was melodically inventive, as if he'd listened to a lot of

Django Reinhardt and Oscar Aleman. His brother played rhythm and could swing even a hokey standard. *Nice stuff,* I thought. After a few numbers they launched into Django's "Minor Swing." It was still derivative, but the guitarist was extending the idiom and making it his own. And when the idiom was defined by the likes of Django, that's an extraordinary thing to do. It's what Louis Armstrong did with the idiom defined by King Oliver.

Then the albino launched into series of standards. From the perspective of thirty years, I can't remember what songs he played next, but I know at one point he was about five feet away from me, and it struck me that I was five feet from actual genius. Every phrase he played had clarity of purpose and he could turn a melodic phrase upside down and inside out and make it sound like play, not pedantry. His playing had some of the same sorcery I hear in Charlie Christian's solo on the Benny Goodman Sextet recording of "Flying Home." On top of that, he was one of the best "touch players" I have heard in person. His control of subtle and expressive dynamics put him, if only for those fleeting moments, in the same sentence as Carlos Montoya, who is the greatest guitarist I have ever heard. In college, when I was assigned to write an imitation of William Carlos Williams, I wrote an embarrassingly obvious poem about Montoya:

> Your guitar is a woman
> Who leaps up to sing and cry
> When you offer her suggestions

As inept as the poem may be, it tries to express what I heard in Montoya on records, and what I heard in the albino's playing that night on Isla Mujeres. Like millions of others, I play my guitar and it makes sounds; rare people like these touch the guitar and it comes to life—laughing, teasing, grieving.

And then it was over. The guitarists just left. They had never been introduced by name. There were no CDs to buy, no T-shirts, no email sign-up list. A few of us in the restaurant clapped when we realized they had played their last song; many were too preoccupied with the moonlight and their dinner companions to do even that.

45
Martine

My friend Peter and I caught the fly-fishing bug in 1972. When we weren't fishing we were tying flies, tinkering with leaders or studying Art Flick's book on trout stream insects in the Catskills.

Peter rented an old stone hunting lodge near the Esopus Creek. We'd fish around Mount Tremper and Phoenicia until nightfall with our friend Gene and then look for a place to land for drinks and dinner. Our regular spot was Tiso's, a family-run Sicilian joint on Route 212. The food was cheap and satisfying, but the red sauce thing got boring after a while. It was a relief when, in 1978, a new place called La Duchesse Anne opened down the road. Our favorite pool to end the evening's fishing was marked by a yellow mailbox, only a half mile from the inn.[7]

The first night we went, a burly, Hemingwayesque guy behind the bar gave us a nod and turned back to the boxing match he was watching on TV. He ignored us for a while and finally I piped up, "Sorry to bother you, but I'd like a Johnnie Walker Red on the rocks and my friend would like a very dry martini." He looked at us funny and pointed to the TV. "Can't you see I'm watching boxing? Get your own drinks. Leave some money on the bar." Peter was playing bartender when a woman rushed into the bar with a babe in arms and deposited it in the playpen in the corner. "This kid shits more than a goose!" she announced to no one in particular. She noticed us at the bar. "You want dinner tonight? I hope I didn't just spoil your appetite. But the kid does shit a lot! I'll get you a menu." That was our introduction to Bruce and Martine.

Over the years, Bruce became a figure of mystery and speculation. Had he been a boxer? A New York City cop? A foreign spy for the Kenyan government? One whimsical rumor had him as a former lingerie buyer for Macy's. Bruce fostered his mystique by never talking about his past, traveling regularly to Nairobi and accumulating a collection of vintage Land Rovers. We knew one thing for certain—Bruce was in the habit of finishing the crossword puzzle in the Sunday *New York Times* before the brunch dishes had been cleared away.

Running an auberge was Martine's family heritage. For generations, her family kept inns along the coast of Brittany, and she carried those traditions with her to Mount Tremper. The kitchen of the inn was also the family kitchen. The bar had some comfortable furniture where the family congregated to play cards, help the kids with homework, knit and share the local gossip. Children and animals roamed free, at least until the youngsters were old enough to clear tables, wash dishes and scrub floors.

Martine had been a student at the Sorbonne during the May, 1968 riots in Paris. Like student revolutionaries everywhere, she was sublimely opinionated and had an ample reservoir of righteous indignation. In later years, when she would go on a tirade about her political views, I would cup my hands over my mouth and call out over an imaginary bullhorn, *"Aux barricades étudiants! Aux barricades!"* That would get her goat.

Speaking of goats, they were among the animals that had the run of the place. The dining room was full one night when a nanny goat wandered in and started to help herself to lettuce off salad plates. She was actually quite polite as she deftly manipulated the greens into her mouth. The patrons thought it was hilarious. Martine was in the kitchen, getting an order together. She heard the commotion, looked through the porthole in the door and came charging into the dining room. She straddled the goat from behind, grabbed an ear in each hand and marched the animal through the bar and out the door, to a round of applause. She reappeared, grinning and waving a napkin triumphantly over her head.

In those days, Kingston was a hub of the IBM empire. Junior executives and their wives made the Duchess a favorite spot for an evening out and for corporate entertaining. It was only a half hour away and yet had the kind of worldly ambiance that reflected well on a young manager on the rise. One evening a well-scrubbed young couple sat with an older couple at the table next to mine. From what I overheard, it seemed that the young fellow was taking his boss out for dinner. While Martine took their orders, he tried to display his sophistication by talking in a loud voice about some inn in Vermont that he and his wife loved for the excellent food.

I paid much more attention to my own dinner than to them, until I saw the kitchen doors fly open and Martine come striding across the dining room with a plate in her hand. She shoved the plate in front of the young man and parked her hands on her hips. "You sent this back to the kitchen, eh?" she challenged.

"Well, yes, actually. You see…"

He didn't get a chance to finish. "Oh, so you are a big expert on French cooking, eh? So you know more than my chef, eh? Well, good for you. Maybe you should go now to Vehr-mon, where everyone is as smart as you and knows everything about cuisine, eh?" She made shooing motions with her hands. "So you go to Vehr-mon now. This lousy food is no good for you, you are so smart and know so much. You leave and go to Vehr-mon to your precious little inn where the food is so *exceptionnel*. You go now." She snatched their half-eaten dinners from the table and piled the plates on a tray with a lot of clatter. The boss' wife was left with her fork in her hand. The two couples sat in silence for a moment. The young man tried to recover his dignity by saying something flippant. Then they got up and left.

The craziest night of all was New Year's Eve, 1985 or '86. A bunch of us booked Martine's package deal: cocktails and hors d'oeuvres, dinner at her nine o'clock seating, rooms for the night and *crêpes bretonnes* and coffee in the morning. Our group arrived in high spirits at eight. Martine had hired a musette group with a terrific accordion player. The Parisian café music and some wonderful appetizers got the evening off to a festive start. Then the wheels started to come off. Martine's sister Marie, who kept the dining room humming, was sick, so Martine had hired two of her daughter's friends to wait tables. The nine o'clock seating turned into ten, and then into ten-thirty. We were finally seated, served a leek, potato and sorrel soup, followed by a cold split lobster with aioli. Everything was grand so far. It was creeping up on midnight when our main dishes came to the table. I took a bite of my *châteaubriand* à *la béarnaise*. Sensational.

I was raising another forkful when the music started. The accordion player and her troupe rushed into the dining room, gesturing for everyone to get up and follow them. We were going to parade down the road and welcome the New Year by singing and dancing on the bridge over the creek. I got a final, forlorn glance at my plate and joined the crowd as we followed the band out the door and into the dark, cold night. Down the road we marched, clapping in time with the music. When we got to the bridge, someone passed around a few candles they had lifted from the tables. We sang "Auld Lang Syne." Martine, who had come with us, led us in "La Marseillaise." Someone threw the flowers they had taken from their table off the bridge. We leaned over the rail to watch them float down the stream and into the darkness. Everybody kissed everybody else. Then we paraded back to the inn as the band played.

It was all great fun. But it had taken a lot of time. All the way back I was thinking about my dinner, turning cold on its plate. *Oh well*, I thought, *I'm hungry enough to eat it cold. It'll be okay*. When we got back to our table, everything was gone. The kids who were serving us had stripped the table down to the bare wood. They were sitting at a table in the corner with two of their friends, enjoying what turned out to be the last of the desserts. We stood looking at one another, incredulously. "Oh shit!" Martine exclaimed. Then she shrugged. "I'll heat up some more soup and bread and get a couple of bottles from the cellar. *C'est la cuisine!*"

That night, the heat was blasting in the spartan bedrooms upstairs. The radiators knocked and banged all night. We slept with the windows wide open to the twenty-degree air and we were still suffocating. When we met our friends downstairs in the morning they told us of their monumental headaches and their tortured dreams. We drank gallons of water and quarts of coffee while we waited for Martine to arrive for *crêpes*. She appeared, fastening her apron and smiling broadly. "We had good fun last night, no?"

For all the hijinks, the Duchess was a serious restaurant. Martine's first chef, Guy, had a gift for turning out *les bon repas*. But he drank a lot and, on a couple of occasions, I heard shouting from the kitchen that carried into the dining room and out into the bar. Guy left after five years, but the kitchen held up well. The Duchess advanced the tradition of French country cooking that had been popularized in upstate New York by Charles

Martine, Bruce and their son, Yannick

Virion's renowned Monblason Inn, across the Hudson in Pine Plains. Like Virion's, uncomplicated dishes with direct flavors were the staples of Martine's menu. The *Cotriade Bretonne* (a Breton fish stew recipe from her family) and roast lamb with rosemary and mustard were my own favorites. She kept a very good, moderately priced cellar. And the place was a visual treat. The rambling front porch, the shellacked pine and mahogany, the dark green floral wallpaper from the 1920s and the enormous wood-stove with isinglass doors made it seem a refuge of warmth in the winter and like woodland shade in the summer. The rooms upstairs were another story. When I first started going, they were eight dollars per night during the week and ten dollars on the weekends. And they were worth every penny: squeaky iron bedsteads, a sink in the corner and the WC and tub down the hall. The place became a favorite refuge for Wood-stock music types who had been kicked out of the house by angry wives or angry girlfriends—or both.

One Monday night, I called Martine from the road. I knew that she was closed on Mondays, but I would be driving by about nine o'clock and needed dinner. Could she feed me? *"Certainement.* You will eat. And we will talk."

The dining room was in darkness, except for a small lamp on our table. Martine brought out a covered pan and put it next to me. "Sorry, *mon petit choux*. Leftovers from family meal Friday night. It's all I have. *C'est tout*. But it's been reheated three times, so it's just right." She opened the lid and started to spoon *coq au vin* onto my plate. Just the fragrance of the dish was intoxicating. I took a moment to admire its glistening, dark brown color. Then I tasted. The dish was transcendent, with subtle notes of smoked, salty meat and an herby cascade of flavors emerging from a rich foundation of butter and wine. I believe to this day it is the best dish I have ever eaten. "I have something special for you," Martine said as she brought a bottle to the table—as I recall, a Châteauneuf-du-Pape from the late 1960s. She poured two glasses. The wine was massive, a splendid pairing with the powerful *coq*.

The mood was set. I ate and, as she had promised, we talked. It was likely the first time we'd spent together without other people around. Martine confided in me that night. The restaurant was thriving, she said, but she was struggling. Bruce had been difficult since he contracted a kidney disease in Kenya. He couldn't or wouldn't cut down his drinking. It would kill him. Her daughter was hanging around with druggie kids in high school. She thought about selling, just getting out. As she talked, I realized that she trusted me, and that we had a deeper friendship than I had realized. I spared her any platitudes that were circulating in my mind. We finished the wine and said good night.

Peter called me early one morning a month or two later. "The Duchess burned down last night. To the ground. It's gone."

Many years later, we had something of a reunion dinner at the Savoy, a lovely place Peter knew in Soho. By design, our table was next to a crackling wood fire to ward off the chill of a windy January night. Martine proudly came with her daughter, who was now a registered nurse, certified in the European Union as well as in the States. She could practice just about anywhere in the Western world and had a limitless future. Martine herself managed the restaurant and bar at some posh yacht club just north of the George Washington Bridge. Peter, his wife Melinda and I sat in the glow of the fire, listening to their stories. A second and then a third bottle of wine appeared on the table. I was beginning to indulge my own sentimentality—a sign that I'd had plenty to drink. But then, at Martine's insistence, some glasses of Calvados from Brittany appeared. We toasted Bruce. We toasted La Duchesse Anne. We toasted the rainbow trout in the Esopus. And finally, we toasted ourselves and our memories.

46
Bugs

Bugs was a gray-and-white Dutch rabbit. She was a friendly, charming little creature that had been rescued from some Easter Bunny display. Bugs learned quickly how to use a litter box, so she pretty much had the run of the house.

Give her a piece of dry spaghetti right out of the box and she was in bunny heaven. She would nibble and manipulate the strand with her rabbity lips as if she were conducting some imaginary woodland orchestra. Sometimes I would put on Herbert von Karajan leading the Berlin Philharmonic in Beethoven's Sixth, "The Pastoral," just to give her the complete experience.

Bugs' life seemed simple enough, and uneventful—until strange things started to happen.

She developed an interest in the basement, which I accommodated by leaving the door open. Down she would go, one step at a time, surveying as she went with those unblinking eyes on the sides of her head. Since she liked it so much down there, I relocated her food bowl and water bottle. *It's cool down there*, I thought. *That's why she likes it.*

Then I found the salamander and the dead mouse.

The house was in Ulster Landing, close to the Hudson, and the basement was pretty damp. One day, on my way to the washing machine, I saw a furry thing crawling laboriously across the concrete floor toward my feet. I recoiled. *What the hell?* I regained my composure, went upstairs and grabbed one of the fireplace gloves to deal with the mutant. I put it in the laundry sink for examination—it was a spotted salamander, covered with rabbit fur. *Ugh.* After a quick rinse, the salamander seemed to have recovered and I escorted it outside.

A few weeks later, as I was coming down the stairs, I saw Bugs banging something against the edge of the bottom step. She'd swing it into the step, swing it back and then bash it again. On closer examination, I saw that her victim was a mouse—quite dead. But Bugs didn't seem to care. She just kept bashing away until I got the fireplace gloves again and relieved her of her burden. Unconcerned, she hopped off to her food bowl and had a snack. *Ah!* I realized. *The mice have been stealing her food.* Bugs was simply enforcing lagomorphic justice. *Steal my food and pay the price, Squeaker.*

That summer, I was one of the directors of a festival called the Great Hudson River Revival. The sponsoring organization, the Clearwater, had

finagled the use of an old Boy Scout camp on the banks of the Hudson in Croton as the festival site. It was my job to be there for the week before the event, riding around in a golf cart with a clipboard and walkie-talkie, doing advance work on a thousand details. Then there would be the festival itself for another three days, and two days of cleanup. What to do with Bugs?

As one of the directors, I got the use of a camp counselor's cabin on the property. All I had to do was bring an air mattress, some bedding and towels, and I would be all set. The cabin even had running water. So I packed Bugs into a carrier and off to the festival we went. When I took her out of the car, her nose was twitching overtime. *She's sniffing a whole new world*, I thought. *How precious*. When I opened the door to the cabin, I realized what she was really sniffing. A huge pile of hay took up about half of the cabin. I put Bugs' carrier on the floor. Her nose twitched faster. She started scratching. She wanted out. I opened the door of the carrier and she bounded to the edge of the pile, took a couple of big sniffs, and dove in. She'd emerge at night to have a snack and chew my hair.

Still, the highlight of Bugs' career came when I visited my mother at Scraggy Neck. Again, what to do with Bugs? There was nothing for it but to bring her along in her carrier. Mother greeted Bugs with her characteristic mix of compassion and judgment: "Oh, she's sweet. And so pathetic. Perhaps she'd like some clover? I think there's a patch growing in the lawn." But Mother clearly had no enthusiasm for the idea that a rabbit would occupy space in her house for a week. Or for ten minutes, for that matter. "Could she go to a kennel?" Mother asked. Not really, I explained. Dogs. Rabbits. Bad combo. "Oh dear," she replied. "What about the basement?"

Now there was an idea with potential. The basement at Scraggy Neck was designed for hurricanes—just a wide, sandy floor to let the water drain out, if it ever came in. I took Bugs down the stairs in her carrier. "No hay this time," I apologized, as I opened the door. She hopped out, sniffed a few times and started to dig in the compacted sand. She dug quickly—and she dug purposefully. Bugs clearly had a plan.

After dinner, I went down to check on her. She was gone. There was an opening in the sand, rabbit-sized. I stuck my forearm in. It just kept going. *What now?* I wondered. *She's got a burrow. A network of burrows by now.* Every day I would go down and replenish Bugs' food and water. She seemed to be emerging at night to eat, which was reassuring, but what was I going to do when it was time to leave? Rabbits don't come when you call their names. I'd have to lie in wait and grab her, or dig her out. *This could really be a pain in the ass.*

The morning came when I was scheduled to leave. I had my breakfast and went down the bulkhead to figure out how to lure Bugs back to the surface. I turned on the light and Bugs was crouching next to her carrier, looking at me—sideways, as she tended to look at anything. The burrow had been neatly filled in and covered over. She had punched her ticket for her trip home.

47
Artie

There's a character in an August Wilson play named Bynum. Bynum's grand purpose in life was to bring people together, often in mysterious and unexpected ways. Like Bynum, Artie had a rare magic with people.

In 1972, I moved to a house on an apple orchard a half hour from Woodstock. I picked up a copy of the *Woodstock Times* to get a handle on what was going on in what seemed, after the bustle of Philadelphia, to be a pretty sleepy corner of the world. There was a small notice in the classifieds: *Songwriter's workshop Tuesday nights. Call Artie Traum*. The ad gave his number.

I had seen Artie and his brother Happy perform at the Main Point and with Joni Mitchell and James Taylor at the Newport Folk Festival. I had their albums on Capitol. I loved their way of forging a new American music from the echoes of the Appalachians, the Delta, Nashville and Washington Square Park. In my mind, their only equals in this project were the Band. Even more than the great playing and passionate harmonizing, I admired the songs. They were intriguing, emotionally complex and very literate. The idea of studying with the person who had written most of them captivated me. I called.

Six of us would meet every Tuesday night. The assignment was simple. Everyone—Artie included—brought a new song to every session. We played our song and listened to critique from the other writers. Sometimes we all pitched in to develop a song on the spot. Everyone was respectful of the process and the work, but it was not always a feel-good exercise. One week, I brought in a song about my father. I knew it was a sentimental mess and I was embarrassed to sing it, but it was my work for the week, so I did. Artie's reaction was direct and constructive: "There's a way to express honest emotion without being so self-indulgent. Get some distance. The first thing I'd suggest would be to take out the words 'I,' 'me' and 'my' and rewrite it from there." That's fine teaching: an honest critique and a pathway to make the work better.

When summer came, the workshop dissolved and didn't regroup as winter approached. Artie started to invite me up to spend the evening once or twice a month. There would always be a fire in the stone fireplace and plenty of strong coffee. We'd talk a lot, and we'd share new songs when we had them. I wrote about those evenings in "Singing Angel Band," a song on my album *Flow*:

You stirred the embers until they glowed
And we both got back in tune
You played another song for me
And I played my song for you
Music kept the winter out
And chased the blues away
First thought is the best thought
That's what you'd always say

The last couple of lines refer to Artie's Zen, catch-lightning-in-a-bottle approach to writing. "When a song arrives, you'd better be ready," he told me once. During another of those fireside sessions, he showed me everything he'd learned the week before when he had taken a guitar lesson from the legendary Clarence White. I was inspired to learn that even an accomplished player like Artie was seeking out new ideas.

That summer, I had gone into a little eight-track studio with Jay Ungar, Neil Rossi and Evan Stover and recorded a demo to shop around to folky record labels. Rounder, Flying Fish and Philo passed on it right away, and I was getting pretty discouraged. Then one night the phone rang well after midnight. "This is John Fahey," a voice said. "I want you to do a record on my label, Takoma. I'll send you a letter and a contract." Fahey was a notorious eccentric and a pretty significant figure in the constellation of folk revival guitarists. He once described his own style of roots-derived music in a funny and honest way as "cosmic sentimentalism." He told me that he'd listened to the demo while his wife was cutting his hair and she told him he should do the project. Three days later, I got a letter with several pages of detailed notes and suggestions about the songs. The contract itself was a very florid affair, with engraved Renaissance angels flying across the pages, tooting their golden horns.

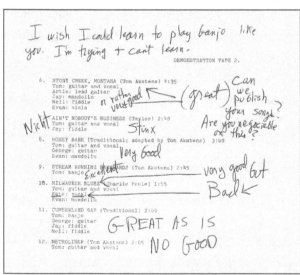

John Fahey's critique of my demo

The next time I was at Artie's house, I told him the news. His response was immediate and direct: "I want to produce it." It would be Artie's first production credit.

We had a budget of $2,500 to get the record done. I had only been in small eight-track studios, and I assumed that we would be recording in one of those, perhaps with a friend or two like Jay, Neil or Evan to round things out. Artie had other ideas. Since this was his first production project, he wanted it to sound ready for airplay. He waved his magic wand. Presto! We could record for four nights and mix for three at the renowned Bearsville Studios, where the Band and Van Morrison had recorded. This was the big leagues. The hitch was that Todd Rundgren was finishing a project, and we would have to work around his schedule. Todd liked to work in the afternoon and go home for a good dinner. We could come in at nine and work until three in the morning. Bearsville would kick in the services of a promising young engineer, Tom Mark, known as "T.M." We budgeted two grand for musicians, three hundred bucks for food and wine, and two hundred for tape. Artie stretched that budget a long way. Billy Mundi from the Mothers of Invention was the drummer, Tony Markelis played bass, Dick Fegy doubled on guitar and mandolin, traditional jazz luminary Peter Ecklund played cornet, Bob Siggins brought his pedal steel to the sessions and Debbie

Artie in the studio. "What? You're asking me? I'm just the producer!"

Green, my old heartthrob from the Cambridge days, was on piano. Jay, Neil, Evan and seventeen-year-old guitar whiz George Langston filled out the band. All I had to do was keep up with these folks.

I loved Artie's style of working on that project. He filled a spiral notebook with notes on arrangements and who would play which instrument on which song. He was organized, which suited the planner in me, but he left lots of space for serendipity. And I loved the studio.

To use an egregiously overused phrase, it was *very cool*—a monument to the '70s rock sensibility. A Bösendorfer Imperial grand piano and luxurious fabric baffles with images of flying geese set an opulent tone in Studio B, the primary recording room. The control room console had a tooled leather and sterling silver armrest. The place of honor was occupied by "Old Grey," a massive sixteen-track Ampex MM-1000 tape machine. Along the wall were racks of dozens of signal-processing effects with their blinking lights and glowing VU meters. I started to call the place Ice Station Zebra.

This nickname became eerily appropriate. The second day of recording, the snow started to come down, and it kept falling for two more days. Some folks did a supply run to the A&P and Overlook Liquors. The last night of the sessions we were completely snowed in and we worked until dawn. The Woodstock Deli made it up the hill with sandwiches just before the roads closed.

We really worked hard on that record. The vintage pool table down the hall didn't get much use. One of the first songs we cut was "Milwaukee Blues." The track that wound up on the album is the first take we did, actually a rehearsal take with everybody playing live and a live vocal. I hadn't played with such a solid live band before, and I felt like I was riding a wave. When we listened to playback on the huge Westlake monitors, I was floored. Magically, the music was tight and loose at the same time. Artie started, in jest, to call me "One Take Tommy." I much preferred that to his nickname for me when I had flubbed an intro: "Sausagefingers."

Mixing was as much fun as recording. In the days before computerized automation, all the faders and pots had to be tweaked by hand during real-time playback. We'd make up a cue sheet and Artie, T.M. and I would be at the console, our arms crisscrossed. It was a choreography of pulling faders, pushing switches and turning knobs. It was nearly as much a performance as laying down the tracks had been. When the song was over, we would all look at one another quizzically. *Did we get it?* The playback of the mix told the tale. An old recording studio saying goes, "If we ain't got it yet, maybe we ain't gonna get it"—but in mixing there were do-overs.

Every week or two for many years, Artie and I would have a phone call in which we would discuss the exquisite absurdities of the world. Toward the end of one of these calls, he unexpectedly said, "Hey, let's start a band. You and me and Chris Shaw. We'll do a concept album. Songs about fishing and the outdoors and such. We'll get John Kirk in on it."

I couldn't say yes fast enough. A name popped into my head: "Let's call it *Big Trout Radio*." As we were hanging up, Artie told me that the last time he had been fishing was in a pond in Van Cortlandt Park in the Bronx when he was nine.

Chris was an amiable guy who had a niche as the Adirondack troubadour. He wore flannel shirts and suspenders, wrote engaging songs about the North Country and sang them in a robust baritone voice. His really strong talent was as a storyteller. He could spin a captivating yarn for five or ten minutes and top it off with a piss-your-pants funny punch line.

I was the wild card. I hadn't really recorded since I had gone back to teaching several years earlier. I had no new songs to contribute. Obviously, Artie held up the lead guitar part of the equation. Chris was a strummer, so he got the rhythm guitar chair. And did we really want a band with three guitars and three baritone lead singers? What the hell was I going to play? It was decided that I would get my mandolin out from under the bed.

I started to dwell on a review I'd gotten in a Toronto paper after a show in the late '80s. The reviewer started out by saying I reminded him of the mellifluous folk singer Tom Rush and the marvelous rootsy guitarist Ry Cooder. I could hardly wait to read more. But I hit the brick wall in the next paragraph: "Unfortunately, Akstens plays like Rush and sings like Cooder." I guess that's why they call it a punch line. With that on my mind, I wasn't feeling very confident about things as we started to rehearse for the sessions. Still, I was determined not to make an ass of myself. I practiced my mandolin about six hours a day for a month and wrote five songs, one after the other.

I soon learned that Artie's approach to rehearsal had changed a lot since we did our first record together. The meticulous notebook had given way to a carefree couple of hours of snacking, storytelling and just enough playing and singing to justify calling it a rehearsal. Nobody seemed concerned about learning the songs—and I really needed to learn the songs, especially playing mandolin, my fourth instrument. Unlike Artie or John Kirk, I have never been a natural, instinctive musician. I've always had to work things out—I'm a bit of a plodder, when you get right down to it.

We recorded in twenty-four-track analog at T.M.'s Make Believe Ballroom outside Woodstock. Artie waved his magic wand again and Cindy Cashdollar, John Sebastian, Robbie Dupree and Abby Newton were in on the sessions. Like the old days, we put almost everything down live so, in the words of the old song, the music was "ragged but right." It was exciting to record live with such accomplished players. So exciting, in fact, that during one of Sebastian's thrilling blues harp solos I spaced out and managed to do the impossible—I blew a chord change in a twelve-bar blues.

I'm a born sentimentalist, and it touched me to record a song live in the studio with Artie and his brother Happy. I had admired their work together since 1969. Their influence had changed my own music, back when it really needed changing. And there we were, just the three of us, playing and singing together.

Artie and I spent a few days working on overdubs to finish the album. As he was putting down a guitar solo on one of my songs, Artie seemed distracted. He was riffing, noodling. On playback, I couldn't find much of

Big Trout Radio is on the air! Connelly, Chris and Artie

the melody in any of it. Through the control room glass, Artie looked perplexed. I hit the talkback switch and asked him, "Hey, Artie, what's your idea for the song? What statement are you making?"

"Statement? I'm not," he responded, with a wry laugh. "You want a statement? Don't forget, we're not getting paid here. For nothing, I'm supposed to make a statement? A statement will cost you ten bucks and a bagel with lox and a schmear."

A few weeks after the album came out, we did a live show at WKZE, a radio station in Connecticut that had us in heavy rotation. The idea was that we would do an interview and play for an hour for a live studio audience of twenty or so. When we arrived, there was a crazy scene going on. Forty people had shown up and were waiting for our car. When we drove up, they pelted us with goldfish crackers and waved rubber fish at us. One guy was wearing waders and carrying a fly rod. Chris turned to me: "What the hell is going on here?"

"We've got fans," I answered. "It's kind of like being in the Eagles—but without the money, fame and beach houses."

One matronly woman who was waving her rubber fish called out, "You guys are a supergroup! Like Blind Faith! BTR!" A few others picked it up and chanted, "BTR! BTR!" That was absurdly funny, but on some hidden level, it felt good. We started to joke about "BTR" when we were on the road. The dinner check would come and one of us would quip, "Forget the credit card. Just sign the check BTR."

After the radio show, we had a photo shoot for the Taylor Guitars magazine at the covered bridge over the Housatonic at West Cornwall. As we were unpacking our instruments on the bank of the river, a young fellow with a fly rod came over, introduced himself as James and asked me, "Isn't that Artie Traum?" I said it surely was and he added, "I just heard you guys on the radio an hour ago! I liked it!" We chatted and signed a CD for him. James and I talked for a bit about different fly patterns and fly-tying materials. He opened his fly box and held it out to me; I remarked that the flies he had tied were beautifully proportioned. He thanked me, and then off he went into the riffle above the bridge to find some trout. About a week later, I got a CD in the mail—*Troutband of America*, featuring the same James— who turned out to be James Prosek, the watercolorist whose book *Trout: An Illustrated History*, was celebrated by reviewers as a continuation of the heritage of Audubon and a new link between art and wilderness preservation. I think he may have been so delighted to meet Artie that he had been reluctant to mention his own music.

As time went on I somehow wound up in the scoutmaster role with the band, which was uncomfortable for me. It seemed to fall on me to make sure we were where we were supposed to be, when we were supposed to be there, and that we were prepared to do what we were supposed to do. For me, it was about being a professional. Perhaps I wanted the whole thing to be more than it was. In any case, the other guys were much more blasé. Set lists were always an issue. I'd put something together and float it in advance, but it always came down to a red-pencil session five minutes before the show. This led to one really embarrassing episode. We were waiting in the wings at a pretty big festival when Artie took the set list and crossed off three songs. "I'm not up for doing these today," he declared. There was no time for discussion. We were on. That left us with four songs to fill our half hour. Usually, at a festival, everyone goes over time. We were done in about twenty minutes. The audience was bewildered when we said our thank-yous and left the stage. Fortunately, they clapped a lot and made quite a fuss until we came back and did two of the numbers Artie had axed.

For a very impatient person, Artie had a surprising capacity to be patient with individual people. He and his wife Beverly and my girlfriend Jane and I used to take lazy afternoon excursions to the town of Hudson to browse the antique shops, bookstores and Italian delicatessens. We had a favorite dinner spot that served Italian and Spanish food. The place was very good, and quite cheap. The complicating factor was the chef, who was an amateur guitar player and songwriter. He idolized Artie and would come out of the kitchen to greet us with a special platter of antipasti. The entire meal was always prepared and served with great care. After our meal, he would reappear with tiny glasses of grappa and his guitar. He'd pull an extra chair up to our table and tell Artie he had a new song he'd like to play for him. Artie would say that he'd like to hear it. The music was dreadful, but Artie knew the guy was sincere and encouraged him. "Hey, not everybody is George Benson," he'd say on the way home.

By chance more than by design, I sat in with Artie at his last gig, a small concert in Glens Falls, New York. He invited me to bring my mandolin along and play his second set. Even when Big Trout Radio was recording and doing concerts, I had always considered myself more of a mandolin *owner* than a mandolin *player,* but I dusted off my old Gibson and did some woodshedding. I had no idea what he would play, and I was apprehensive about tackling some of the jazz numbers he had written with sophisticated chord progressions.

As it turned out, Artie's show that night was a return to his early days, the Sunday afternoon folk sessions in Washington Square Park in the late 1950s and early '60s. I knew some of the songs, and the ones I didn't were

Artie's last concert. Those amazing hands!

pretty much of the "three chords and a cloud of dust" genre of American homemade music. We did "Diamond Joe," a song about nefarious doings and frontier justice. It has a wonderfully cynical last line that Artie loved: "Give my blankets to my buddies and my fleas to Diamond Joe." We also did "The Cuckoo," a song both of us had learned around 1960 from an old recording by Clarence Ashley, who played it in a haunting modal banjo tuning. Artie's version, on the guitar, borrowed from Ashley's banjo frailing, some flamenco flourishes and a lot of down-home Travis picking. The audience was blown away. I was, too. Throughout the show, he showed that he was a complete master of the coffeehouse format. His patter between songs led gracefully from one song to the next, but always with a sensitivity for the absurd and the tragicomic.

After the concert, we went for dinner at a bistro around the corner. Artie was delighted with the show, the audience and the old brick building that had been an ideal setting for his journey back to roots music. I told him he should consider the kind of album we used to do—what I called a weekend album. Book three days with a good engineer and cut everything live. Why not do a record of songs from the Washington Square days? I suggested that he bring in just one or two great players and a female harmony voice. Keep it really simple. It would be a revelation to listeners who thought of him mostly as a guitar virtuoso. I was also thinking, without saying so, that it would be a piece of his legacy, that it would bring things full circle. He had been ill for months, and his response chilled me: "I might like to do that. If I had time."

Artie was notoriously picky about restaurant food, and that night he barely mustered enough interest to push things around his plate. "It's the medicine I'm on. Can't eat much," he explained. Two days later he got very bad news from his doctor. He knew.

Chris and I said a few words at Artie's memorial service. I talked about the snowy nights at the songwriters' workshop, what a fine and generous teacher Artie had been, and that he would still be my teacher for as long as I played music. After the event, Levon Helm, with whom I had little more than a nodding acquaintance, came up to me and told me with a dash of Southern courtliness, "Fine words. Fine words. Spoken like a preacher." As we shook hands, words came out of my mouth that sounded oddly formal but echoed my respect for him as one of my musical elders, as Artie had been: "Thank you, sir."

Pat Alger said it best at the memorial: "I came here today thinking I was Artie's best friend. I found out this afternoon that all of you thought you were his best friend, too. I think all of us were right."

Where Real Music Was Played II

Smitty's, New Paltz, New York

Smitty's was a bluegrass and country music bar, erstwhile dude ranch, occasional fried chicken joint and flourishing hippie nirvana down a lonely road in the Shawangunk Mountains outside New Paltz, New York. It was the domain of Wilbur Smith, a Black entrepreneur with a nose for money and a strong distaste for governmental authority.

Smitty's property included a stretch of Coxenkill Creek and Split Rock, a natural swimming hole that was a popular skinny-dipping spot. On a hot summer night, Smitty's bar could be stifling. No worries—off to the creek for a moonlit plunge in the chilly water.

Smitty's business was a pure product of his imagination. One of my friends insists that he took an old chicken coop and just kept adding on until he had a bar. Someone else told me that the place was made of a half-dozen house trailers welded together with the walls knocked out. Whatever the case might be, Smitty's had a low ceiling and a floor that oscillated in time with the music when the crowd started to dance. The entire building bounced, like a dancing house in a kids' cartoon from the '40s. And that's exactly what happened every Wednesday and Friday night, when the Arm Brothers played. From the first note to the last, the floor was jammed with stomping dancers and the joint was literally jumping.

The Arm Brothers were led by Dan Del Santo, who sang with a bottomless bass voice and strummed fiercely at a Martin D-41 guitar. He could drive a band like few rhythm guitar players I have ever heard. Del Santo had a portly, almost comical presence, but in his unique way he was oddly charismatic. His dedication to his music was absolute. That commitment seemed to draw people along for the ride.

Evan and Dan Del Santo, who has a knife between his teeth

My friend Evan was the fiddler in the Arm Brothers. Sometime in the fall of 1972, Evan invited me to come out and hear the band. Whatever I might have expected, Smitty's took me by surprise. The band started their set with one of Del Santo's satiric originals, "Bar Hound." The song was funny and the band kicked ass. I looked around at the crowd and everyone in the place seemed to be smiling. Someone handed me a very cold longneck Rolling Rock. I couldn't imagine a reason to be anywhere else at that moment. I came back often.

Smitty's went the way of all good things. Del Santo moved to Austin, where he became an unlikely legend for his quirky mix of soul music, western swing and what he called "world beat." Then he got tangled up in a drug bust and escaped to Mexico. The Mohonk Land Trust hobbled Smitty with lawsuits over title to his land. Then people started to dance to Blondie, not Bob Wills. But on some of those summer nights, with the band driving hard, the dancers stomping and the whole place rocking, it did seem like it would go on forever.

The Yellow Door, Montreal

The Yellow Door was run by the folk music club at McGill University in Montreal. It was the classic campus coffeehouse, a few steps down in an old building, with steam pipes running along the ceiling, square brick pillars in the middle of everything, a cramped stage and an espresso machine that was louder than some of the performers. I played there once a year for quite a while in the '70s. They paid chicken feed—and in Canadian dollars, no less—but they treated performers very well, and Montreal was a fun city. After the shows we'd go to some Mexican restaurant in Outremont where the beer was cold, the food was plentiful and cheap, and there seemed to be no hangups about cannabis.

The university evidently had a special deal with the Ritz-Carlton on Rue Sherbrooke. I stayed there a couple of times when the rooms weren't otherwise spoken for. One night I was on my way to the club when I encountered Jerry Garcia and Bob Weir of the Grateful Dead in the elevator at the Ritz. "Musician?" Garcia inquired, pointing to my guitar case. I told him where I was headed. The door opened, and we were going our separate ways when he called over his shoulder, "Rock on, brother!"

One year, I was booked to play the club on December 27. It struck me as odd, since students would be away on Christmas holiday, but I figured the Yellow Door folks knew what they were doing. I arrived as scheduled, settled in, tuned up and waited for the crowd to arrive. I had a coffee and chatted with the waitress. I waited a while longer, had another coffee, and chatted some more with the waitress and the manager. Then we all waited some more. No audience in sight. *Maybe booking this for December 27th wasn't such a great idea,* I was thinking. It was almost an hour after show time, and I was putting my guitar back in the case and was looking forward to an early night when the door opened. Two guys came in with a gust of wind. They looked confused. "Is this the place for the music?" they asked.

I wasn't enthusiastic about getting up on stage for an audience of two, so I sat with them at a table and we talked a while. They were Kuwaiti graduate students at the university. They had seen a poster at some foreign students' association. They thought the show was to provide something for students who didn't celebrate Christmas and were far away from home. The waitress brought coffee and cookies. "On the house," she said. "Merry Christmas! Oops, sorry."

The two guys didn't flinch. Instead, they asked me if I would sing a Christmas song—but not a religious one. The only thing that came to mind was "Rudolph the Red-Nosed Reindeer." I did my best with it but forgot a bunch of the words and filled in with nonsense. We all laughed. Then they wanted me to sing some of "the old American songs." I did a few blues and ragtime numbers. They wanted to know the story behind each song I sang. By now the manager and waitress were sitting at the next table. The manager took my guitar and sang something. We were having a party.

One of the fellows explained, "When there is music in Kuwait, we dance." He hummed something and tapped the table like a drum. I tried to pick up the beat and follow it on the guitar. The two guys stood up and started a syncopated clapping. They swayed together for a moment. But the music was all wrong. They got giddy. We all laughed again. The other fellow told me I should get an oud. He told me there were many drummers and oud players in his clan, and that I should listen to Kuwaiti music. I promised to try to find some records the next time I was New York.

Then the manager said something about the Mexican restaurant. We decided to call it a night. We asked our Kuwaiti friends if they would like to come with us. They looked shyly at each other, paused a moment, and then said thanks, but no. It was snowing as the manager, waitress and I drove up the hill towards Outremont. Thousands of Christmas lights were glowing in the city below us.

The Towne Crier Café, Beekman, New York

Right out of graduate school, I taught for three years at the very progressive Poughkeepsie Day School, which had been the laboratory school for Vassar. The school followed the English Summerhill model; there was no set curriculum, and learning was supposed to be student-initiated. Every morning, we would have a big meeting to decide what everyone wanted to do that day. That's a fine ideal. But in reality, many of my students wanted to do three things that most high school kids in the '70s seemed to want to do: make out, get high and play guitars. There wasn't an abundance of focus left for studying "The Love Song of J. Alfred Prufrock" or *Wuthering Heights*. Nevertheless, I had some very capable students, most of whom left the school after twelfth grade with confidence in their own imaginations and a remarkable capacity for self-direction.

While there might not have been as much time or energy as the faculty wanted for geometry, French or Shakespeare, there always seemed to be plenty of both for music. I spent an hour or so every day playing bluegrass, old-timey music and songs of the Flying Burrito Brothers—Grateful Dead genre with a group of students, several of whom would go on to become noteworthy professional musicians: Paul Glasse, Michael Gold, George Langston, Lisa Mandeville and the renowned early music scholar and performer Ruth Cunningham.

Concert at James Earl Jones Theater in 2017 with former students Paul Glasse, Michael Gold and George Langston

We had a joyful reunion at the James Earl Jones Theater in early 2017.

One of the musical students was a wonderful kid called "Grits" Stover, who was learning the fiddle. His older brother, Evan, was an accomplished bluegrass and swing fiddler. Evan and I were talking music one day when he told me about a coffeehouse that had recently opened down a back road, off a side road in Beekmanville, a forgotten hamlet in Dutchess County. It was called the Towne Crier Café.

The Café was in an old stagecoach stop, a Colonial-era building that had served as a general store and inn. A big front porch made the place inviting, and the warm wood interior made the space seem very cozy. All the wood surfaces and the nooks, crannies and shelves of the old country store conspired to make this the best-sounding room I have ever played. One week, Jean Ritchie might be delicately plucking a dulcimer melody. The next C. J. Chenier and his band might be torching some zydeco jump tune. It didn't seem to matter; quiet or loud, music always filled this space comfortably, with startling clarity.

Phil Ciganer owned the club. A refugee from Wall Street, he had the instincts of a trader and the spirit of a rebel. And he knew food. Phil roasted his own coffee beans before anyone else even knew you could, and the baked goods on the counter were themselves worth the trip to the Café. And he knew music. The Towne Crier was one of a handful of clubs where you could take a roll of the dice on any given Friday or Saturday night and be confident you'd hear something genuinely worthwhile.

Phil had an amazing nose for Celtic music, Louisiana music and Appalachian string band music. When I recall the bands and solo performers I saw at the Towne Crier from 1972 to the mid-'80s, I realize how essential the club was in expanding my own musical awareness: De Dannan, the Bothy Band, Martin Carthy, the Boys of the Lough, John Renbourn, Richard Thompson, Alistair Anderson, Buckwheat Zydeco, Queen Ida, the Balfa Brothers with Nathan Abshire, C. J. Chenier, Beausoleil, The Red Clay Ramblers, Martin, Bogan and Armstrong, Ralph Stanley, Hot Rize, Bela Fleck, Buck White and his daughters, Elizabeth Cotten, Tracey Nelson, John Hartford, Norman Blake, Hazel Dickens and Alice Gerrard, Dr. John, Steve Goodman, the Holmes Brothers, Leon Redbone, the New Lost City Ramblers, Jesse Winchester and one of my own favorites, the Highwoods String Band, a loosey-goosey, Galax-style old-timey band from Ithaca. I can't imagine how Phil managed to book these performers into a club that might have had at most eighty or ninety seats. And I'm grateful that he avoided the usual coffeehouse fare of twenty-something singer-songwriters crooning about how miserable their lives are. In all the years the Towne Crier was my local place to hear music, I don't believe there was a single night when I left before the show was over.

I played the Towne Crier three times myself, once with my friend Neil on the hottest weekend in decades and once on a bone-chilling weekend with Debby McClatchy, a fine old-time banjo player from San Francisco. Phil and I got friendly, and he invited me to be his associate director for a new festival, the Great Hudson River Revival. The festival was a project of Hudson River Sloop Clearwater, an environmental organization that had been started by Pete Seeger. The initial board meetings to plan the project were very interesting—we'd all be around Pete's kitchen table, talking nuts and bolts about budgets for promotion, the number of parking spaces or what we'd need to do to get a license to have food vendors. Pete wouldn't seem to be paying attention to these details. Then, without warning, he would launch into an extended rumination about having music from up the river and down the river be a force for uniting all the peoples of the earth in harmony. I realized that I was, probably for the first time in my life, in the presence of a true visionary. I also realized that visionaries don't concern themselves much with parking spaces or food service permits.

Phil would call me at eight or nine at night and ask, "Can you be here in an hour? I'm headed to the city to check some things out." These were Phil's scouting expeditions for ethnic music and food to expand the scope of the festival way beyond the board's somewhat provincial idea of the music and culture of the Hudson Valley. He'd point out to me, "Hey, the fuckin' Hudson flows by ethnic neighborhoods in the Bronx and Hoboken, right?" He had a point. A typical scenario for these excursions might take us to some Guatemalan restaurant in Yonkers just as the lights were going out. Phil would tap on the glass, and someone would peek suspiciously through the curtain, realize that it was Phil and break into a broad smile. The door would be flung open to welcome "Señor Pheeel" and his companion. Food and beer would appear, people would be called on the phone, instruments would come out of cases, recipes would be discussed. The end result, though, was always the same—a slightly stoned voyage up the Saw Mill River Parkway at dawn, with the feeling that I had gotten to know people and had seen and heard things that night that had made my life a little richer.

The festival itself was much the better for these excursions. Phil brought in West African kora players and griots, Japanese koto players, Iranian oud players, Argentinian *nueva canción* and klezmer musicians. He enlisted an African American church group to sell soul food as a fund raiser. There was Central American food and Asian food. There were craftspeople who were serious professional artisans, working in different ethnic and regional traditions. In 1978 there really was no term for what we were doing. On one of our late night-drives up the Saw Mill, we brainstormed and came up with the moniker "cross cultural." So the Revival became known as a cross-cultural event. We might have come up with the term together, but the concept itself was all Phil's. For that, he deserves enduring credit.

The Swimming Pool Casino, Saratoga Springs, New York

I was only in this place once. As I recall, it was in a motel of some sort, or perhaps it was a ranch house turned into a bar—somewhere on Route 9, south of Saratoga Springs. I was playing at Caffè Lena for the weekend, and a friend came in between sets and told me I had to get to this place after my show. Paul Siebel would be there, singing Hank Williams songs. Siebel was an enigmatic figure who had recorded two intriguing albums for Elektra Records at Bearsville Sound in the early '70s. He had then fallen victim to booze and drugs and hadn't performed for years. In the meantime, his songs had been covered by Linda Ronstadt, Emmylou Harris and Waylon Jennings. This was going to be a first step on the road back, my friend assured me.

I got to the place about midnight. Inside, the Formica tables and fluorescent lights made it look like an Elks Lodge in some Minnesota iron mining town. There couldn't have been twenty people in the room, and most of them seemed to be there by accident. Siebel was sitting on a barstool singing Hank Williams, Ernest Tubb and Jimmie Rodgers songs in his signature nasal whine. I asked him to sing one of his songs that was a favorite of mine for its wry irony, "Pinto Pony." He seemed surprised: "You know that?" He sang it with all the pathos it deserves. Then he went back to the comfort of the country classics. I was happy a few months later when my friend Artie got him into the studio to record the Hank Williams classic "Weary Blues" for the *Woodstock Mountains* album.

49
The Bloodbath

In the early 1980s I shared an office in Woodstock with Harris, an entrepreneur who did talent acquisition for colleges and universities. His nickname in the music industry was "The Ayatollah"; he was effective, abrasive and uncompromising. We worked independently, but collaboratively, from offices in the lower level of his house. Our business was to advise the schools on the availability of talent, and then negotiate contract terms on their behalf. We did a lot of dates with acts like Tom Petty, Huey Lewis, Pat Benatar, George Carlin and James Taylor. From fall through spring we were really hopping, talking nonstop to agents and managers and traveling around the country to cover major concerts. We were on site to confirm that the lighting company showed up on time, the checks had been cut for the proper amounts, and that the student activities folks had sorted the M&M's in the bowl in the dressing room so it had only the colors prescribed in the band's rider (no greens—that was either Cheap Trick or J. Geils, as I remember).

During one busy week, Harris had a run of Hall and Oates shows at colleges in Pennsylvania. He and his wife, Nancy, decided to make a trip of it. They set out on Tuesday and planned to drive back from the last show in West Chester late Friday night. I covered the office for the week by myself. On the way in on Friday, I stopped at an auto supply store to get a replacement for a headlight that was on the fritz. After lunch, I went out to the car to do the repair. I gripped the damaged headlight, gave it a tug, and it came apart in my hand in long, lethal splinters.

I didn't feel much of anything, but when I looked down I saw blood spurting from my wrist. Lots of blood. I ran into the office bathroom to grab a towel to try to stem the bleeding. I applied pressure. The blood kept coming. I grabbed another towel. More blood. Now I was panicky. Another towel. It wouldn't stop. I went to my desk, got a handful of rubber bands and put them around my wrist tightly and grabbed another towel. I ran to my car and started to drive as fast as I could for Kingston Hospital, about twenty miles away. I dashed down our road and onto Route 375, a narrow, twisting two-lane. I roared along for a mile or so. Then, in a flash, I had to slam on the brakes to avoid rear-ending a car that was going about twenty miles an hour. At the wheel was a very old fellow with a wild, hippie-ish mop of gray hair. A large poodle was in the passenger's seat. The old guy was leaning over and talking earnestly to the dog.

There was no room to pass—just a double yellow line for several miles. I honked my horn. I flashed my one good headlight. I yelled. The guy looked in his rearview mirror. He slowed down to ten miles an hour. He'd show me. No one was going to rush his joyride with his poodle. After all, they had urgent matters to discuss. I honked and screamed some more. Meanwhile, the towel was getting saturated with blood, and I was starting to feel lightheaded and out of touch with reality. Finally, I waved my bloody towel out the window and honked the horn. The guy saw the towel. He must have thought I was threatening mayhem. He swerved onto the shoulder to escape me. I flew past. After a few hours in the emergency room, I was sent home to rest with a couple of downers to help me sleep. I unplugged the phone and went to bed.

Harris and Nancy arrived home at two in the morning. Harris went down to the office to check phone messages. Nancy heard him screaming and rushed downstairs. There was blood everywhere—the bathroom floor, the walls, the hallway and all over my desk. They were stunned by the carnage. Only one shocking conclusion was possible. I had been savagely murdered. My killer had dragged my body outside and escaped in my car. Harris called 911 and reported the crime. Nancy called my home number. The phone just rang and rang. *Oh God...*

The state police had a cooler, more forensic approach. They came to my house and found the car. The bad news was that the dashboard and steering wheel were covered with gore. The good news was that I had obviously driven myself. But where was I? They banged on the door. No response. Finally, one of the officers went around the house, knocked on my bedroom window, called my name, and shone a bright light in my face. I sprung from bed, naked. Dazed from the shocks of the day and the drug-induced sleep, I brandished my bandaged hand in the glare of the flashlight. "It's him!" I heard the officer call to his partner. "He's alive."

50
No Respect

There's an old Mickey Mouse cartoon in which Pluto rescues a kitten from an ice floe. The kitten follows Pluto home. Mickey makes a huge fuss over the little guy. Pluto gets insanely jealous and a Pluto-devil appears over his head, urging him to do away with his rival. Then a Pluto-angel appears, encouraging him to be kind to the poor, helpless creature. The disputation between the devil and the good angel has been a device of psychological drama since the medieval mystery plays and Marlowe's *Doctor Faustus*. The premise is that the good angel and the bad angel dwell in all of us.

When I was doing talent acquisition for colleges, my associate and I got a lot of invitations. Once, I was treated to a splendid meal at the River Café in Brooklyn by an executive at William Morris. I assumed he was headhunting. We had a grand evening, and I expected a job offer. Before the meal was over, I was measuring the drapes for my brownstone on the West Side. The offer never came. But the seared rack of lamb was sublime. There are always mighty letdowns and small consolations in show business.

One day, we got a call from the manager of Catch a Rising Star, the hot comedy club in Manhattan, inviting us to a showcase the next night. There will be a great buffet, he assured us—like nothing you've ever seen—stone crab flown in from the Keys—and of course an open bar for you wonderful people. Nothing but the best, and thanks for your interest in these wonderful young talents, I'm sure we can do business, blah, blah, blah.

After the office closed the next day, my associate Harris, his wife, Nancy, and I headed to New York in Harris' BMW. The showcase was to start at ten, and we arrived more than an hour early. We were shown to a table. The waitress greeted us by name and asked us for a drink order. "Johnnie Walker Red, please," I replied.

A moment later she appeared with a fifth of Johnnie Walker Red and a glass with two ice cubes. She set the bottle on the table. "Enjoy!" she said.

In those days, I was never one to look askance at a bottle of Scotch, so enjoy I did. But I hadn't had lunch, so I kept looking around the club for the buffet. It was pushing ten o'clock when I flagged down the waitress. I was still sober enough to manage *'Scuse me. The buffet? Stone crabs? 'Surround here summwhere?*

She shrugged. "I heard the kitchen fucked up or something. I dunno. Sorry. Maybe I can get you some peanuts or something."

'Sgood idea. No lunch. Peanuts. Love peanuts. Good. My speech was becoming monosyllabic.

A couple of lame comedians came on. "But seriously, now, folks, let me tell you about my ex-wife" kind of stuff. I got bored. So I had a little more Scotch. *Where were those goddamn peanuts, anyway?*

The waitress appeared again. No peanuts. Instead, a bottle of Perrier Jouet in a shiny ice bucket and three flutes. Champagne? Sure. *But 'bout dose peanuts? Dinnent haf lunsh.* She'd check into the peanuts. In the meantime, a little blast of Perrier Jouet to ward off the demons. *Dasvidania.*

Then Judy Tenuta came on. I was so loaded by that time that her act seemed like the funniest thing on God's green earth. Tacky prom dress, weird eyeglasses, accordion, jokes about her cat puking up a hairball. Yuk, yuk, yuk. Funnier than Imogene Coca ever *thought* of being. *Judy Tuna is the fuckin' best.... Any luck with doze peanuts, Miss? Oops, 'scuse me, gotta pee.*

On my way to the toilet, I passed the bar. Rodney Dangerfield was perched on one of the stools. His arm was around a young lady who might easily have been mistaken for a nineteen-year-old lingerie model. They seemed to be engaged in intense conversation, tête-à-tête. I stopped a few feet away and surveyed the situation through my alcoholic haze. My evil angel spoke up first: *Gotta talk to Rodney. Just say hello. Just for a second. Just tell him how hi-larious he was in* Caddyshack. *He'll like that. He really will. Go ahead.* My good angel urged me: *Don't. Just don't. Just go to the john. Right now. This is the most assholish idea you've ever had. I'm begging you...* The evil angel won.

I went up to Rodney and his companion. "'Scuse me, Miss. Jus' need to talk with Rodney fer a sec. Just a sec. Rodney, just a sec, Okay, Miss? Thanxsh. Just need ta tell ya Rodney, Okay? You are the greatest fuckin' comedian ever been in movies. Or on television. Whatever. Rodney, you're the *best*. Okay?" He looked right through me. The girl was laughing. "Okay, Miss," I intoned, focusing my blurry attention on her. "You have been extraordinarily gracious and indulgent. Your perspicacity overwhelms my temerity and inspires me to curb my loquaciousness." Suddenly, my slur had vanished and my speech had become extremely polysyllabic. I made a courtly bow. "Oops. Gotta go take care of some biznezz." I resumed my course to the loo.

When I returned to our table, the peanuts were waiting for me. Shells were flying and I was gorging myself like a wolverine on an elk carcass when Rodney himself took the stage. He adjusted his tie, maneuvered his neck in his collar and began: "You never know what weird assholes will come up to you when you're minding your own business on a barstool. I tell you, I don't get no respect!"

51
Pat

I was at Artie's house, talking with him about my next "tour"—a swing of a few college dates in upstate New York and a coffeehouse show in New Jersey. "Pretty good money this time. At least at the colleges," I told him.

"Good," he replied. "You're taking Pat with you."

"Pat? Who's Pat?"

"A new guy in town. From Georgia. Great guitar player. Great song-writer." There were no quibbles to be had when Artie had made up his mind. "He'll be okay with fifty bucks a show and meals—Oh, and he insists on his own room."

"His own room?"

"Just do it. You'll love him. It'll be great."

I went to Pat's house a day or so later for a bit of rehearsal. Well, not exactly a house. More of a converted chicken coop, actually. A low, angular kind of place—painted with a lot of white, with a drafty porch and almost no furniture. There was a six-pack of Molson on the only table. Pat opened one for himself. He drank it while I watched.

We played a bit. Artie was right. Pat might be short on the pleasant-ries, but he picked up on what I was doing by instinct and blended in like an accomplished session player.

Money was really tight, Pat told me. How much would he make, and when did we leave?

On our way out of Woodstock the next day, Pat gestured for me to pull into a convenience store. "Got ten dollars?" he asked. I forked it over, and he came back to the car with a six-pack of Molson, a huge bag of Doritos and a copy of *Penthouse*.

I tried to spark some conversation as we rolled west on Route 28, but Pat was preoccupied with his Molson, his Doritos and his *Penthouse*. I turned the radio on. "Would you mind turning that off?" he asked. "I'm reading."

After an hour or so, I thought I'd try a little levity. *Penthouse* was no-torious for ridiculous fake letters about sexual exploits: "Well, you could at least read me some of the letters." He looked at me like I was nuts. Silence. I kept driving.

After another hour or so, I stopped for gas. Pat kept reading his mag-azine. After I had finished filling the car up, I suggested, "Maybe you could drive for a while?"

He had his answer prepared. "No. That wouldn't be a good idea. I've been drinking beer." Back to *Penthouse*.

So on I drove.

I don't remember much about the college gigs, except that one had a huge spotlight in the back of the theater that made me feel as if I were the damsel in a Dudley Do-Right cartoon, tied to the tracks by Snidely Whiplash as a locomotive bore down on me. Blame my oddball imagination. Anyway, as Artie had promised, Pat played great guitar. He sang a couple of his own songs, which were literate, musically sophisticated and catchy as hell. *This guy isn't going to be on the road much longer for $50 a night*, I thought.

Our fourth night was at the Stanhope House, a club in an old stage-coach inn and former speakeasy in northern New Jersey. I had played there once before, on Artie's recommendation. "They'll treat you like the Beatles," he told me. "They don't get it that we're washed-up folksingers on the fringes of show business. Or maybe they just dig what we do."

I concluded it was the latter. They laid out an excellent dinner, nice wines, top-shelf booze and—yes—plenty of cold Molson. Pat seemed to be enjoy-ing himself. He was suddenly quite jovial, animated, funny. I started to like the guy a lot. We were click-ing. *This is going to be a great night,* I thought.

With Pat at a festival, mid-1980s

Just before we went on for our first set, the woman who was involved in running the place came over to me and warned me about a large table toward the back that was making some noise. She explained that it was some guy's fiftieth birth-day party, and they were living it up a bit. He was a regular customer, she said. She had asked him to keep it down during the show. She assured me it shouldn't be a problem once we got started.

Well, it was a problem. "Living it up a bit" evidently meant getting loaded and telling shitty jokes with boisterous, hardy-har-har punch lines. The audience in the front of the house was getting more and more restless as this guy got drunker and louder. I tried to keep the show moving, playing bluesy shuffles and ragtime numbers. At the break, the woman came up to me, apologized, and assured me, "I'll handle this."

But Pat was already on the case. He marched up to the table to con-front the guy. *Shit, don't do this*, I thought, and scrambled after to restrain him. But he was in high dudgeon and in no mood to be restrained.

"What do you do for a living?" Pat demanded.

The guy was flabbergasted and tried to act like it was a joke. "Hey, well, if you *really* need to know, I'm an attorney. A tax attorney. Hardy-har-har."

Pat glared him down. "Want to know what I do for a living?" he challenged.

Now the guy was really uncomfortable, as if Pat's answer might be "mob enforcer." He stammered, "Ah, I g-guess so."

Pat leaned forward, over the table. "I'm a professional musician, and you will treat me with respect!" he bellowed in the guy's face.

That was the moment I learned that Pat, who is my friend to this day, is not someone to be trifled with.

A few years ago, Pat spent some time with us in the Adirondacks. We fished for bass and pike on Indian Lake, cooked good meals and read a lot. One rainy evening Pat delighted us with his captivating guitar settings of standards and show tunes.

I had hired a couple of local guys with a Caterpillar D-7 bulldozer to dig boulders out of the north field. When the glacier passed through ten thousand years ago, all that crunching and grinding left a hell of a mess, and it was beating up my John Deere diesel tractor. The guys were scraping away and shoving boulders around as Pat and I got organized to head out for an afternoon. I checked my wallet for cash for lunch and said absently, "Hey, I've only got thirty-five bucks…"

Pat, who is an articulate scholar of Robert Frost and Rockwell Kent, can still slip into a Georgia hill country accent. He was quick: "Thirty-five bucks? Them 'dozer boys is gonna be wantin' more than that!"

52
Snapshots II

An Omen

A trombone player friend of mine was on his way home from a gig at Joyous Lake in Woodstock when an owl crashed into his windshield. A lover of birds, he felt heartsick. He stopped, picked up the inert bird, placed it in the back of his truck, covered it with a tarp, secured it and drove home. His girlfriend was deeply into the New Age movement and kept him up most of the night with disturbing lore about the terrible things that befall people who kill owls. Perhaps there would be some hope, she suggested, if they took the owl to a shaman friend of hers in the morning. He would know what to do. At sunup they drove over the mountain to Big Indian to seek the counsel of the shaman. The shaman came out to greet them. "A dead owl is a very bad omen," he intoned. He lifted the tarp. The owl was sitting there, looking at them, swiveling its head, blinking. Then it sprung out of the truck and flew into a tree. "This is a very good omen," the shaman declared.

Fog

After several years in the Adirondacks, I decided I needed a dose of salt water. I had grown nostalgic for everything I remembered about the ocean—even the way my eyes used to sting when I opened them underwater. I found a 1930s bungalow on Quonochontaug Pond in Weekapaug, Rhode Island, and booked it for a week in September. I took my solo canoe, my fishing gear and a heavy cast-iron pan. I also took the old index card with my mother's striped bass recipe, the one she had gotten from her Portuguese housekeeper, Sylvia Sylvia. No, that's not a typo. Sylvia married Manny Sylvia—and there you have it.

"Quonny," as it's known locally, is a salt pond, connected to the ocean by a narrow breachway. The ferocious currents that build up when the tide races through the breachway stir things up and make for some good fishing. I'd had a grand week—walking the barrier beach, reading on the porch, and cooking dinner and fishing with my friend Paul Geremia, the country blues guitar master. My final night at the bungalow, I resolved to try Quonny one last time, early the next morning.

I woke at six to find the pond blanketed in one of the heaviest fogs I could remember. *It'll burn off when the sun gets up*, I convinced myself, and loaded my gear into the canoe and shoved off. I paddled in the general direction of the breachway. I couldn't see ten feet, but I knew if I kept the sound of the surf off my right shoulder, I'd at least be headed in the right direction. After a few minutes, I stopped to listen and get my bearings. I heard the whooshing rumble of the surf, but there was another, much subtler sound. It was almost mechanical, like a series of chattering, staccato splashes. As I listened, it got closer. When the sound got within the length of my paddle, I could see large forms slicing through the fog and the water. A very big school of very big bluefish. Suddenly, they were bumping against the side of the canoe in their frenzy. I grabbed my rod and lobbed a streamer fly into the melee. A fish grabbed it and towed my little canoe through the fog until I landed it.

In spite of my cast-iron pan and recipe card, I keep very few fish for the table, but this one was hooked deeply and wasn't going to make it. I have a rule that if you keep a fish, you'd better put it to proper use and eat it. My quandary was that I had to be out of the cottage by eleven, and I had a six-hour drive back to the mountains. While I was considering what to do about the fish, the sun got higher and the fog suddenly lifted. There's an old stone wharf in the pond and a young father was fishing there with his son, who might have been four or five. The boy was fishing with one of those kids' Zebco sunfish rigs that has a little plastic rod and Mickey Mouse's head for a reel. I paddled over and called, "Would you like a bluefish?"

"Sure," the fellow replied. "But I'm from Indiana, and I don't really know what that is."

I reached into the bottom of the canoe, grabbed the blue's tail and held it aloft. It was an impressive fish, a yard long and likely twelve pounds. "It's this! Enjoy it for dinner," I said as I tossed my catch onto the wharf.

When he saw the fish, the young boy began to wave his arms over his head and skip around it in circles. "I'm going to tell Mommy I caught it!" he yelled.

The Way We Were

Shortly after my first record came out I got a call from the manager of a well-known club in Pennsylvania. He'd heard the album on Philadelphia radio and was excited to get me on his schedule, but he explained that he wanted to put a "local group" on as opening act to make sure I got a good crowd my first time at the club. I told him I understood; "No problem," I assured him.

The night of my performance, the club started filling up early. I was particularly happy to see some older folks and a lot of kids. *Nice crowd*, I thought. *Nice to have youngsters in the audience.*

I had it wrong. The youngsters, as it turned out, were my opening act. The older folks were their grandparents. To pad the house, he had booked a variety show of winners from the local middle school talent competition.

The place was packed when the show started with a fledgling folk group that did three or four numbers. They were followed by a juggler. Then two girls in spangly outfits did some baton twirling. Then a kid with a ventriloquist's dummy came on and did a routine, which he followed with quite a few magic tricks. Some of the tricks didn't work very well, but it didn't matter to the grandparents; Instamatics were clicking away in every corner of the room, regardless. The opening act was well into its second hour when an eleven- or twelve-year-old diva took the stage and sang selections from the Streisand songbook, to the accompaniment of a cassette recorder. She belted out "The Way We Were" to close the show and took her bows to sustained applause.

Then they all left.

Dawn Patrol

In the mid '70s, I would sometimes set my alarm for 4 a.m. and drive a half hour to a spot I had discovered on Shawangunk Creek, near Mohonk, south of Woodstock. In the first light of a May or June morning, I'd wade a mile or so upstream and fish my way back to the car. By 5:15 or so, the air would be filled with the lowing of dairy cows and a cacophony of songbirds. Big burlap sacks of sweet corn, picked the afternoon before, would be cooling in the riffles, waiting to go to market later that morning; an ear or two would somehow find its way into my pocket. Many mornings, I'd come upon a raccoon—more brazen about pilferage than I—busily washing an ear of corn in the shallows. I'd often hear foxes yapping in the field. Most mornings, I'd encounter muskrats, painted turtles and snakes along the banks. I might spook a doe with her fawn as I waded along the creek. A solitary bat would likely zip overhead, catching the last bounty of darkness. Kingfishers, redwings, cedar waxwings and songbirds I couldn't identify flitted about. The creek was full of crayfish and dragonfly nymphs. And there were the fish: belligerent smallmouth bass, pickerel, redeyes, sunfish, catfish and monstrous carp that made me jump when they tried to cruise between my shins. The abundance of life in this little creek was a revelation.

One morning, as I got to my favorite pool at an oxbow far up the creek, I was startled by a large animal swimming purposefully in my direction. I backed out of the water, but the animal kept coming. When it got to the bank, it raised its head and made threatening, chattering sounds. It was an otter, demanding that I make myself scarce. Then I saw that the otter's babies had obediently arranged themselves on a downed tree at the far end of the pool and were watching intently as their mother defended them.

When I was young, I had a few books in the Golden Nature Guides series. Each had a fanciful painting in the manner of a diorama, a sort of Peaceable Kingdom illustrating simultaneously all of the animals and birds that might be found in any given habitat. Shawangunk Creek just after dawn on an early summer morning was like one of these paintings come to life.

Nicknames

The key to surviving in an old house way, way out in the country is to find trustworthy local folks who know how to do things that you don't know how to do yourself. Shortly after I bought the Adirondack farmhouse, I was lucky to find Pinky, a zip-a-dee-doo-dah carpenter, electrician and plumber. He had a real name, but he told me that everyone had called him Pinky since he was a baby, when he had the worst diaper rash anyone had ever seen.

When I needed some driveway work done, he suggested I call his friend Charlie Brown. Pinky explained that Charlie Brown also had a real name (Fred, short for Fredrick), but had earned his nickname by being the class clown in grammar school. Charlie Brown arrived a few days later with his dozer, extended his hand and said, "You can just call me Chuck." Only way, way out in the country do nicknames have nicknames.

There's Too Loud, There's Ridiculously Loud and Then There's...

I had a nice boat on Lake Champlain for five years, named *Nobska*. She was a Sisu, which I have been told means "fortitude" (or more colloquially, "balls") in Norwegian or Finnish. She was a trim twenty-two-footer with a roomy berth in her cabin, a little galley and a big cockpit. With her ninety-horsepower motor, she moved along nicely. I'd often go aboard in the evening with provisions for a day or two, fishing gear, a few Nat King Cole Trio cassettes, some books and my Weems & Plath brass lamp to read them by. I liked to cruise at low throttle north from my dock at Chimney Point on the Vermont side, enjoying the sunset over the Adirondacks. After nightfall, I'd sometimes pass quietly through rafts of hundreds of waterfowl sleeping in the middle of the lake, away from the shore and predators.

I'd follow my whim, often anchoring about ten miles up the lake around Essex or Westport. If it was a particularly lovely night, I might go the thirty miles or so up to Burlington. I'd tie up and walk up the hill to nose around town for a while before turning in. One night I was passing Hunt's, the music club in town, and saw Johnny Winter's name on the marquee. That sounded like a lark, so I paid the cover and got a drink. The show started almost immediately. I've heard a lot of loud music in my life, but I simply could not believe the sound level in that club, nor could I comprehend how anyone could endure it. I lasted for less than two songs and then headed down the hill to the refuge of the boat, my ears shattered.

As I lay in my bunk that night, I remembered something a sound engineer friend had told me once: "You want to know about loud? There's too loud, there's ridiculously loud, and then there's Johnny Winter loud."

"How do you know something is Johnny Winter loud?" I had asked.

"Your eyeballs hurt."

Fire Alarm

Susanne's father was a retired dairy farmer with a refined appreciation for the pleasures of inertia. In other words, once he was settled in his chair, he was not inclined to get up. One afternoon, he was ensconced in the easy chair in our living room, snoring away, when the fire alarm sounded. I figured I'd better wake him up and get him moving toward the door right away. "Hey, Ed! The fire alarm! We've got to get outside. Let's go!"

He opened one eye and peered at me. "I'll move when I see the flames," he said.

Drawing by Susanne of her father, Edwin Murtha, 1980

53
Forces of Nature

Horseshoe Shoal

When I was in high school, Father and I would take the sea skiff out to Horseshoe Shoal in Nantucket Sound. We liked to anchor near the buoy when the tide was on the ebb. As low tide approached, the current grew fierce, ripping over the bar that was awash. Big "gorilla" bluefish, in the twelve-to-fifteen-pound class, would trap baitfish against the shoal and go into a wild feeding frenzy. The action would continue until slack tide, usually for an hour or so. We loved catching these pugnacious fish on Stan Gibbs pencil poppers, which danced across the surface and provoked slashing strikes. I caught my first fly-rod bluefish on a freshwater Hula Popper during one of these blitzes. Sometimes we would put our rods down and just stand at the gunnel and watch as the blues flashed through the shallows in the sunlight and the silvery baitfish skipped across the surface to escape them. Just the sound of the hundreds of rampaging fish was awesome. We could hear their jaws snapping above the squawking of the gulls that fluttered overhead, looking for a safe moment to dive and grab a scrap.

Montauk

Peter and I were fishing off Montauk with Paul Dixon, the famous fly-fishing guide. It was a bluebird day in October, with wispy clouds and a soft breeze. We had been catching striped bass all morning and were eating lunch as Paul set a lazy westerly course along the beaches. Suddenly he cut the engine and pointed over the side. We were in about ten feet of clear water, over a clean, sandy bottom. Below us a mass of stripers moved in formation, headed for their winter grounds in the Hudson and the Chesapeake. I thought of a film I had seen of African wildebeest, driven by their primordial instinct to migrate in the

Fly fishing for stripers near Race Rock Lighthouse

Serengeti, plunging down a steep embankment and into a rushing river. I thought of the geese, passing over our Adirondack farm in chevron formations of dozens—sometimes hundreds—and how, for some reason I couldn't understand, their lonesome calls always made my heart ache. Peter's whispered "A force of nature" nudged me out of my reverie. The phalanx just kept coming. Hundreds of stripers, likely thousands. As we watched, a weird, keening sound came from the cliffs ashore. Then a droning chord. Then a melody. I looked. A bagpiper was playing for the entrance of a bride in her brilliant white gown and wind-tossed veil at some cliffside wedding. We watched the fish, moving, moving, moving, and listened to the piper. "What's the tune?" Peter asked. His question made me smile. "A very appropriate tune for both occasions," I answered. "'Comin' Thro the Rye.'"

The Blowdown

Something shocked me awake at dawn. I rushed out in my underwear and stood on the front lawn, looking toward Gore Mountain. The sky was an impossible yellow—like the color of a Triscuit box. The air was dead still, but I had a sense that some terrible natural violence was at hand. Then I realized. It was the sound. Ten seconds closer to sleep, I might have mistaken it for distant thunder. I heard it now as a ripping, thrashing sound. Something of great force was doing great damage, and it was getting closer. It was Saturday, July 15, 1995.

The sound, I now know, was "the Blowdown" hitting North Creek, eight miles away, shredding the forest in its path along the Upper Hudson River and cracking tens of thousands of mature trees in half. I have read that five campers were killed and 150,000 acres of forest were annihilated that morning, as a wind event known as a derecho moved swiftly from west to east. Across the Adirondacks, some ten million trees were destroyed.

I had sat the summer before on the porch and watched a monumental thunderstorm come over the rise of Eleventh Mountain. Thunder miles away was loud enough to shake the house. Lightning shot from the black clouds to the ground with terrifying rapidity. As it approached, the sheet of rain sounded like the sizzling of bacon in a hundred skillets. I had walked outside at midnight the previous winter when it was twenty-seven degrees below zero and it hurt to breathe. I looked up at the primeval sky, saw more stars than I could have imagined existed, and listened to the maple trees cracking and splitting as they froze from within. The winter before, I had sat snowbound in the house for days, waiting for rescue from a four-foot blizzard and ten-foot drifts. But I never understood the fierce majesty of the northern wilderness until I saw that yellow sky and heard that god-awful sound.

The Green Drakes

The Green Drake hatch is the main event on the West Branch of the Ausable River near Lake Placid. This large mayfly emerges from the sections of the river that have a mucky bottom. The real action happens on warm, still nights in mid-June when the Coffin Fly appears. This is the final, "spinner" stage of the Green Drake's life cycle. These insects converge in huge swarms, and they're big bugs. The trout get very excited when they come down to the surface of the water to lay their eggs and die. My fellow guide Rachel and I made a long trek into the bush country stretch of the river one June afternoon, hoping to catch the spinner fall, which is always an iffy proposition. We staked out a wide pool and waited for the big show. We fished idly for an hour or so, catching little brookies from the feeder stream at the head of the pool. But there wasn't a sign of the kind of big brown trout we were after.

The Green Drake hatch on the Ausable

About seven, Rachel pointed to the sky. "They're here," she said. Overhead, a swarm of insects, nearly transparent against the evening sky, was moving upstream steadily at the pace of a slow walk. The swarm stretched from bank to bank, probably sixty feet. It was as long as I could see, both upstream and down. We stood and watched, anticipating the actual spinner fall when the bugs would mate, lay their eggs and collapse in the surface film. We waited for about an hour. I wouldn't pretend to calculate the numbers of insects that passed by us during that hour, but there were certainly millions. In a word, it was biblical. Then, as darkness set in, the air temperature quickly dropped a few degrees. This was the trigger for the Coffin Flies. They began to undulate up and down and to mate with partners. Within a minute, the river was carpeted with exhausted spinners. The pool exploded with large browns. We each caught three before things turned off. The fish were beauties, but what I remember most is the swarm of Coffin Flies and the feeling I had of a grand purpose in nature to which we were an insignificant footnote, if we were anything at all.

54
Jennifer's Dress

I was browsing the shelves at Montana Books in Saratoga Springs some-time around 1990. I glanced over the top of the six-foot bookcase and an attractive woman of about my age met my gaze. I assumed she was stand-ing on a stool. She wasn't. She stuck her head around the corner of the bookcase and said, "Boo!"

Jennifer was six foot five, the female equivalent of a seven-foot-tall man. She was one of those small-college graduates who never quite seem to leave town. In her case, it made sense. People in the town knew her and had stopped staring. She had carved out a pretty comfortable niche for herself.

We talked a bit, discovered we knew some of the same people in the music world and decided to go for drinks at the Adelphi—one of the old-line Saratoga hotels, gracefully renovated into a fern bar and restaurant with excellent Rob Roys and Billie Holiday on the sound system. I asked if she had a boyfriend. She said she did, but that it was over. He had been arrested for shoplifting. *Shoplifting?* "He was caught stealing cosmetics at CVS," she explained. "He's into women's clothes and stuff. He'd like to wear my things, but he's only five-nine!" I laughed at the idea of Jennifer with a short guy. "I'd actually love it if he could, but he's positively swimming in them!" We laughed together. The door was open. I told her my story. She told me hers.

Jennifer was from a moneyed family in Connecticut, with a yacht at Dodson's in Stonington and the social expectations that go along with it. "Let me tell you about my mother," she began. Her mother could never cope with having a daughter who was taller than every boy in every grammar school class picture. She'd packed Jennifer away to some exclusive girl's school like Miss Porter's. Her parents were happy enough when she chose an artsy liberal arts college in upstate New York. "My mother buys me stuff. She can't help herself. Anything that she thinks would fit me. I go home and there are bags of clothes, coats, gloves, shoes. Things I will never wear. She even bought me a wedding dress. Know what sucks? To be a thirty -something unmarried woman and have your mother buy you a wedding dress. Always hoping, huh, Mom? Hey, it would look good on you!"

A few weeks later, Jennifer came to visit. She pulled up the driveway in a station wagon bursting with boxes and bags. For someone with my interests, she was Santa and the station wagon was the sleigh. It took hours to go through the clothes. I tried things on. She tried things on. We took Polaroid pictures. We cracked a bottle of wine and made a game of it. The wedding dress itself was magnificent, with big puffy shoulders and a square mile of radiant white satin. Honestly, the dress was intimidating. I felt uncertain, as if merely by touching it I would intrude into a domain that women hold sacred. But Jennifer went first, and after some encouragement from her, I tried it on. When she fastened it up the back, I felt as if I had gone airborne. We took a lot more pictures. Over dinner, we plotted and planned for Halloween. We argued playfully over who would be the bride and who would be the maid of honor. We decided there had to be two Halloweens that year.

Jennifer's dress—Halloween, about 1989

The fun didn't last long. We enjoyed our time together, but we never had much of a romance. "Why isn't this working?" I asked one day.

"You only like me because I'm tall."

That was absurd, but she'd made her mind up about it and there seemed to be no way to convince her. Still, a few weeks later, I decided to try. I called her after dinner one night. She picked up the phone and I could hear a male voice in the background, howling like an animal in distress. I thought it was some horror movie on television. "What the fuck is that?"

"Can't talk now," she shot back. "Got to go. It's someone I'm involved with. He's acting out very badly. Don't call back. I'll call when I can." *Click.*

Someone she's involved with? Acting out? Howling like an animal?

The next afternoon, she called. "Things are okay now," she assured me. "Look. Stray dogs and abandoned kittens, get it? You're much too together. I need someone who needs me to get from Tuesday to Wednesday. Goodbye." *Click.*

Me? Together? I wanted to laugh, but there was nothing to laugh about.

55
Monday Night Football

I was a fan of the Chicago Bears, back in the days of Jim McMahon, Mike Singletary and William "The Refrigerator" Perry. In contrast to the corporate football that was starting to take over the NFL, the Bears were a throwback to the muddy, bloody game that had been played by Gino Marchetti, Chuck Bednarik, Jim Brown and Dick Butkus in the '50s. *Monday Night Football* was also in its prime, with Howard Cosell and Dandy Don Meredith bickering at each other before, during and after the game. Their commentary was usually as entertaining as the game itself.

So put the Bears on the tube Monday night, give me a bowl of stew and a glass of Garnacha and I was ready to ward off the November sleet in the Adirondacks.

The first half was ending and I was thinking about another glass of wine when I heard the signature squeak of the back door hinges. I couldn't imagine who would be calling on me at the end of the road at 9:45 on a stormy night. I called out "Hello?" No answer. "Who's there? Hello?"

As I stood up to investigate, my cat Stella bolted from the back hall, bounded onto the kitchen counter and dove head first behind the refrigerator. Not a good sign. "Hello? Hello?" Still no answer. Gingerly, I tiptoed through the kitchen and peeked around the corner into the back hall. The door was open, but the hall was empty. "Helloooo?" Nothing. Carefully, I approached the door and looked outside.

A yearling black bear was on the back porch. He looked back at me blankly. I froze for a moment and then recalled some bear lore I'd heard somewhere or other. I ran into the kitchen, grabbed two pans and started banging them together and yelling for all I was worth. As I watched from the window, the perplexed bear lumbered down the steps, across the grass and up the hill. Then he started to run, crashing through saplings and underbrush.

I told my friend Betsy about the episode a few days later. "Good thing he didn't get inside, freak out and trash the place. Stella must have scared him off," she joked. "Must have been a young one without a territory. Looking for some quick calories before denning up." Betsy knew all that kind of stuff. "But you really ruined his night," she added.

"How so?"

"The Bears, right? His team. He just wanted to catch the second half."

56
A Cover Story

On one of my occasional expeditions for women's finery, I discovered a little women's wear and formalwear shop in Gloversville, New York. It was a
holdover from the era, thirty years earlier, when upstate towns each had a
thriving main street with a row of specialty shops.

The owner, a young woman who had inherited the business, went all
out to stock beautiful clothes and accessories. She even had an Estée Lauder
counter. My first time in the shop, I was stunned by the quality and selection in this little store in a small town whose heyday had long passed. I was
browsing through the racks of Pendleton, Eileen Fisher and Ursula clothes
when she came over to say hello.

"Shopping for your wife?" she asked.

I explained that, at the moment, I didn't have a wife, and that, actually,
I was shopping for myself. Maybe a nice sweater or something?

"Oh, I'd love to help!" she exclaimed. "But first I've just got to tell you
a story."

It turns out that she had a regular customer, a man in his fifties. He
would come in and explain carefully that he needed to buy a formal gown
for his wife. She was a shut-in and couldn't get out to shop for herself. Fortunately, he was exactly the same size as she, so he could try on the clothes
and then buy what he knew would please her. The woman who ran the shop
would dutifully pull out some selections and hand them over the door of the
dressing room for the fellow to try on. He'd come out and swirl around in
front of the mirror and ask her opinion. After a while, he'd choose something and pay cash. A month or so later, he'd be back for another gown.

They must go to a lot of parties, the owner thought. And then, suddenly, it dawned on her: *Why would a woman who is a shut-in need a closet full
of party dresses?*

57
Busted at the Border

My friend Billy played guitar and dobro with me on the road for several years in the late 1970s and early '80s. He also traded in guitars, mandolins, ukuleles and violins. Billy was from Texas, and his sense of style reflected the outlaw rocker sensibility of the time. He was partial to leather bomber jackets, fancy boots, mirrored aviator shades and silver-and-turquoise jewelry.

Billy had a taste for high-end vintage guitars and Volvo 240 sedans. We had a show scheduled at a university in Quebec, and Billy used the opportunity to close the deal on a very rare D'Angelico New Yorker jazz guitar from the 1940s. We were to meet the seller in Montreal. The agreed-upon price was $9,500.

We were working on an album at the time and we had a photo shoot the day before our trip. During the shoot, Billy asked me several times how much cash he could legally bring into Canada. He kept saying, "I don't want any hassles at the border." I didn't either, so I called Canadian customs and got

an unequivocal answer: $10,000. Billy confidently put $10,000 in his trucker's wallet for the next day and agreed there was no cause for further concern.

But the next morning, Billy seemed to become more and more nervous about "getting hassled" as we got closer to the border. "Nothing to worry about," I jokingly

With Billy and red guitars, 1988

assured him. "You're dressed like a drug dealer in an episode of *Starsky and Hutch,* so we should breeze right through." That observation didn't seem to alleviate his anxiety.

I had been in and out of Canada dozens of times, and the routine at Canadian customs had always been pretty much the same. A cordial officer would ask my place of birth and the reason for my visit to Canada. The pro forma answer was "vacation." Then the officer would smile, say, "Welcome to Canada," and wave me through. I prepped Billy on the procedure. "Just be honest," I said. "Never lie to a customs agent. They don't like that. And if they ask you about bringing cash into Canada, just tell them the truth. But they won't. Or at least they never have. Just stay cool." Billy agreed that he would stay cool. But I saw him bury his trucker's wallet deep in his kit bag.

We got to the customs booth. Something was different. The officer wasn't cordial. He didn't ask our countries of citizenship. He didn't ask the purpose of our visit to Canada. He stared at Billy and told him to remove his sunglasses. Then he asked him directly, "How much United States currency are you bringing with you into Canada?" I was stunned by the question. Billy was completely discombobulated. He rubbed the back of his neck, attempted a weak chuckle, and began a verbal tap dance "Ah, well…yes, let's see, currency? You did say currency? Ah well, let me think now. Ah…*four hundred dollars.*"

I knew we were screwed. The officer knew it, too. He pointed to a building a few yards down the road. He told us to park the car, have our identification ready for inspection and await further instructions. We parked. I sat in silence. Billy said, "I just didn't want any hassles, that's all." After a while, two officers escorted us inside. They split us up and took us to different interrogation rooms.

The investigator who interviewed me was actually quite nice. She examined my driver's license and passport, asked me how many times I had crossed the border in the past year and whether I was bringing any illegal substances into Canada. I gave direct answers, and she seemed satisfied. Then she asked about cash. I told her I had about $300 and that my friend had $10,000, with which he was intending to buy a vintage guitar. She asked where the guitar had been made. "New York. The model is called a New Yorker. It has a label inside that says so." In that case, we would be returning it to its country of origin? I assented.

She directed me to a waiting room and I turned my attention to a handy copy of *Drug Facts for Young People.* An hour went by and Billy appeared, escorted by a stern-looking customs agent. I thought for an uncomfortable moment that he had been arrested. I was relieved when the officer smiled, shook Billy's hand, and reminded him to get a signed and dated bill of sale for the guitar and to declare it at U.S. customs on our return. Then he told us to have a good show and to enjoy our stay in Montreal.

When we got back to the car, I ribbed Billy: "Looks like you have a new pal. Kind of a roundabout way of making friends."

Billy adjusted his aviator shades before answered nonchalantly, "Hey, the guy's a guitar player. Really into old jazz guitars. He's only sorry he didn't know the New Yorker was for sale, himself. Like I said before—no hassles."

58
Eateries and Dives II

An Unknown Brasserie, Paris

Things were going badly for me at a certain point in the '70s. My shame about my gender confusion had started to take me over and subvert my relationships. *I ought to be able to get over this*, I'd say to myself. But I couldn't. I'd torpedoed my marriage to a patient and loving woman with senseless infidelities. More shame. I kept dwelling on the college teaching career it seemed I would never have. I had lost faith in myself as a person of integrity and value.

I found some comfort in the little toy bull that my aunt Rufina had given me when I was in grade school. I'd press on the base and he'd fall into a forlorn heap. But when I released my thumb he'd spring to his feet, chipper as ever. Resilience. The little bull might make me smile for a moment, but he couldn't take away my hurt or erase the contempt I had for myself.

My girlfriend of the moment and I were growing restive with each other, and I assumed all the blame for that. My first album had flamed out. I was playing a lot of gigs, but I realized I was doing it by the numbers much of the time. Then one night, to my alarm, I found myself utterly bored with my own show halfway through the first set. I needed to do something very different. So I went to Paris.

I stayed for a week or so at a little hotel on a little square somewhere not far from the Panthéon and the Jardin du Luxembourg. The place was comfortable, clean and completely without pretense. Out my tiny window, I could see the postcard rooftops and garrets of Paris, and the square four stories below. The first morning of my stay, I opened my window and stuck out my head. I was delighted to see that there was a market in the square. The rich colors of the vegetables and flowers energized me. I hurried downstairs, grabbed a pocketful of tiny pears from one of the stalls and went exploring. I wandered through Marie de Medici's gardens in the morning and wound up in the afternoon among the medieval art at the Musée de Cluny, where I spent a long time in front of a fifteenth-century wooden sculpture of Mary Magdalene. The extraordinary composure of her face gave me a deep sense of peace. I left the museum wondering about redemption.

At the end of the day I passed a little brasserie a few streets from the hotel. There was a chalkboard in the window: *POULET FRITES, 25FR.* A cheap chicken dinner in Paris seemed like a righteous idea. And it turned out to be a very nice meal indeed. With a demi of wine and a bowl of escarole soup, I was out maybe ten bucks. It was a lovely night, so I took a walk and splurged a bit to catch a set of Memphis Slim at Aux Trois Mailletz. I felt really good for the first time in months.

I returned to the little brasserie almost every night, sometimes just to drink wine at the bar and listen to the jukebox. Most of the music was schmaltzy French pop from the '50s, but that suited my mood just fine. The crowd seemed to be mostly locals, middle-aged or older. They talked with one another and ignored me completely. On the last night of my stay, I mustered up the pluck to play the jukebox myself. I walked over with a few coins and started to make my selections. One of them was Edith Piaf's "Non! Je Ne Regrette Rien." *How Parisian,* I thought. I congratulated myself on my acumen. I had barely returned to my stool when the song started to play:

> No! I don't regret anything
> I don't feel sorry about any of it
> The debt is paid, it's swept away
> I don't give a damn about the past

Soon I noticed that a few of the locals were singing along softly. Then I realized that two women across from me had started to cry. I couldn't imagine what I had done when I had chosen the song. Which is exactly the point. I thought I was being clever, but I had no appreciation for the impact the song had on Parisians of a certain generation. I know now that it meant the loss of youth and loss of Piaf herself, a tragic genius who had stood for the struggles of ordinary people to reconcile themselves to their thwarted hopes and loves. I spent a long time trying to absorb my lesson in humility.

John's Pizzeria, Greenwich Village

I was in New York quite a lot in the 1970s and '80s. Regardless of my itinerary, uptown or down, I always made my way to the Village to play the vintage Martin and Gibson guitars at Matty Umanov's shop, and to grab some pizza at John's on Bleecker Street. Chubby, the owner, was the master of the classic Neopolitan pie—a paper-thin crust with lovely brown bubbles around the edges, the perfect accent of oregano and just enough sweet tomato sauce to make a base for the salty, sinfully gooey mozzarella.

Chubby was a big fan of the astronauts. The walls of the place were covered with autographed pictures of Alan Shepherd, Gus Grissom, John Glenn and other space explorers. They were a quirky contrast to the photos of Joe Namath, Bette Midler and Bella Abzug that were predictable elements of decor in other Manhattan eateries of that era.

One particular frame had a place of honor. Chubby had evidently written to Neil Armstrong, congratulating him on his voyage to the moon. The frame proudly displayed Armstrong's reply. It was addressed to Mr. John S. Pizzeria and began, "Dear Mr. Pizzeria, Thank you for your letter. As we reach for the stars…"

Hattie's Chicken Shack, Saratoga Springs, New York

Hattie opened her chicken shack in 1938, when Saratoga Springs was, in her words, "Real fast, man. Real fast." She was from Louisiana. Her husband, Mr. Bill, had been a Pullman porter and a tap dancer in the 1930s. He had worked with the renowned Bojangles Robinson, who did marvelous tap routines with Shirley Temple in a number of films. Autographed photos to Mr. Bill from Bojangles were framed on the walls.

To be honest, the food at Hattie's was pretty bad. The chicken was decent enough, but the watery grits, desiccated cornbread and canned vegetables were what you might expect in the chow line at a minimum-security prison. But who really cared? Hattie's was a scene, full of folkies, dancers from the New York City Ballet and hard-core gamblers. I mean, the food at Max's Kansas City sucked, too. That didn't stop Lou Reed, Blondie, Warhol and Candy Darling from hanging out there. By the way, did anyone ever order the "chick peas" that were trumpeted on the sign at Max's? (Given the urgent trendsetting at Max's, the joke was that they were actually *chic* peas.)

During the Saratoga track season, Hattie's was open twenty-four hours, seven days a week. Hattie would be in the kitchen, out on her feet, rattling pans and plates, cooking and getting orders out all by herself. Mr. Bill would catch five or ten minutes of sleep on his cot in the corridor next to the kitchen. Then he'd spring to his feet, say "Yessir" to no one in particular, and go back to sleepwalking among the tables. Hattie's was a couple of doors down from Caffè Lena on Phila Street, a center of the folk music world at the time. When the music was over at Lena's, we'd walk down Phila to the "Exec" (a dive bar rather grandly known as the Executive Café), close that place down and stumble our way back up Phila to Hattie's at four in the morning for dinner or breakfast, or a little of both. Mr. Bill would greet us with a glassy stare. I'm convinced that you could eat three meals a day at Hattie's all summer long and by Labor Day Mr. Bill would still have no idea who the hell you were. It must have been a hangover from all that time as a Pullman porter, tending to the needs of thousands of faceless White people, year after year.

The Hunan Diner, Kingston, New York

My friends Tom and Betsy recently bought a classic stainless-steel diner from someplace in the Midwest. It arrived on a flatbed, and they plan to set it up as "The Blueliner" at a busy crossroads in the Adirondacks that doesn't have a decent restaurant for thirty miles around. It ought to be a real hit. I learned from my friends that there is quite a market for the classic enamel-and-stainless diners from the '30s, '40s and '50s. After decades of wretched fast food, some people seem to have rediscovered the charm of the roadside diner.

That wasn't the case in the 1970s and '80s. In my travels as a performer, I'd pass many old diners. The lucky ones were sealed up with plywood, with NO TRESSPASSING signs to discourage looters. Some others looked as if they had been completely ransacked. They were a sorry sight, particularly when I was passing through small towns in Ohio or Pennsylvania, earnestly looking for a place for a decent lunch.

One of the boarded-up ones was on a busy corner in Kingston, New York. I'd pass it from time to time and wonder if and when anyone might take the place over and try to make a go of it. One frosty evening I noticed that the plywood had come down. There was a light on inside. In one of the fogged-up windows was a shirt cardboard written on with Magic Marker: HUNAN DINER. Wherever I was going and whatever I was planning to do could wait.

I went inside. A cloud of steam was billowing from the kitchen area. A small, round woman was at the stove, tending a huge kettle. She was humming as she stirred whatever was inside. It smelled richly of pork, cabbage and garlic. I said hello and asked if she was open. She shook her head and waved her hands. She had no idea what I was saying. She called out, and a suave-looking guy appeared from the back of the place. "My sister. She's only been here two months," he explained as he gestured in her direction. He extended his hand and introduced himself as Charlie. "You're our first customer! You got beer? Go get beer. You want beer with this food."

I headed down the street for beer. I stopped on the way to call some friends from a pay phone, told them about my discovery and said I would hold down a booth until they arrived. When I got back, I offered one of my beers to Charlie. We cracked them open and he told me his story. He had been manager of a well-known Chinese restaurant near the U.N. Since it was in a diplomatic center, it had to be good. It was also very expensive, since the customers were mostly on expense accounts. He made a lot of money. "Did you see my Mercedes parked in front?" he asked. "All paid for." He used some of his wealth to get his sister out of China, through Hong

Kong. She had been head cook on a commune in Hunan province. He said she was a genius with food, but she didn't know how to do anything else. She didn't know a word of English and didn't care much to learn. What was he going to do with her, now that she was here? He started looking in the real estate section of the *Times* for a restaurant to buy and saw a listing for the diner. They rode up in his Mercedes to look it over. He made an offer for half the asking price and bought it for cash, fully equipped. He fixed the place up, and she got ready to cook. Charlie told me that when he took his sister to an American supermarket for the first time, she couldn't cope with the abundance. She stood, looking silently at the vast selection of fresh vegetables and fruits. Then she wept.

When my friends arrived, Charlie brought us a platter of cold noodles with sesame garlic sauce. He told us it would be a fine preface for the main course he insisted we order, a smoked pork and black bean stew with whole chiles and whole garlic cloves. The noodle dish was standard fare at Asian restaurants at the time, but I had never tasted anything like this version. My guess is that the clear, brown sauce had strong tea and sesame oil as its base, with soy, roasted garlic, rice wine, chiles and sesame seeds toasted very brown. Wonderful! I pestered Charlie for the recipe every time I was in the place, but he always replied with the same charming fib: "I'd be happy to give it to you, but my sister won't even give it to me!"

Saranac, Manhattan

When I had my little antiques shop in the Adirondacks, I got friendly with a woman who was a traveling researcher for Ralph Lauren. She'd stop in twice a year and buy me out of my old yachting, tennis and golf magazines. She explained to me that they would be piled on a big table in the middle of a loft. The Lauren designers would scour the magazines for inspiration, cut out images and pushpin them to the Homasote walls of the loft. "It might not sound like it, but it's actually a very creative process," she assured me.

Her job was to keep the designers supplied with retro fodder, and the magazines were her main source. She also paid top dollar for photographs that showed clothing, luggage and accessories from the 1920s and '30s. She once paid me a ridiculous amount of money for a framed photo of the University of Ottawa hockey team, from 1925 or so. I asked her what was so desirable about the image. "See the three stripes on the sleeves of their sweaters that are the same as the stripes on the cuffs? Our designers will do something wonderful with that." I could only take her word—and her check.

We got talking one day about how remote my shop was and how far away I was from a good restaurant. She invited me to Manhattan and promised that she'd lead me to some great food. One very rainy fall week-end, I drove to New York. I met her at One Fifth, a cocktail bar that had a glamorous ocean liner theme. My friend told me that the mahogany bar was from the *Lusitania*, or maybe it was the *Andrea Doria*. She couldn't remember. I pointed out that both of those ships had sunk. "Oh, well," she said and shrugged. We looked at each other and couldn't seem to think of anything to say. The check came for our two rounds of drinks and appetiz-ers. She grabbed it. "Expense account," she explained.

We headed way uptown to 94th and Madison. "You will *adore* this place," she assured me. As we parked, I noticed a sign over a door across Madison: SARANAC. "That's the place?" I asked. I had thought the idea of this excursion was to get the rube (me) away from the boonies and to show me the bright lights.

"It's so *you*," she gushed.

We crossed Madison and entered what is unquestionably the silliest restaurant I have ever been in. Someone with, as they say, more dollars than sense had thrown money at a decorator who clearly had never been north of the Tappan Zee Bridge.

The "Adirondacky" menu at Saranac was just foolish. Frankfurts and beans, flapjacks, pan-fried trout and s'mores for dessert. I'm not kid-ding—s'mores in a Manhattan restaurant. They also listed a lobster roll—made with the very rare Adirondack lobster, I guess.

Our waiter appeared, decked out in a checked flannel shirt and sus-penders. Somehow the outfit looked much more Lauren than L.L.Bean. He introduced himself as Dorian and launched into what I took to be an im-pression of Serge, the art dealer in *Beverly Hills Cop*.

The decor was laughable. A fiberglass Old Town canoe hung rev-erentially from the rafters as if it were an heirloom guideboat by Grant. The walls were covered with pictures of anglers with tarpon and barra-cuda, fish that have never been caught within a thousand miles of the Adirondacks. The hefty tackle to subdue these tropical monsters hung next to the photos. A taxidermied head of a mountain goat loomed over the bar. The unfortunate creature must have wandered somehow over the Rockies and blundered into the sights of a hunter on the other side of the continent.

"You've got a strange look on your face," my host suggested.

"Sorry," I replied, and started to chortle. "But is this place a put-on?"

We split and took a cab over to Il Vagabondo to eat a plate of car-bonara and watch the bocce players.

Wagamama, London

There are Wagamamas from Belfast to Dubai now, as upscale noodle bars have become trendy. I think the crazy Japanese movie *Tampopo* might have had something to do with it, as well as the fact that you can get a satisfying postrecession meal at Wagamama for about fifteen bucks. The name means "Little Bastard," and the original Wagamama in London did have something of an upstart attitude.

Celebrating the way
of the noodle, 1996

Susanne and I discovered it after spending an afternoon at the Tate, much of it in the astonishing Rothko gallery. We were up to our eyeballs in art, and very hungry. From the moment we entered, Wagamama seemed to go out of its way to declare that it wasn't going to be like anyplace else we'd eaten. Long tables and benches filled the sparse dining space. Servers circulated with little computers, relaying orders to the open kitchen. We sat at a table with an older, bearded gent who had a philosophical turn of mind. He engaged us in conversation about the origin of the universe and the meaning of life. The philosopher was entertaining, the place was fun and the food was very satisfying.

We found ourselves in the same district the next evening. We were again very hungry and decided to go back to Wagamama. We sat at one of the long tables with some other diners and placed our orders. Soon we were joined by an older, bearded gent who engaged us in conversation about the origin of the universe and the meaning of life. *Déjà vu?* No, it was a *different* philosopher. I began to wonder if Wagamama employed retired philosophy professors to entertain the diners while they slurped their soba.

J&J's Foxx Lair, Bakers Mills, New York

This place was a mean-looking roadhouse about five miles from my Adirondack farmhouse. I never actually stopped and went inside, and there's a reason for that. When I was moving in, I got my first load of firewood from a local fellow named Nate. It was late in the day, and I asked Nate if the Foxx Lair might be a good spot to run down and grab some dinner, since I was still unpacking. "Wouldn't think so," he responded. "That crowd in there? They get one look at you and they'll be fightin' each other to see who gets to fight you first."

Penns Valley Meat Market, Millheim, Pennsylvania

Peter and I were on the road in Centre County, Pennsylvania. He was working on a *New York Times* story about food, farming and the emerging restaurant scene in the "real" Amish country. As I sometimes did when Peter was on assignment, I was tagging along as his photographer. These jaunts always meant lots of good food, good laughs, some nice fishing and a hundred and forty-five bucks whenever the *Times* ran one of my shots.

Peter on Penns Creek

But being a photographer among the Old Order Amish meant lots of aimless pictures of barns, mules and empty buggies. No photos of the Amish themselves. I got that message our first afternoon in Centre County. We had been invited to a noontime dinner of chicken and dumplings at an Amish farmstead. A woman in a bonnet and apron approached us as we pulled in the driveway. Her first words admonished us: "No cameras. No pictures. None." Then she added cordially, "Welcome to our home." So the camera stayed in my rucksack for most of the trip, except when we managed a couple of days of trout fishing on the limestone spring creeks that well up from the ground in that part of Pennsylvania.

We were passing through the little hamlet of Millheim one morning, when Peter swerved into a parking space in front of a ramshackle market. He pointed at a placard in the window. "Look. Homemade bologna. And they make sandwiches. We'll get some for later." Peter, who is very fond of cured meats and sausage, was nearly in the door when I

Waste not, want not?

glanced to the left and saw a sign above the other entrance to the building: YEARICK'S TAXIDERMY STUDIO.

I thought this called for some discussion. "Peter, ah, look. Bologna and taxidermy under the same roof. Whaddaya think?"

"Think? I think they probably have very good venison. I also think we need sandwiches for later."

So in we went. I looked around and found some solace that there didn't seem to be a connecting door between the two enterprises. Meanwhile Peter was at the counter, engaged in a lively conversation with the butcher. Before I knew it, two overstuffed sandwiches appeared. Bologna, with horseradish mustard. We ate them that afternoon, sitting among the wild rhododendron on the banks of Penns Creek. They were delicious.

The Italian Village, Chicago

Susanne and I were in Chicago for a metropolitan ramble, including a couple of days at the Art Institute. We had tickets for *West Side Story* at the Lyric Opera—a production with the original Jerome Robbins choreography and a full orchestra playing the complete Bernstein-Sondheim score. Curtain was at 7:05, and the fine print on the tickets was emphatic that late arrivals would not be admitted until intermission. Since the tickets cost more than my first car, we determined that we'd plan a relaxing, very early dinner and get to the theater with plenty of time to spare. We made a reservation for five o'clock at a place near the river with an interesting-looking menu and great reviews. It looked inviting from the outside, with a sweeping, curved wall of glass running the length of the restaurant. But when we pushed the doors open, the din from the dining room felt like a physical assault. About a hundred young professionals were getting a head start on the weekend, all vying to be heard above the loud music and each other. That lovely curved wall of glass amplified the tumult like a parabolic reflector on an NFL sideline. I gave my apologies to the maître d'—he just shook his head, gestured to his ear and mouthed the words "Too loud."

On the way out, a young woman suggested we "try the Italian place four blocks down." By now the clock was ticking and a chilly wind had kicked up. When we saw a towering, '50s-era neon sign for THE ITALIAN VILLAGE, we felt as if the universe had tossed us a life preserver. We scooted up the stairs and encountered a distinguished-looking fellow in a black bow tie and vest and black jacket. I explained that we had to get to the theater. Could he seat us? Would it be possible at all to get a quiet, relaxing table? He nodded to a younger fellow in a black bow tie and vest and snapped his fingers. "Number thirty-four," he directed. The younger guy nodded back and led us through rooms that seemed like a dreamscape. The walls were covered with murals of Tuscan hillsides. Stars twinkled in the artfully painted plywood skies and lights glowed in tiny farmhouse windows. Our waiter seated us at a booth that was like a little private room. Cozy as could be.

So what did we order? Something "artisanal" and "locally sourced" with "nuanced flavors"? Hell, no. We went right for the comfort food.

Eggplant Parmigiana, Chicken Marsala, string beans with garlic instead of pasta, an enormous platter of excellent sautéed spinach, a bowl of splendid roasted potatoes with lots of herbs and a glass of hearty Montepulciano. It was a joy to order dinner in a big city without having to know a coulis from a confit from a croustade. As our very professional waiter had assured us, we were out the door in time for the theater, in the afterglow of a fine meal.

It seems that everyone these days is eating avocado toast and poke bowls—certainly not lasagna, which is about as far from trendy diets like paleo and keto as you can get. And now, with the scourge of the coronavirus, I'm fearful for the future of the old-line, family-run Italian joints that for decades have worked hard to turn out rewarding meals at fair prices, places where you can taste the pride in the food. I'm thinking of a few right now: Carlo's in Allston (my favorite restaurant in Greater Boston), Parillo's in Amsterdam, New York, and Monty's Garden in Leominster, Massachusetts, an unspoiled treasure from the 1930s that was bulldozed

Susanne at the Italian Village, 2019. Look at that spinach!

to make way for a Walgreens. At their best, restaurants like these are places where tables get pushed together, voices are joined in laughter and people celebrate, not just eat. Reading the back of the menu, I learned that the Italian Village has been serving up good food and celebration since 1927. I wasn't surprised to read that Frank Sinatra once held a wedding celebration under the plywood Tuscan sky with the tiny twinkling stars.

O Dinis, East Providence, Rhode Island

Fado is the Portuguese word for "fate." It is also the name for a kind of passionate, melancholy music that is sometimes called "the Portuguese flamenco." I have been in search of fado since we bought our little house in Rhode Island several years ago. I romanticize the small part of my bloodline that springs from an Azorean whaler who settled in New Bedford in the early nineteenth century. It's a harmless indulgence. I make *caldo verde* a few times a year, drink robust red wine from the arid hills of the Douro region and listen to recordings of rapturous Portuguese guitar music by the great master Carlos Paredes. But live fado has eluded me, even in a region that has such a strong Portuguese heritage.

Manny, our skilled Portuguese carpenter, suggested O Dinis, a restaurant in East Providence where his family went to celebrate birthdays and christenings. "They've got fado sometimes on Monday nights," he told me. "But I don't like that kind of music. Too sad."

A few weeks later, my friend John and I decided to discover O Dinis on our way back from the Herreshoff Museum in Bristol. It turned out to be the epitome of the neighborhood joint, complete with Formica tables and paper placemats with a quiz about the U.S. presidents. Everyone in the restaurant was speaking Portuguese. A charming young woman introduced herself as Natalia and showed us menus. When we explained we didn't know anything about the food and needed help, she offered to order for us. "*Bacalhau na Brasa*," she suggested. "It's salt cod, the Portuguese staple. And *Bife*, a nice sirloin with garlic and a fried egg on top. And a bottle of Alentejo." Gratefully, we threw ourselves on her mercy.

A moment later, a voice came from the next table. "Don't listen to her. You should have ordered this: *Carne de Porco Alentejana*." As we turned, the fellow picked up his plate and brought it to our table. He sat down and put the plate in front of us. "This is what you want at O Dinis. Come on, try it," he insisted. Gingerly, John and I dipped our forks into corners that didn't look too picked at. It really was very good. Before I could ask what it was, he was calling Natalia back to our table. "Cancel the *Bife*, Natalia. They can get a steak anywhere. Bring them an order of this. Pork and littlenecks. Look at their faces. They love it." As he was leaving a few minutes later, he stopped at our table again and said, "Welcome to Little Portugal," and dropped a twenty on our table to pay for our wine.

The meal was very satisfying, and we were discussing how everyone in Portugal must be diabetic—bread, potatoes and rice with every dish, and not a green vegetable in sight. Then we heard another voice from a different table: "You shouldn't have listened to that guy. Okay, the *Porco* is good, but when the special is sea bass at O Dinis, you gotta order it." He pointed to the head and mass of bones on his plate. "The best anywhere."

"I thought about it," John ventured, "but I thought it might be frozen sea bass from Chile."

"My friend, my friend," our neighbor replied with an admonishing wave of the finger and a tone of voice that might be used for a well-meaning but wayward child. "You are in a Portuguese restaurant in East Providence, Rhode Island. We know fish." He beckoned across the room and called, "Natalia, hey, bring us a sea bass—from the refrigerator. Yes, from the refrigerator. We have an unbeliever here." A moment later, Natalia came out of the kitchen with a black sea bass on a plate. It glistened in the fluorescent light and looked blankly toward the ceiling with a glazed eye. "Smell it," our mentor directed, holding the fish under John's nose and then under mine. "What do you smell, huh? *Nothing.* Right? That's fresh! That's a black sea bass from the day boats in Point Judith. Next time, you'll know." He leaned back, crossed his arms and smugly rested his case.

"He does this every night," Natalia joked.

Before we left, I made a quick detour to the restroom. When I emerged two minutes later, John was at the bar with Dinis, the owner, who was regarding him with glassy eyes as he poured him a shot of Portuguese brandy. "For John, my countryman!" he exclaimed. "I look at him, I know he's Azorean. Stocky. Dark. I know his face. I know his people. From São Miguel." Dinis' drinking companions nodded their agreement. "São Miguel," one repeated. John, who is one hundred percent Scots and the grandson of a Presbyterian minister from upstate New York, just smiled a bemused smile.

I interrupted, "Actually, *I'm* the one with Azorean blood."

Dinis looked me up and down—tall, thin, fair-skinned. "You? Azorean? You're funny. A comedian. I like comedians. Have a brandy." Portuguese brandy? I wasn't expecting much, but it was perfect for the moment, like a young, untamed Armagnac. I asked Dinis about fado music. "I'm a fado singer!" he declared. "You don't know me?" Without waiting for an answer, he showed us a picture on the wall. A younger Dinis, in full-throated song. It was a still from the movie *Mystic Pizza.* "That's me. With Julia Roberts. I sang in the movie, the wedding scene. Everybody loved it. You like fado? Come some Monday night when I sing. For now, have a little more brandy."

As we walked to the car later, John asked, "Do you think I should get one of those DNA tests?"

59
The Haint

I was sitting in my favorite chair by the window one fall night during my first year in the Adirondacks. I was reading a John Dickson Carr mystery novel that was filled with strange and ghoulish goings-on. A fire was crackling in the woodstove, the cat was sleeping on the hearth and I had coffee and a little glass of Armagnac at hand. Suddenly, I was aware of something spherical and yellow, glowing in my peripheral vision outside the window. I turned to look, and it seemed to hang there for a second or two. I couldn't tell whether it was the size of a baseball and a few feet away, or the size of a basketball and maybe a hundred feet distant. Then it started to move, quite steadily, toward the north field. Then, in a blink or two, it was gone. It was fascinating and somehow quite disturbing.

The next morning, George showed up with a delivery of firewood. I'd heard someone described as a "bear of a man" before; George really was one. He even moved like a bear, with a rolling, hunched gait. Every movement he made conveyed power. He had been born down the road about sixty years earlier and had gone to the one-room schoolhouse that was now some stockbroker's ski getaway. He had trapped, run a sawmill, logged with a team of horses for most of his youth, and worked on the family dairy farm until the cows got sold off in 1958. George was a walking, talking *Foxfire Book*. He was expert in all kinds of things about which I had no knowledge. He showed me how to orient my firewood stack so the prevailing wind would dry it out and keep it dry. He told me that mothballs would keep the porcupines out of my shed. He showed me the little patch of ginseng on the hill behind the house. When I mentioned that I had heard he was a fine woodsman, he replied simply, "I'm just a pilgrim, brother."

George spoke in a lilting, archaic style that suggested he didn't have much exposure to radio or television—or even to people who lived thirty-five miles away, in Glens Falls. He'd say, "Eye kin be bact wit nather five cohd a wood a Tuesdey nixt." or "'Tis been a quit a whieyl sinct aye been in this hare dooryahd." The only other time I had encountered the word "dooryard" was in Walt Whitman's 1865 elegy for Lincoln. Listening to George, I was hearing a voice from the mountains, a century past.

I was eager to describe to him the strange thing I had seen. He listened carefully, his head cocked to one side. He took a moment to digest my report. Then he said something that sound like "'Tis ain't."

I started to protest, "Well, I really *did* see it, George…"

He shook his head and repeated what he had said, as if to make himself understood to someone who was slightly dense. After a few tries, I heard it differently: "'Tis a haint."

"A haint?" I remembered the word from *To Kill a Mockingbird*. "You mean a ghost, George?"

Indeed he did. He'd seen them himself, he told me, hovering over the fields, looking in folks' windows. They were a bad omen. "Some'v dieyd after se'en 'em." He gave me the chills. I imagined a long winter of slow, unexplained decline. On my headstone would be carved "Seen a haint."

With the help of George's wood, I survived that first winter. I told my tale to my friend Betsy, the font of all obscure knowledge. "Ball lightning," she declared. "A very rare phenomenon. But you're not the only one. Czar Nicholas saw it." I recalled what George had said, *Some'v dieyd after se'en 'em*. Remembering what had happened to the czar, I didn't find Betsy's words a comfort.

The Adirondack farmhouse where I lived for thirty years

60
The Panty Club

I've always hated men's underwear. Boring, bunchy, droopy, cotton and white. Built neither for comfort nor for speed. Was there something about tidy-whities I was supposed to like?

When I was in grammar school in the 1950s, girls wore dresses to school. If they stumbled at hopscotch or swung a bit too high on the swings, we bystanders might catch a peek of something pink or blue—something pretty. The boys in the schoolyard would sing a ditty when these events happened (as long as no teacher was within earshot):

> I see England
> I see France
> I see Sally's [or Lucy's or Mary's] underpants

The girls on the playground even adopted it as a skip-rope song.

Not having sisters, I didn't know much about panties—but I was certainly curious, and I explored the topic in the Sunday *New York Times Magazine*, known in those days as the "Girdle Gazette" because of all the lingerie advertising. Later on, I was to discover that girls' bungie-boos (as the slang of the time called them) were not only colorful, they were soft, and designed to kind of *hug*—not just sit there on your body until they needed a wash.

As an adult, I came to realize that there was a connection between undies and mood—but a somewhat mysterious connection. Kind of like music. Do you put on Sinatra because you're melancholy? Or do you put on Sinatra and become melancholy? Anyway, a chipper pair of knickers can give the day—and whatever else might need it—a bit of a lift. Living alone through a few Adirondack winters, there were times when I certainly needed a lift.

One particularly gloomy March afternoon, I set out in search of a new pair of feel-good undies. The closest town was Glens Falls, which is no shopping mecca. (The mere mention of "Glens Falls, New York" served the comic team Bob and Ray as a punch line for many years.) The only thing resembling a department store in Glens Falls was a J. C. Penney.

As I considered my options among the racks at Penney's, a very nice saleswoman came over and asked if I needed any help. I told her no, not right now, anyway. She replied in a conspiratorial tone, "Well, you just go ahead and *have your fun,* dear. I'm right here if you need me."

This lady was obviously tuned in to my project. I felt emboldened that I was browsing the panties without shame or the need for a cover story. For the first time, I was fearless in the lingerie department. After a while I chose three pairs of stretchy, colorful undies and went to the counter to make my purchase. My enthusiastic new friend pointed out that there was a promotion going on in her department. "You bought three pairs. So you qualify for our Panty Club! Would you like to join?"

"Sounds like fun," I replied. "When are the meetings?"

I don't think she got the joke.

61
Leaping Clear of the Water

I fished for many years in the Adirondacks with Pete Hornbeck, a canoe builder and watercolorist. We both grew up in the era of fanciful illustrations on the covers of *Field and Stream* and *Outdoor Life*. These paintings often depicted a pike leaping clear of the water with a plug in its jaw, a smallmouth bass leaping clear of the water with a popping bug in its

Hornbeck, looking at life from the fish's perspective

mouth or a brook trout leaping clear of the water with a delicate dry fly pinned in its lip. *Leaping clear of the water* was the common theme, and as corny as they seem now, those pictures fired the imagination of a suburban twelve-year-old. The back pages of the same magazines were a bazaar of ads for all kinds of wonders that appealed to middle-aged men in the 1950s: folding canoes, worm farms, trusses, pipe tobacco, live pheasant eggs, Canadian whiskey, naughty playing cards, fly-tying materials, Bowie knives and cottages to rent beside lakes and rivers from the Ozarks to Maine.

Hornbeck and I were reminiscing one night about these magazines and about our shared fascination with the ads for rental cottages. We decided it would be a hoot to rent one, maybe on the Saint Lawrence near Clayton, New York, where there was good smallmouth bass fishing. If it got stormy for a day, we could always spend time at the antique-boat museum in the town. I hadn't seen *Field and Stream* for years, but Hornbeck had a copy. We flipped through to the back pages, and there they still were—ads for rental cottages. One place was a mile or two from Clayton. It had two-bedroom cottages for $215 per week, including a fourteen-foot aluminum boat and one tank of gas. We called and booked one.

In anticipation of our trip, I boned up on the Saint Lawrence. Everything I read sooner or later turned into a rhapsody on the river's muskie fishing. I saw pictures of the world record muskie, an astonishing seventy-pound fish, caught there by Arthur Lawton in 1957. I started to dream about the big muskies on those old magazine covers, *leaping clear of the water*.

The cottage turned out to be a little wobbly and a little musty, but it was cozy enough and directly on the river. We spent our first afternoon settling in, had a good dinner and set out for an evening's fishing. We decided to try for a muskie right away, with big swimming plugs. The only complication was that we didn't know much of anything about muskie fishing. "Well, when you get right down to it, they're pretty much supercharged pike," Hornbeck ventured. "They like to hang around weed beds, right?"

"I guess so," I ventured and steered us in the direction of Grindstone Island to find a weed bed. It didn't take long. There was a stand of what looked like huge pickerelweed, running parallel to the shore for as far as I could see. I pulled up, cut the motor and got ready to cast. "I have no idea what I'm doing," I confessed to Hornbeck as my plug flew through the air.

They say the muskie is the fish of ten thousand casts. Couldn't prove it by me. The plug landed, I took two turns of the reel handle, and the water exploded. A muskie of maybe thirty pounds *leaped clear of the water*, hung horizontally for an instant, shook her head and threw the plug about twenty feet.

We looked at each other. Damn.

Those few seconds played themselves over and over in my mind like a flipbook for the rest of the week. That evening we cast until we couldn't see what we were doing. The next day we cast all day, and the next, and every day for the rest of the week. We barely ate. We didn't sleep much. We forgot completely about the plump smallmouth bass that were likely swimming right under our boat. We just threw big swimming plugs and monstrous things with whirling propellers on heavy wire leaders. We were on a maniacal mission to hook another muskie. For the next six days, we never lost hope. And we never saw another fish.

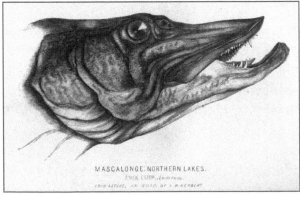

A muskie, from an 1855 print

62
The Worms

The listing in the Saratoga Springs paper read *Luther Allison and His Band.*
Direct from Chicago. Friday Night. The location was a roadhouse dive whose
name I've long forgotten, in Edinburg, New York. I knew that Allison had
played with Freddie King, Howlin' Wolf and James Cotton. I'd read somewhere that he played the blues "like his life was hanging in the balance." I
called a friend of mine who listened to the blues all day and all night. We
made a plan to go.

Edinburg is the least likely place I can imagine to see a Chicago blues
legend. It's a sleepy upstate lakefront town that seems to be over the bridge
from nowhere in particular. The club was hard to find. There was no sign
and just a few lights in the window. Ours was the only car in the parking lot.
Two women who appeared to be mirror images of each another greeted us.
They were the first people I had ever seen dressed in the Goth style. They
had a ghostly pallor, dramatic eye makeup, huge jewelry, black clothing of
a vaguely Edwardian design and opera-length lacy gloves. My friend and
I sat on barstools and, since there was no band equipment set up, I asked
about the notice I had seen for Luther Allison. "Oh, he screwed us," one of
the women replied. The other one continued, "Just blew us off. But we've
got a great band coming later tonight from Saratoga, The Worms. See, we
made a stage and everything." I looked in the direction she was pointing.
Four sheets of plywood on cinderblocks. A good Chicago drummer would
shake that to pieces in four minutes.

I confided to my friend that I wasn't too keen on waiting around for
any band called the Worms. She was of the same mind but suggested
that, since we'd driven an hour, we have a drink anyway and check out
the space-age Seeburg jukebox in the corner. The bar was very strange.
One bottle of Scotch, one bottle of bourbon, one bottle of gin, one bottle
of vodka, one kind of beer. No food. But lots of Baggies tacked to the back
wall with pushpins. The bags were carefully labeled and filled with material
that looked like twigs and dried leaves. As my friend and I sipped our one
kind of Scotch, I asked about the Baggies. "We gather plant material and
sell it. They're for making potions and distilments. We know all about that
because we're witches," she explained, cheerfully. She added that there
were "no animal body parts" in any of the Baggies—perhaps she was trying to shake off the bad rap left from the "eye of newt" line in Shakespeare's
Macbeth. The two women went on to explain that they were sisters and had

just opened the place with their husbands. Their mission was to enlighten Edinburg and its environs about witchcraft and the Chicago blues.

I was thinking that a sign in front of the place might help manifest these lofty ideals when their husbands made their appearance. They were muscular, stripped to the waist and shiny with some kind of oil. They had meticulously groomed, jet-black hair and wore gold chains around their necks. They kissed their wives in unison. "Bodybuilders," my friend whispered to me. One of the bodybuilders announced that they had just gotten a call with the bad news that The Worms had canceled. They could double their fifty-dollar guarantee by playing a private party. "They screwed us," the first witch said. Her sister added, "Just blew us off. I heard they sucked, anyway. How could a band called The Worms do anything but suck? Right?"

Realizing that the question was directed to me, I assented: "I'm sure you're right. They must really suck."

"Hey, you must really like the blues, huh? Coming down here to see Luther Allison and everything. Sorry he screwed us." "He just blew us off," her sister echoed. "But let's play the juke and have some laughs, anyway. It's all stuff from our own collection of 45s. We lived in Chicago and got them at the Maxwell Street flea market." She went up to the machine and started to push buttons. The music was incredible: Magic Sam, Junior Parker, Johnny Young and Shaky Walter Horton, with a dose of Little Anthony and the Imperials and Vito and the Salutations thrown in. At one point, the couples started to dance. We watched in fascination as the bodybuilders cradled the witches in their arms and they slow danced to Otis Rush's "Got to Be Some Changes Made," T-Bone Walker's "Mean Old World" and Muddy Waters' "I Just Want to Make Love to You." My friend and I looked at each other, shrugged and started dancing, too.

63
The Marines Have Landed

For most of my life I lived in fear of discovery. I was convinced from childhood that if anyone discovered my gender identity issues I would be humiliated, ostracized and sent to a reform school or an insane asylum. I survived by the most rigid compartmentalization imaginable. The compartment that held my gender conflict was the most camouflaged and scrupulously hidden of all. I did what my instinct told me to do to protect myself. But without realizing it, I had grown up developing the skills of an addict, bigamist or con artist. Not exactly consistent with my core values.

When I was fifty-five, I decided I didn't want to live like that anymore. As I explained to my spouse Susanne, "I've been closeted for fifty years. I suppose I could go for another fifty, but then I'd be—let's see now—a hundred and five. So…" She agreed that it was about time to find some community. But where?

The internet was the obvious starting place. In 2002, a Google search for "transgender" yielded a strange gumbo of websites: reviews of obscure Scandinavian films, rip-off artists selling large-size clothes and shoes at exorbitant prices, cheesecake photos of nightclub "female impersonators" from the 1950s, homepages of desperately lonely people, solicitations from "escorts" and "models." On the positive side, there were links to websites of a few organizations that seemed legitimate. I knew nothing about any of them, so I settled on a group called "Tri-Ess" for my first contact. The name was an acronym for Society for the Second Self. The group billed itself as "an organization for heterosexual crossdressers." *Well,* I pondered, *that sort of describes me…I guess…maybe…*

I didn't recognize the homophobia implicit in their statement of purpose. I didn't realize that "crossdresser" was already under critique as a reductive term. And why *second* self? Why not an integrated self? Anyway, my thinking wasn't that evolved in 2002. I just wanted to connect with somebody to talk with and maybe befriend. I sent an email and after a rather byzantine security process, I was invited to attend the group's upcoming convention in Manchester, New Hampshire.

I registered for the event, booked a room for the weekend at the Holiday Inn and spent the better part of a week deciding what clothes and accessories to bring. That was a challenge, since I had little fashion sense and no personal style to fall back on. "Keep it simple," Susanne suggested. So I packed lots of basics. Everyone looks good in black, right?

I had thought that Manchester was an odd place to have a convention, and when I surveyed the scene, it seemed even odder. The hotel was marooned in the middle of a vast, icy parking lot, like a vessel aground on an asphalt sandbar. The façade was unwelcoming, the lobby was cold and my room was shabby around the edges. I began to wonder what exactly I was going to do for the next three days. I pulled the curtains to get a better view of my dismal surroundings. Like a mirage, a big red MACY'S sign loomed at the far end of the parking lot. If all else failed, I could at least shop.

The scheduled event for Friday night was a cocktail hour and dinner at a big Italian restaurant near the river. I spent the afternoon getting ready. I learned at least one thing during my fledgling attempt to glamorize myself—shaving a toe is like trying to shave an okra. Every outfit I tried looked worse than the last. Basic black? *Drab. Boring.* Something bright and colorful? *News flash—it's winter.* Something a little glamorous? *Is there anything more hideous than a fifty-something floozie?* The mirror was not my friend. Before I knew it, it was after six o'clock. I was already late. I threw on something. I combed my hair and grabbed the first jewelry I saw. I rushed out the door.

Well, *almost* rushed out the door. I had never been in public before in anything other than conventional male attire. When my hand reached the doorknob, I froze. *Can I actually do this?* I opened the door, peered up and down the corridor and listened for footsteps and voices. So far so good. I made my way cautiously to the elevator. The coast seemed to be clear. I pushed the button. There was a *ding* as the elevator reached my floor. The door opened. I was face-to-face with four young marines in khaki uniforms. "Our floor," one of them said. And then, "Excuse us, ma'am," as they swept past me. No smirking. No irony. Four marines. My first time out.

I couldn't begin to process what had just happened, so I followed the example of sharks that keep moving forward through the water, no matter what. I drove to the restaurant, rushed inside and found my group, huddled together in an alcove sort of space. I introduced myself and people were cordial enough—the women more so than the men. Women? Yes, as it turns out I was the only person in the group who did not have a wife in tow. Here were "heterosexual crossdressers" with a vengeance. I had a Scotch in honor of the Halls of Montezuma and pledged to myself to do more listening than talking. I tried to gauge the group, looking to see how I might fit in. It didn't seem promising.

We went in to dinner, and one of the wives sort of adopted me as her protégé. She was calling me "dear" as if I were eleven years old. She manufactured a compliment about something I was wearing. Then there was an anticipatory silence. It took a moment before I realized that she was indoctrinating me into a female ritual in which compliments are exchanged.

I responded with the first thing that popped into my head. "Your hair looks nice," I ventured.

She tilted her head, smiled coquettishly and confided in a loud whisper, "Tons of spray. Feels like a Brillo pad on my head." I laughed out loud—to the evident annoyance of her husband, who was sitting next to her with her own tonsorial Brillo pad. We went back to our girl talk. She told me the marines were as surprised to see us as we were to see them. Their commanding officer had put them on their best behavior, "or it's a blindfold and a firing squad at dawn." She had a zany streak. I was having fun.

It was too good to last. As the meal got under way, the "heterosexual crossdressers" began to completely dominate the conversation. Maybe the booze was beginning to kick in. One of the "ladies" began a sentence, "So I told the son-of-a-bitch…" Her wife shushed her. Tension was building. Gradually, the wives retreated into silence. I realized then that you can take an obnoxious middle-aged professional man, put him in a wig and a dress and what you get (drumroll, please) is an obnoxious middle-aged professional man in a wig and a dress. I finished my scampi and apologized to my new friend for departing early. "I know," she confided. "I've had my fill, too." And she wasn't talking about the food.

I made my way back to the hotel, thinking that a nightcap would suit me just fine. But the lobby was full of young marines, this time in fancy dress uniforms. They had been joined by pretty young women in party dresses. Somewhere a band was playing. Forget the nightcap. I took a deep breath and plunged toward the elevator. I pushed the button. *Ding*. The door opened. This time I was face-to-face with two young marines and their dates. One marine said, "Excuse us, ma'am," as they swept past me. The other added, "Have a nice evening, ma'am." The girls smiled pleasantly as they passed me. I wondered if I were dreaming the whole mad episode.

The answer came at about three in the morning, when I was awakened by shouts of "Ooh-rah! Ooh-rah!" I thought the place was on fire. I grabbed the powder-blue robe I had bought at Macy's that afternoon and opened the door. The hotel was built around an atrium, maybe five stories tall. A few of the marines, who had loosened up a whole lot since had I last encountered them in the elevator, were in their boxer shorts, rappelling down from one floor to another on ropes. Some of the pretty young women had lost their party dresses somewhere along the way and were swimming in the pool in their underwear.

I watched the kids having their crazy fun for a few moments, hoping they wouldn't get hurt or busted. Elsewhere, in the bowels of the Holiday Inn, Brillo pads were resting on wig stands and "heterosexual crossdressers" were snoring the night away.

64
The River

Ha!

I spent twelve summers as a fly-fishing guide on the West Branch of the Ausable River, near Lake Placid. I worked a lot with Rachel, an excellent guide and a gifted painter with an MFA from Yale. We share an enthusiasm for the abstract expressionists of the 1950s, and would kick the can around about Kline, Motherwell, Krasner, Newman and Rothko over beers at the lodge after a hard day's fishing. I'm afraid our conversation bewildered some of our clients, who were more inclined to discuss the Yankees and the Giants.

Rachel is very competitive. At least when it comes to fishing, I'm not. A few years after my guiding days, she and I had a little reunion. We fished some of our favorite runs and pools on what felt to me like a long, lazy afternoon. I think that to her it felt like another challenge.

My favorite technique on the Ausable is to fish a local fly called a Usual with three different looks on the same drift: a dry fly, a fluttering caddis and an emerger. I tie my version of the Usual with the lustrous fur combed from our beautiful ginger cat with the huge feet, Snowshoe. That after-

noon, Rachel watched as I worked on a big brown trout. I gave the fish a couple of different looks at the Usual, mending line to give the fly a dead drift. He wasn't buying it. So I rested the fish for ten minutes and came back with a presentation I had learned many years be-

Rachel on the Ausable

fore in the Catskills from Leonard Wright, "the sudden inch." As my Usual drifted into the trout's cone of vision, I gave my wrist a sharp little twist. The fly hopped. The trout surged. We both saw it coming. At the last instant, it refused the fly. I heard Rachel beside me: "Ha!"

"Well, I guess he's seen my act. Let's move on," I suggested.

"Not so fast. I'll get 'im," was her response. She waded into the position I had just relinquished and ran a little green and black streamer fly in front of the fish's nose. She wiggled her rod tip to make the fly dance. The trout slammed it. "Ha!" She raised her rod tip and the fish was on.

Space Patrol

I guided off and on over the years with Ray, who had worked on the big rivers in Montana and Idaho. He told me about a client that he'd taken down the Yellowstone in a drift boat. "The guy was a total head case," Ray told me. "We're drifting along. Suddenly the guy stops casting and says, 'I want to ask you a question.' Ask away, I say, expecting an ordinary question about the kinds of insects in the river, or the birds, or something like that. The guy says, 'See that island we're passing?' I said I did, what about it? So he comes back with a question: 'How much does an island like that weigh?' *Weigh?* The fuckin' island was a half mile long. *It's attached to the fuckin' earth!* So I'm thinkin' this guy's a joker. But no, he wasn't a comedian. He was on genuine space patrol. Completely on space patrol. A half hour later he comes up with another question: 'So tell me, what time of year do the deer turn into elk?' *What?* I wanted to tell him to get out of the boat and wade his ass back to Livingston."

Kehrazin'

Rachel and I used to guide a big junket from ESPN on the Ausable every year. One day I drew some bigwig from the network and one of the corporate sponsors, a pleasant fellow who owned a company in Tennessee. The sponsor had never caught a trout on a fly, and he was itching to get his first. It was a miserable day to try—hot, still and bright. I took them to a stretch of water we guides called "the petting zoo," where the trout were generally cooperative. I managed to find a spot of shade over a promising run against the far bank and tutored the fellow on how to fish a nymph downstream, swinging it at the end of the cast. He worked the run for a while, and he hooked and landed a pretty nice fish. He lit up with delight. A few minutes later, he checked his watch. "Hey, it's pushin' four. We've got an event back at the hotel at five. Better get goin'!" We packed up and rushed them back to their car at the lodge. The fellow shook my hand earnestly as we said goodbye.

Later that night, I was having dinner at the bar at the lodge when someone tapped me on the shoulder. I turned and saw that my client from the afternoon had extended his hand in my direction. I reached to shake and felt a few bills settle into my palm. As I discreetly slipped them into my pocket, he poured out an apology. "Ah know yew folks do this for a livin'. Ah had a great day and Ah didn't do mah share. That was darn rude."

I told him I was paid well by the lodge. Anyway, I understood he had been in a hurry to get back to Lake Placid. Not to worry. "That sure is nice," he continued. But a little gas money always comes in handy, right?"

We shook again and he started to walk away. Then he turned and asked me a question that sounded like, "Yew evah been to the kehrazin'?"

Kehrazin'? I must have looked very puzzled. "Kehrazin'. Yew know. NASCAR." Oh, *car racing*. Yes, he went on, he and his company did a big thing at Talladega. He glanced at the ring on my left hand. "Now why don't yew and yer lady come down for the kehrazin' in a few weeks. Yew just get yourselves down to Birmingham, and we'll send a kehr to fetch yew. The hotel's all taken care of. We always got a hospitality suite goin'. We set out some fine drinks and some fine Southern cookin'. We get some of the Nashville folks down there. We had Clint down there. We had Randy down there. We had Reba down there. Damn, yew lissen to me now, Reba is *good people*." He handed me his business card and told me the date. "Now yew call my gal first thing Monday and she'll get ya'll set up, y'hear?"

At the end of the night, I remembered the new money in my pocket and reached for it to settle my dinner and bar tab. I found five crisp, neatly folded hundred-dollar bills.

Susanne and I had something planned the weekend of the race, so I called the number on the card and asked the secretary to convey my thanks and regrets. A while later, I was talking to my friend Pat, who is wired into the music scene in Nashville. I told him the story. "Hard to believe he was for real," I suggested.

"You Yankees just don't get it. Never will. No Southerner is going to extend you his hospitality without meaning it. Damn, son, you should've gone!"

Le Diner Est Servi

On a very hot May afternoon I guided Marc and André, two genial Montrealers. We didn't start until 4 p.m., since we'd be fishing in what could pass for midseason conditions—low water and bright sun. I worked with Marc on his nymph fishing technique. At one point, I lengthened his leader so the fly would move more naturally in the water. He became fascinated by the motion of the nymph and began to talk excitedly about *le ballet de l'eau*. At six, Marc announced that it was time for dinner, and the way he said it made me understand he wasn't talking about a handful of peanuts and a PowerBar. By the time I got back to the truck, they had covered the tailgate with a white linen tablecloth, gathered a little bunch of wildflowers and stuck them in a glass, and laid out a serious meal. There was a venison pâté, three cheeses, ham, cornichons, stone-ground mustard, a green salad, a remarkable-looking loaf of *pain de campagne* and a chilled bottle of Chenin Blanc from the Loire. The meal was eaten with the leisure and savor that it deserved. At one point I went down to the river and reported that the trout had started to rise. They looked at me with indulgent smiles as Marc broke off another bit of bread and André filled the glasses. This was a meal that was not about to be rushed. Suddenly I was feeling very Type A.

After dinner, I took them to a spot where brown trout usually rise to caddis flies on warm, early summer evenings. Marc took a nice brown almost immediately and followed it with a very pretty native brook trout. He yielded the prime casting position in the pool to André, who promptly landed and released two lovely browns. I was beginning to think there was a lot to be said for a good dinner. I noticed a trout starting to rise at the head of the pool that was easily the largest fish of the night. We let her feed until she established a rhythm. In the clear water I could follow the fish's rise, which was quite deliberate until she was within an inch of the surface. Then she erupted in a slashing motion as she took a fluttering caddis. She was all of eighteen inches, the kind

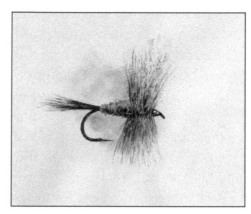

Richard Harrington watercolor of an Ausable Wulff dry fly tied by me

of Ausable brown trout that made the reputation of this river in the 1930s in the popular books of Ray Bergman and Lee Wulff. We worked on the fish carefully for twenty minutes, casting a few times, then letting her settle down, then casting again. On one drift, André's imitation and a natural caddis floated down the feeding lane two or three inches apart and the fish took the natural with an explosive splash, throwing spray. Was she getting reckless? Finally, the trout made her mistake, and Andre hooked up. The fish took off immediately. André wasn't ready for the surging run of a three-pound trout. The fish made it into the next riffle downstream, where the fast current helped her escape. When André reeled in his line, we saw that the hook on his fly had been bent into an L shape. Marc's comment? *"Tres, tres formidable!"*

The Cookie

"You've got to take my client and his son today," Rachel announced as she swept into the shop. "After two days, I can't handle any more. The guy's a super-obnoxious orthopedist from Palo Alto. The kid's only eight. He's terrific, but the guy's on his ass all day." She imitated a nasal, complaining parental voice from the place where childhood nightmares dwell: *"Stop that dilly-dallying, Daniel Piper. Right now. This is fly fishing, not some silly child's game. It's costing a lot of money for this vacation. Stop daydreaming and pay attention.* Dammit, I could slap his face right now." Like it or not, I had a client for the day.

At the river, I quickly abandoned the orthopedist to his own devices, sending him upstream to pound a barren stretch of water. I took Daniel under my wing and led him to one of the best runs in the river. While I was giving him a casting lesson, his line dangled in the water for a moment and Daniel felt a sudden tug. The fish was off as quickly as it had been on. Daniel responded by putting on his game face. "I'm going to catch one," he declared. For the next two hours, he fished with the kind of focus that would have done credit to someone four times his age, while I worked hard to connect him with a trout. But it was turning into one of those really tough days as the sun got higher and brighter. Finally, as the day wound down, Daniel rolled another fish. It was a dandy, at least sixteen inches.

"Did you see that?" I asked him. He hadn't. "Do you want to make another cast? I think you can catch this one. It's a big trout."

Daniel narrowed his eyes and stared at the water while he considered his options. "You know," he explained carefully, "I'm tired. I think I'll go back to the car and just eat my cookie. I hope it hasn't gotten wet while we've been fishing." He reached into the pocket of his waders and held the cookie out for me to examine. "It's still dry!" he exclaimed with delight.

With some fly fishing clients, about 2010

65
Phobia

The Adirondack house had a big, screened-in porch that looked across a pristine valley to the mountains. It was a perfect spot for a gathering on a sunny September afternoon to celebrate the turning of the leaves. I invited the usual cast of characters and their spouses: my editor from *Adirondack Life*, the local boatbuilder, a whizbang carpenter and an Adirondack guide. Quite an outdoorsy group. Lots of flannel shirts for the guys, and turtlenecks and puffy down vests for the women. Everyone brought a dish to share, and some wine and beer. Vivaldi's "Autumn" was on the stereo and the party got off to a jolly start.

After a few rounds of drinks, the conversation turned to phobias. I confessed my fear of heights. Someone else talked about their morbid fear of spiders. One of the women told us that she lived in dread of the cotton balls that are packed in bottles of aspirin and other medications. Then Barney, the guide, revealed his terror of snakes. Even talking about snakes seemed to make him shaky. I realized that his pride was on the line. Fourth generation Adirondack guides just shouldn't be frightened of snakes.

My girlfriend at the time had a Maine coon cat named Rita. Rita was a powerhouse hunter. We usually kept her in because we were dismayed by what she would sometimes bring home—half-grown grouse and adolescent snowshoe hares were among her specialties. But this day she was on the loose, scouting her favorite territory by the stream at the end of our long, curving driveway.

As Barney went on about his phobia, I heard a muffled cry from the clump of birches at the bend in the driveway. Then I saw Rita, dragging a three-foot black snake toward the porch, trying to howl as she held on to the serpent writhing in the grasp of her jaws. Barney saw it, too. In midsentence he jumped from his chair, ran through the house, burst out the back door and scampered up the hill. We went after him, calling, but he just kept going, headlong into the thousands of acres of woodland behind the house.

Meanwhile, Rita had given up on her quarry, which had evidently slithered off into the underbrush. I could hear voices from up the hill: "It's okay, Barney. The snake's gone. Everything's okay. You can come back..." The voices went on for a long time. An hour after dark I heard Barney's truck as it pulled down the driveway. Next to the woodstove, Rita was snug in her cat bed, twitching in her sleep, dreaming of her big conquest.

66
Anne

I met Anne in Chicago at a transgender event called the Be All, as in "Be all you want to be." Some of the conferences I went to were held in chain hotels, with dismal banquet food and a pedestrian deejay who thought playing "Man, I Feel Like a Woman" must be just the ticket for *this* crowd. But not Be All. Whoever ran this thing had it down cold. The venue was a premium hotel with a surprisingly fine kitchen. Jugglers, magicians and mimes wandered through the cocktail hour as a jazz piano played. A string quartet was the soundtrack for dinner. A funky soul band with

Anne, with a friend

about a million horns played for dancing. A hot blues band from the South Side did a midnight set as fireworks went off over the lake. There were poetry readings, film screenings and a session on how to do improv for personal growth. No wonder a thousand folks converged on Be All from all over the world every year.

Anne had a spot in the vendor area. She sold stylish leather shoes in sizes up to 15. Did I hear someone say "big shoes"? I was drawn into her booth as if by an invisible force field. She appraised my feet.

"Let's see 'em, Sugar," she drawled, and gestured to me to take off my shoes. "My word, but they *are* big 'uns, aren't they? Well, let me just see what I can rustle up." She started to rummage through her piles of shoeboxes. A lot of laughs and $250 later, I had three pairs of shoes I really liked and could actually wear. I went to dinner that night with Anne and her beau. Anne had a whole repertoire of saucy jokes about two Southern ladies sitting in a porch swing—sort of a regional variant of the "a priest and a rabbi get into an elevator" genre. She was a hilarious storyteller.

Anne told me she ran her business out of her converted garage in Lafayette, Louisiana. She started it because she wore size 12s herself, and figured a lot of other women did, too. She was surprised at the outset that about half of her customers were men. One of her first was someone that she knew had a high profile in Baton Rouge politics. "She was a great customer and nice enough, but kind of a windbag, like she knew everything about everything. Every time she came in, she'd be talkin' about some bar in New Orleans where she went as 'Darlene.' The place had shrimp étouffée, great oysters, live jazz, everybody knew her, she had the best time ever, blah, blah. She was always tryin' to get me to go along. One day, I agreed. I had just gotten a new car and wanted a road trip anyway."

As they drove from Lafayette to New Orleans, Darlene was in high spirits, talking about her adventures in the Big Easy. Anne was looking forward to an eventful night. They parked the car a block from the club.

"Okay, let's go!" Anne said, and started to open her door.

Her companion froze. "I can't," she sobbed. "I've never been anywhere dressed like this before. I just can't."

"Never been anywhere? What? But you told me..." Anne had no patience for this kind of jive. "Now you listen to me, bitch. I didn't drive two hours to get an earful of your blubberin' and whimperin'. You've got exactly three minutes to fix your makeup, pull up your big girl drawers and get outta this car. We're goin' into that bar and we're gonna stay until closin' time. I'm gonna have a big ol' time, and you better make up your mind to have one too. Now get movin'!"

Anne paused for dramatic effect and took a sip of her Appletini. "Now you know, I had to haul that ol' gal out of there at 3 a.m., she was havin' so much fun. The sun was risin' in my rearview mirror before we got home to Lafayette. All she needed to get her goin' was a little dose of Cajun tough love. Right, Sugar?"

At the Chicago Be All Gender Conference, 2004

67
The Connelly Nose

When I was a child and adolescent, I was convinced that I was the only person in the world who had the thoughts and feelings I kept so secret. In my twenties, thirties and forties, I tried to research information on what was known in those days as "gender dysphoria" and its manifestations. In the Van Pelt Library at Penn, I found a book from 1928 called *Venus Castina: Famous Female Impersonators Celestial and Human*. It dealt with "the yearnings of feminine souls trapped in male bodies." But stories from Roman mythology and the *en travesti* escapades of the eighteenth-century Italian singer Farinelli didn't have much to do with my effort to make sense of myself.

When the internet arrived, everything changed. In a moment, I discovered that there were actually millions of other people who had the same thoughts, feelings and questions that I had. I became particularly interested in how "gendernauts" and "femulators" (to use two clever internet terms) found outlets for self-expression and managed their relationships.

One of my discoveries was a flamboyant character from County Tyrone, Northern Ireland, with the aristocratic name Raymond Saville Conolly de Mountmorency Lecky-Browne-Lecky. Lecky, who was born in 1881, lived alone in a sprawling manor house with a private theater. Evidently, Raymond's mother had dressed him as a girl into his teens. He called himself Tibby and wore as his typical everyday outfit a jacket of mauve silk velvet, a silky cravat, ruffles and diamond rings. Tibby was renowned for his impersonations of women in amateur theatricals. As the magazine *Irish Life* reported in its Christmas number for 1913:

> In the sketch, "Her New Dressmaker," Mr. Raymond Browne-Lecky fairly brought down the house, appearing in the role of a young widow, "Mrs. Forbes," his "make-up" and disguise being so perfect that many of the audience were completely mystified, and refused to believe that the charming lady was, after all only a "mere man." Mr. Raymond Browne-Lecky's gown was as follows: The "jupe" very full, "en cloche" draped with a "Volant" of "point d'Alencon"; the "corsage" in "crepe de chine," encircled with a "cincture of passementerie," "manches en gigot," veiled with a "Volant de dentelle."[8]

Whatever all that might mean, it's clear that Tibby took his wardrobe very seriously.

It was Tibby's elaborate name that really caught my attention. More than thirty variant spellings of the name Connelly are recorded in church registers in Ireland and also in Ulster where, under whatever spelling, the Conollys were well established by the sixteenth century. What's more, a branch of my mother's family named Lecky (sometimes spelled Leckey) emigrated from Northern Ireland, first to Halifax and Digby, Nova Scotia, and then to Boston and New York. When I misbehaved, my mother would jokingly warn me that she would "send me back to Novy with the rest of the herring chokers in the family."

Raymond Conolly Browne-Lecky

So Tibby's ornate moniker contained two of my own family names— the same Tibby who was celebrated for his impersonations of women. *Coincidence*, I said to myself. *Lots of people have those names. And lots of people impersonate women—or quite a few do, anyway...*

Fa as a young lawyer, about 1910

Still, there was something eerily familiar about one of the photos of Tibby, one of the pictures when he's out of costume. He's staring into the camera, his right shoulder slightly forward. I have a picture of my grandfather, who was born a year later than Tibby, at about the same age. He's standing in much the same pose, also staring into the camera. They have the same high forehead and full jaw line. The shape of the mouth is the same. Most remarkably, Tibby has my grandfather's nose—distinctively long and straight—what my mother always called "the Connelly nose."

Before we all start humming the theme from *The Twilight Zone*, of course none of this means that I'm related to this eccentric Irish aristocrat. And even if I were? I wouldn't begin to speculate that some rogue chunk of DNA might somehow bind me to Tibby and his excursions into femininity. Nevertheless, I do feel an affinity with the person in the photographs, and the story behind the pictures—the story of a fellow gendernaut and femulator, finding a place for himself in the world a hundred years ago.

Snapshots III

A Typo to End All Typos...

Among the thousands of student papers I have graded in my thirty years of college teaching, one title stands out above the rest: an essay on Dylan Thomas' famous poem about his father's death, "Do Not Go *Gentile* into That Good Night."

...and a Malapropism to End All Malapropisms

Comparing Henry V to Richard III, a Shakespeare student of mine made the point that at the end of the play Henry is "so *self-defecating* and passionate. I assume this is another example of his calculating deceitfulness."

...and a Voice from the Back Row

In my drama theory class, I was teaching some challenging ideas from Bert States' exceptional book *Great Reckonings in Little Rooms: On the Phenomenology of Theatre*. I presented this problem for consideration: "Shouldn't the purpose of art be to discover truth, not engage in pretense? Let's envision what happens in the theater when the lights go down in the hall and the lights come up in the performance space. People appear, dressed up in borrowed clothes, pretending to be characters in the play. They start talking in words that we know someone else wrote down for them to say. They display emotion on cue. Why don't we all just stand up and say, 'Hey, wait a minute, this isn't real. Plato was right when he complained that theater is just fakery. And because it's not real, my consciousness is too preoccupied with real stuff to let it in'?"

There followed quite a lot of discussion about suspension of disbelief and the psychology of enactment. It was a good discussion, but it seemed to have run its course after a few minutes. I was about to ask another question when a hand went up in the back row. It was a young woman who hadn't spoken for weeks, who seemed to be dangling off the edge of the cliff as far as this class was concerned. Then she said one of the most powerful things I have ever heard in a classroom: "For me, and for all of us if we allow it to happen, theater is a dream in which we can all share."

The Royal York

I have a fondness for the old-line Canadian Pacific hotels. It must run in the family. My great-aunts, Grace and Mary, would send us colorful postcards in the 1950s from Château Frontenac, Château Laurier and the Royal York when they were on their annual train trip from Quebec City to Banff and Lake Louise.

Susanne and I checked into the Royal York in Toronto late one evening and decided to eat in the dining room. The dinner wasn't up to expectations, so the manager sent a bottle of wine and a fruit basket up to our room, with a personal note that we wouldn't be charged for the meal. It was the kind of nice touch you'd expect from a real hotel.

During the night there was a lot of ruckus in the hallway. Security didn't handle it well, so I lost patience about 2 a.m. and decided to confront the rowdies and tell them to put a lid on it. I threw open the door. Oops. The hallway was filled with a half-dozen rappers—lots of gold chains and New Era 59Fifty hats. I shudder to think what my fate might have been in a hotel corridor in Chicago or New York. But, fortunately for me, these were very polite Canadian rappers who apologized sheepishly and took the party back to their room. I mentioned the episode at the front desk in the morning and when we got back to our room after breakfast there was a large floral arrangement and another personal note from the manager. Dreadfully sorry, he said; we wouldn't be charged for the room that night and he hoped we would enjoy the rest of our stay.

I took a moment in the bathroom before we headed off to the zoo to see the snow leopards. When I flushed the 1929-era toilet, a geyser shot up from the ancient porcelain bowl, and it exploded in pieces on the floor.

I reported the mishap to the front desk, and a mob descended on our room with buckets, mops and wrenches. The phone rang. The manager was on the line. He was so frightfully sorry; while we were out, our effects would be moved to another room and our entire stay would be on the house—and please do stay an extra night if we would like. That evening, we were shown to a suite at the top of the hotel. On the way up the elevator, the bellhop let it drop that the Dalai Lama, Cary Grant, Duke Ellington and Frank Sinatra were among the guests who had enjoyed the suite. When he opened the door for us, there were more flowers, another bottle of wine and another personal note, apologizing for the "unfortunate chain of circumstances." Outside the picture window was a stunning view of the harbor and the sailboat races on Lake Ontario. Not being dummies, we took the manager up on his offer and stayed the extra night.

The Voice of an Angel

John, Ray and I went to the Cape for a few days to fly fish for stripers and blues. The first morning we hit Nauset Marsh at dawn and fished hard for three hours. When the tide changed we headed to Wellfleet. John and Ray decided to trek about a mile down the beach to a jetty on the point. Walking miles in waders has never been my idea of fun, and I was feeling lazy. I decided to stay put. The sun was high enough to be deliciously warm

John at Nauset Marsh, dawn

against the cool breeze, so I put my tackle bag under my head for a pillow and caught a nap on the sand. I was in a deep sleep when I heard a melodious, angelic voice: *Oh fisherman...oh fisherman...*I opened my eyes and it seemed that a lithe young woman, backlit by the sun, was leaning over me. Her arm was outstretched, pointing toward the bay. I stumbled to my feet and saw dozens of gulls swooping and squawking, low over the water. A school of big bluefish was rampaging in the shallows twenty feet from the sand. I grabbed my rod, cast a streamer fly into the middle of the melee and hooked up. I was still half asleep as I played the fish. John and Ray had seen the commotion and the bend in my rod and came running down the beach in their waders. When the blitz was over, I told them the story of the lovely voice and the woman who pointed toward the water. "What woman?" they asked. They hadn't seen any woman.

Wild Kingdom

Our Adirondack house was on thirty acres, surrounded by thousands more acres of undeveloped land. Susanne and I took a nightly walk to the waterfall at the end of our dirt road, with our eyes open for critters. We saw fishers pouring themselves over the trunks of downed trees, otters swimming exuberantly through deep snow, owls in the trees, praying mantises and giant water bugs, ravens, bobcat sign, beavers and muskrat preparing their winter dens, and a great blue heron devouring a field mouse. We loved our happenstance wildlife discoveries. On one of Susanne's first visits, we were cleaning out the bluebird houses. I opened the top of one of the houses and we were both startled when a small brown animal with very large eyes scampered out and up the utility pole. It climbed about ten feet rapidly and then launched itself into the air and glided forty feet to a tree and quickly disappeared around the other side. A flying squirrel!

All I Wanted Was Some Chicken Jalfrezi

As I was checking into the hotel for the big Chicago gender event called Be All, I saw my friend Anne and her beau talking with some other folks I knew. Anne came over and said, "We're headed out for an Indian dinner. One of the gals knows a great place. Drop your bag and come along." I joined the crowd and we drove to a rather posh Indian restaurant in Arlington Heights. We were seated, given menus and then we waited. We waited a long time. Anne flagged down a waiter and asked for water. He just stared and walked away. Something was seriously askew.

After about twenty minutes, a man who seemed to be the manager rushed up to our table in a very agitated state. He started to snatch our menus away. "Not for you!" he declaimed in a thundering voice. Everyone in the restaurant could hear him, and they all turned to see what the disturbance was about. Now he was pointing and shouting: "This place not for you. No food for people like you here. Leave now. Leave now."

So we left, but not until Anne had let loose some Cajun fury and given the guy a serious talking-to. Afterwards, we would joke about getting all dressed up to deliver a dressing down. "What now?" she asked as we got back in the car. I suggested we head down to Naperville; I recalled seeing an Indian joint down there at some point in my travels. We found the place and were greeted warmly by an older lady who showed us to a table. I ought to mention at this point that Anne's companion dressed a bit like Zsa Zsa Gabor—think Gene Hackman doing Zsa Zsa. A very cordial young waiter came to our table and asked her in halting English, "Would like cocktails, sir?" I suggested gently that it might be easier if he just referred to everyone at the table as "ma'am." He nodded earnestly and assured me, "Oh yes, sir. Absolutely, sir. Not to worry. I will call you ma'am, sir."

High Anxiety

I get panicky when I have to get on a ladder to clean the gutters. Heights are not my thing. Susanne, on the other hand, loves to be up in the air. One of her favorite jobs was painting billboards from a narrow scaffold high above NASCAR tracks. She pounced on the chance to ride in a glider piloted by one of my former students. I stayed on the ground, taking pictures. When we visited Toronto, our first destination had to be the CN Tower, 1,815 feet in the air. After some coaxing, I did go up the tower with her to the LookOut level, a wimpy 1,136 feet aloft. I stayed well away from the windows while she devoured the view. "Let's go higher," she urged. I took a deep breath and held her hand as we rode up to the Sky Pod level at 1,465 feet. Here, angled windows allowed her to lean gleefully over the abyss. I plastered myself to the wall near the elevator, nervously eyeing the pendulum that shows how the building is swaying in the wind. My inner voice whined *Get me down from here!* Things evened themselves out a bit that evening when we went to see *Spiderman II* in an IMAX theater. I sat calmly as cars whizzed by in 3D and careened into one another; Susanne gripped my arm in both hands until I was black and blue.

"People Like You…"

I was on my way home to the Adirondacks from Manhattan and decided to try a little Italian joint in New Jersey that a friend had recommended. I was seated at a deuce in the middle of the dining room—not my favorite seat in any restaurant—but the meal was good and I was feeling relaxed. Without warning, I was struck a forceful blow on the right side of my head that knocked my glasses askew and nearly tossed me out of my chair. I turned in time to see a boy of fifteen or so scurry back to his seat in a booth, across from a woman who was glancing furtively in my direction. I took her to be his mother. I crossed the room and told them I wanted an apology. The kid was looking away. She faced me and said, "You're not going to get an apology. He's autistic. He can't control himself."

My head was starting to throb and I wasn't feeling very compassionate. "I'm sorry, but if he attacks strangers in restaurants, you'll be held accountable. He's a big kid. What just happened could have been pretty serious. An older person would have wound up on the floor."

She lashed out. "Don't give me a lecture, queer!"

I realized I was trembling and felt unsteady on my feet. I retreated to my seat. I was waiting quietly for the server to bring my check when she stopped at my table on her way to the door, with her son in tow. She shook her finger in my face and said in a mocking tone, "Don't forget. They used to lock people like you up."

Rogue Wave

It was what they call a bluebird day in early October. I was off Napatree Point, between Watch Hill, Rhode Island, and Stonington, Connecticut. I had called my fishing friend John an hour earlier on the cellphone. "You ought to be out here," I had told him. "It's sunny and warm. I'm catching stripers like crazy. Big ground swells from some storm out at sea, like a slow-motion rodeo ride." Even in my little sixteen-foot aluminum skiff, gentle ground swells didn't bother me. I had grown up with the six-to-eight-foot swells that rolled into the southwest side of the Vineyard from the open ocean.

Fish were busting in the wash near the end of the point, chasing sand eels. I was a hundred and fifty feet away, picking at the edges of the school and carefully nudging closer. Suddenly a fisherman on the shore started screaming and pointing. I turned and looked behind me. One of the swells was cresting at eye level, just astern. Then it broke over me. I was on my knees and the boat was half full of water. I got partway to my feet, grabbed at the wheel and gunned the motor, trying to get my bow into the waves. Then another wave broke over me, broadside, and knocked me flat. The boat was swamped. Then the largest wave of all picked my boat up in its crest and hurled her into the rocks. I jumped for it. I saw the propeller turning in the air over my head.

I made it to a sandy patch and the fisherman helped me set two anchors to secure the boat in a tiny rocky cove. The pump was dead and the boat had a dent near the bow, but it looked fixable. I thought I might be able to float her out at high tide, if I could pump her out and get the motor running. I started the long trek down the beach to search in town for a hand pump.

When I returned, the tide was up and the boat was careening wildly in the cove, tossed by wind and waves and bouncing from rock to rock like a billiard ball. *What had happened to the anchors?* Then I realized that in the two hours I had been gone, someone had stripped

The wreck

the boat and stolen the anchors. What was left looked like a beer can that had been crushed underfoot. I was ashamed that I had lost my boat. I'd failed the first rule of seamanship: Keep the water out. But I was dumbfounded that anyone would steal anchors off a crippled vessel. It was no consolation when Peter told me that our friend Paul Dixon, a professional captain and fly-fishing guide, had been swamped off Montauk that same morning by another rogue wave.

Golf

After fifty years away from the game, I decided at age seventy to take up golf again. I like walking the course for exercise, and I enjoy trying to puzzle out why one shot can be pretty good and the next a "worm burner," a "moon shot" or a slice that threatens passing cars.

There's a nice course a couple of miles up the road from our house, in Goddard Memorial Park. Designed in 1939 by Donald Ross, it's a classic little New England course, close by Narragansett Bay. One fine June afternoon I was on the fairway of the eighth hole, about to hit my approach shot to the shallow, elevated green that is well-guarded by bunkers. It's a tricky shot, the kind that nearly always turns out to be an exercise in humility. As I started my backswing, something rather large fell out of the sky and hit the ground with a *thud* a few yards to my right. I walked over to investigate. A bluefish! Out of the sky? I looked up. An osprey was hovering overhead. She whistled a warning at me to let me know she wasn't happy about having dropped her lunch and intended to get it back.

Ham

When we relocated from the Adirondacks to Rhode Island, we were suddenly close to theaters, museums and galleries in Providence, Boston and New Haven. I started to go to a lot of plays, some of them were at The Players, which stages productions in a marvelous old, lop-

A still from the *Richard II* video, 2020

sided theater on Benefit Street in Providence. I had no acting experience, but out of curiosity I enrolled in a scene study class organized by the astute directors Patricia and Alan Hawkridge. I found myself drawn into the mystery of acting.

For The Players virtual festival in 2020, I worked up part of Richard II's speech from act three, scene two of Shakespeare's play: "For God's sake let us sit upon the ground / And tell sad stories of the deaths of kings." In the speech, Richard is struggling to come to terms with the loss of his crown and the inevitability of his own death. My friend Brian, who is a cinematographer and producer, helped me with the video. He even superimposed a medieval castle for a backdrop.

During our last take, I really felt the power of acting. It came on unexpectedly and just took me over. Richard has a line, "All murdered!" and from that point on, I heard his voice, not my own. By the time the speech got to "As if this flesh which walls about our life / Were brass impregnable," I felt as if I were having an out-of-body experience. It's probably awful, hammy acting, but it was great fun.

The Journey, Not the Destination

They say it's about the journey, not the destination. They also say fishing isn't just about catching fish. Hornbeck and I didn't have those shopworn aphorisms in mind when we loaded his truck and set course for our secret smallmouth bass creek on the Canadian border.

As we drove over the causeway at Tupper Lake, a gigantic snapping turtle blocked the middle of the highway. We slowed to a crawl to avoid hitting her, and I pulled over to the side of the road. "We really should try to move that gal," I said. "If someone hits her going fifty, it will be bad for her, but really bad for the driver. It would be like hitting a boulder."

"It's a long way to the border," was Hornbeck's chilly reply. But we grabbed my heavy wading staff out of the truck and approached the beast. "Watch out!" Hornbeck admonished me. "Those things crawl slow, but they strike fast. And once they've got your arm or hand, they don't let go. Very bad news." Then he set himself up to direct traffic around the turtle.

My wading staff is an old ash tool handle, three quarters of an inch in diameter. I held it close to the turtle's mouth. If you're waiting for me to say she bit it in half—sorry, I wish I could. But like Hornbeck said, she struck blindingly fast and seized it with her vise-grip jaws. I pulled on it with the

The snapper

intention of sliding the critter off the highway and into the swamp by the side of the road. Forget it. The turtle had embedded its inch-long claws in the asphalt and was holding on with incredible strength. "I can't budge her!" I called to Hornbeck. He came over to help and put a canoe paddle under the turtle's rear end to act as a lever. The idea was that he would scoot her along while I pulled. Forget that, too. The turtle was stronger and more determined than the two of us.

Meanwhile, a guy pulled over and told us we should get behind the turtle, grab its carapace right behind the head and lift. "That way she can't git ya," the guy insisted. *Right. And then what?* The turtle probably weighed a hundred pounds, and it looked like it could rip you up with those claws.

Another guy stopped and suggested we tie a rope around it and drag it off the road with the winch on the front bumper of his truck. *Sure. Tie a rope around it. You first.* The convocation about moving the turtle was verging on the ridiculous.

Then, unexpectedly, the snapper decided she had listened to enough nonsense about how to move her and decided to do it herself. She dropped the wading staff and lumbered purposefully back toward the swamp. The guy who had advised us about grabbing her by the shell scampered out of the way as if Godzilla were after him.

An hour later we were driving on Route 11 near the border, only a few miles from our beloved creek. A cat dodged in front of us, carrying a kitten. She made a beeline for an old barn by the side of the road. I told Hornbeck we ought to pull over in case she had to cross the highway again with more of her babies. "You're going to stop traffic for a cat?" he grumbled.

"Not exactly," I answered. *"We're* going to stop traffic for a cat."

Hornbeck took charge of the eastbound lane while I flagged down a westbound logging truck. Sure enough, the mother trotted across the road and then returned with another kitten. As she did, a sedan with Ontario plates pulled to a halt. The elderly couple in the car smiled and made playful little gestures to act out what the cat was doing. As the cat crossed again, the logger was telling me how his wife took in every stray cat in Clinton County. I looked up just in time to see a car barreling down the road toward the old folks. I cringed when I saw that the driver was reading a newspaper.

The collision was enormous. The old couple's car sprang forward about a hundred feet. Amazingly, no one seemed badly hurt, but both vehicles were demolished. As we gathered to comfort the elderly lady, the cat scooted past us and through the wreckage, another kitten in her mouth.

"Pretty good day so far," Hornbeck quipped. "We saved a turtle. We saved a cat and her kittens. We caused forty thousand dollars in property damage. We nearly got two old Canadians killed. No matter how good the fishing turns out to be, it can't possibly top this."

70
The Headstone

Halfway down the row of winter rye, the rototiller stalled and died. *Jammed on a rock,* I thought. But when I hauled it out to free the tines, I saw that they'd caught on a curved, triangular chunk of rusted metal—a moldboard plow.

Gardening on an old Adirondack farm can be a kind of accidental archeology. During the winter, frost pushes all sorts of discarded, lost and buried objects toward the surface. Over the years, my spring tilling unearthed spoons, bones, spark plugs, shards of blue-and-white crockery, an intact medicine bottle from a North Creek apothecary and a jumble of wagon parts.

These finds always made me wonder about the Wescotts, the family who worked this land for a century, beginning in the 1850s. It's no great feat of the imagination to extrapolate the rusted plow to a horse's breath steaming in the chill air of an early planting season, but I found it much more difficult to envision the people. I tried to picture them tending the animals, hanging the wash or playing with the children, but I lapsed too easily into sentimental clichés from nineteenth-century genre paintings. My gut told me that clichés wouldn't do justice to the realities of their lives.

During my first summer in the Adirondacks, I got a surprise visit from Elmer Heath, the last farmer to work this place. We talked in that North Country kind of way, leaning against the fender of his truck, looking down at the toes of our shoes, watching as they nudged the gravel. He told me about the night in 1958 when the barns burned. I told him about the 1905 penny I'd found under the front doorsill while I was renovating. "It'd be the Wescotts that laid that penny down when the new house went up," he said. I asked if he could tell me much about the Wescott family. He responded with a question: "Been to the graveyard? That headstone just about tells it all."

The graveyard is just beyond the west field, a five-minute walk from the spot where I found the penny. The gravesite itself is shaded by a canopy of ancient maples. It's framed by a fieldstone wall that forms a square about seventy feet on each side. The single marker, a blunt obelisk at the center of the square, bears witness: Jarus J. Wescott, born in 1843, served in the Civil War in the 96th New York Infantry—the illustrious Adirondack Regiment. His wife, Francis, was born in 1841 and died on April 29, 1881, nine days after giving birth to a girl, Maud. Baby Maud outlived her mother by only a month, dying on May 27. Her two sisters had both died on Christmas Day, 1880; Alice was fourteen, Edna was nine.

The Jarus J. of the headstone is known in all the local historical records as Jarius Cornelius Wescott. Those same records spell his wife's name more conventionally as Frances. If some snowbound Faulkner were writing the tale sketched out on the stone, the name Jarius would fit the character very well. For in the Bible the distraught Jarius implores Jesus: "My little daughter lies at the point of death. I pray you come and lay your hands upon her that she may be healed and she shall live" (Mark 5:23). In the gospel story the twelve-year-old dies but is brought back to life by a miracle. There was no miracle for the daughters of Jarius Wescott.

The Wescott headstone

Research told me there had been a diphtheria epidemic in the North Country in 1880 and 1881, perhaps brought to the area by itinerant peddlers. It's likely that Alice and Edna Wescott died of this disease. Frances Wescott bore her last child soon after tending to her two young daughters in their fatal illness. She may have contracted diphtheria herself although, given the timing of her death, she could have succumbed to "childbed fever," a common complication of childbirth in the nineteenth century. At that time giving birth at forty was a very perilous experience even for a healthy woman.

How did these catastrophic losses affect Jarius, who had as a young man endured the horrors of battle at Williamsburg, Seven Pines and Cold Harbor? My elderly neighbor Eleanor would sometimes relate the local legend of how, in old age, Jarius sat by the upstairs bedroom window for entire afternoons, looking out over the graves of his wife and daughters. In this telling, Jarius is like the gothic characters in Robert Frost's poem "Home Burial," who are connected through the window to the bleak landscape of their child's grave and their own deep grief.

When the legends and historical records have all been heard from, the wall of stones that Harry Wescott built to enclose the graves of his parents and sisters makes the most eloquent statement. The wall flows with the contours of the land. By my reckoning, it may hold 40,000 stones or more. I wonder that a subsistence farmer took the time and effort to build such a wall. It's a testament to devotion and endurance. It's a monument to an Adirondack patriarch, made from the very stones he must have cursed as he guided his moldboard plow across the bony fields—perhaps the very plow I found in my garden plot.

I walked to the old cemetery often. Ironically, it always seemed to me to be full of life. I never stopped there without seeing some creature or its sign. In winter there were hare and deer tracks, squirrels, jays and chickadees; in summer, goldfinches, chipmunks and dragonflies. Some of the maples had been blasted by lightning over the years and woodpeckers, both the smaller downys and the big pileateds, liked to tap at them for larvae. Next to the grave marker, the flag, always fresh and crisp, fluttered in its star-shaped bronze holder. I must have read the inscription on the stone a hundred times. Alice, Edna, Frances, Maud. What beautiful names. How sad.

71
You Can't Put Anything Over on Me

For a few years in the 1980s, I had a market garden on my farm property in the Adirondacks. I grew vegetables and sunflowers, mostly for a wonderful inn on the back side of Gore Mountain called Highwinds.[9] Next to the gardens I had an antiques shop in a rustic little building that had once been a barn for hogs and poultry. I kept the shop stocked with the best antiques, art and antiquarian books I could find on wintertime buying trips to Canada, the Hudson Valley and southern New England. I had some great stuff.

Word got out soon enough, and I had a pretty steady stream of customers during the warmer months. Rita, the shop cat, liked to greet the customers at the door. If there was a chill in the air I'd have a little fire going in the woodstove, with a tea kettle chugging away. Bix Beiderbecke or Count Basie were usually on the stereo. There was a comfy reading chair with a good lamp. Some afternoons I'd set out a bottle of wine and some nuts, or a bowl of apples. A nice basket by the door was stocked with squash, beans, tomatoes and peppers for sale. It was a very friendly and homey shop.

HEYDAY ANTIQUES

Adirondack books, photos, and paintings, select country items, and the unusual.

Thurs.-Sat., May-Oct., or call.
Located 1 mi. off Rte. 8 on Bartman Rd.

BAKERS MILLS, NY · 518/251-2217

I ran the place on trust. If I was in the middle of cooking dinner when a car drove up, I might just say, "Browse as long as you'd like. I'll be in the kitchen up at the house. Just knock on the back door if you need help." People were completely disarmed by that degree of trust. To my knowledge, I never lost an item to theft.

But I did get a bad check once, for about $350. I really felt burned and resolved to be more vigilant. A dealer friend urged me to get a driver's license number for every check—particularly from any car with out-of-state plates. Girded with my new policy, I was ready to crack down on the evildoers.

It was nearly closing time the next Saturday when a car came slowly up the drive. An older couple got out—dressed very nicely for some sort of social function, but in a style that might have been in fashion in 1962. She was wearing a floral sheath, pearls and a white sweater over her shoulders; he had on a seersucker suit and a bow tie. Rita greeted them at the threshold, and they made a fuss over her. While this was going on, I noticed their car: an older Mercedes with Delaware plates.

They seem like nice elderly people, I told myself. *But you never know. They could be clever professional thieves, or just kleptomaniacs. But I'm on guard now. Vigilant. No more rip-offs.*

The gentleman took an interest in the paintings on the wall behind the display cases. One was a lovely oil-on-panel of a woodcock, in its original frame. I had dated it about 1890, and had priced it at $950. He asked his wife if she thought it would go nicely in the upstairs study. She agreed that it might, and he announced, "We'll take that one." He hadn't asked about the price. Meanwhile, the lady had taken a fancy to an art nouveau pewter vase. "We'll take this, please." She hadn't looked at the price either: $265.

"We're expected for dinner at seven," she reminded her husband, who was exploring the book nook.

"We'd better go," he agreed. "But I think I'll take this book." Another $30.

He approached the counter with a benevolent smile and took out his checkbook. "How much will that be?"

"With tax, $1,332.15, please."

I expected he might fall over, but he didn't flinch. He simply started to write the check. I was immediately on the alert. After all, only scam artists wouldn't care about the prices, and no scam artists cleverly disguised as a nice older couple were going to take advantage of me that afternoon. "I'm sorry," I chimed in, "but would you mind putting your driver's license number on the check?"

"Oh, certainly not. Not at all," he replied. He fumbled with his wallet, wrote the number on the check and handed it to me. With my eagle eye, I scrutinized the check. Then I noticed the name and address: *E. I. DuPont. Wilmington, Delaware.*

In front of the shop with Rita the greeter cat and my 1937 Chrysler

72
All Around the Mountain

Like a lot of the kids in the Boston suburbs in the early 1960s, my high school friend Neil and I had our own little bluegrass band. It was a lark, but we went on to separate colleges and drifted apart. He was a much better musician than I, and more seriously dedicated to discovering and playing traditional and old-timey music—what is now fashionably called American roots music. Neil wound up at BU and lived at Old Joe Clark, a sort of co-operative boarding house for traditional musicians and friends on Fayette Street, near Inman Square in Cambridge. He'd started the Spark Gap Wonder Boys, an old-time string band that was making a name for itself around New England. The Wonder Boys were a great band, particularly after the addition of Dick Fegy, a marvelous guitar, fiddle and mandolin player who went on to record with Dylan and Frank Zappa. Their rendition of the old breakdown "Little Rabbit" would rattle anybody's rafters. The Wonder Boys were the first northern band to win the World Champion string band competition at the Union Grove Old Time Fiddlers' Convention in North Carolina. Neil came home with a trophy that was three feet tall and a smirk that lasted several months.

I'd go to parties at Old Joe's and Neil and I would get together from time to time and play a few songs. We went to Union Grove together and to Newport, but we were both preoccupied. We reconnected musically when Neil played on my first record in 1976. After the record came out, I invited him to back me up on some shows at colleges and arts centers. Soon, we were playing some of those concerts as a duo. But then Neil got busy as a member of David Bromberg's band, and the tide went out again. In 2002, we played together at a memorial gathering for Dick Fegy and decided that maybe we ought to do some concerts and a bit of recording. Before we knew it, we had a dozen shows booked. The more we played together, the more we liked it—and audiences liked it, too.

We set up a recording studio in the great room at the Adirondack farmhouse and invited my friend Joel Hurd, an excellent engineer, to come in for a few days and record us. We cut everything live, experimenting as we went with new approaches to some of the songs we'd been playing off and on for decades. All three of us were energized and very confident about the project. I set everything aside for a few weeks and then gave our twenty hours of recordings a careful listen over a long, snowy weekend. I was pleased with much of what I heard, but there was something missing—

namely, an audience. The recordings lacked the immediacy and spark that seemed to happen when we played for a crowd.

About the same time, I stopped by chance at a little bookshop in Keene Valley, in the heart of the Adirondack High Peaks. As I was browsing, the owner came over and introduced himself as Dennis. There was something familiar about him, but I couldn't quite place him. He told me that I had played a festival at his college in the late '70s. He reminded me that he had asked me a question about playing guitar in open tunings, and I had given him an impromptu guitar lesson for an hour or so. It turns out that he was married to Martha Gallagher, the renowned Celtic harper. I told him about playing with Neil and about the recording project. "We do house concerts," he replied. "You can record at our place. It's a lot of fun!"

It was fun, indeed. Dennis and Martha got a bunch of delightfully loony people together for an audience, laid out a splendid table of food and wines, and turned us loose. We wound up doing two nights, and I think they were as good as any shows that Neil and I had ever done together. We decided to call the album *All Around the Mountain* because we'd gone around the mountain a few times before we found the spirit of the project, and around the mountain to Dennis and Martha's house for two memorable nights. And it so happened that Neil knew a modal lament from the back pages of Appalachian music by that same title. I was gratified when I took the final mixes to Tom Mark's Make Believe Ballroom for mastering. Artie and I were at the console when T.M. rolled the first track, "Nashville Blues." At the end of the cut, when applause suddenly appeared, Artie was surprised: "This is *live*? Really good!"

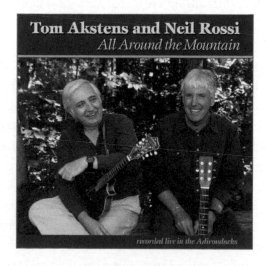

73
The National Geographic to the Rescue

After a couple of years in the "transgender community" I decided the whole thing ought to be about more than shopping, parties and grappling with my inner sense of shame. I had gotten friendly with Mara, who ran the National Center for Transgender Equality. Mara had a razor-sharp wit and magnetic enthusiasm. Her favorite word was "amazing!" She had spoken at a few of the conventions I attended, and what she had to say motivated me to do something positive for other transpeople, who were often fired from jobs, kicked out of apartments, given lousy medical care, denied credit, abused and assaulted. Whatever self-pity I harbored had been purged after ten minutes of hearing her speak. There were vulnerable people out there who needed to have their rights protected.

I decided to attend the NCTE lobby days in Washington, an annual two-day effort to make grassroots connections with legislators about transgender rights. The first day was devoted to training. After all, if you're going to try to convince someone of something, you really ought to have some idea what you're talking about. After the daylong training on employment issues, there was a reception at the National Press Club. Mara spoke for a few minutes. She managed to be both inspiring and funny as hell. In the morning, we set out for Capitol Hill. I visited Mike McNulty, an upstate New York congressman who was a fellow Holy Cross graduate. We had a cordial visit and he pledged his support for the employment rights bill the NCTE was pushing. In the afternoon, I was scheduled to gather with other New Yorkers and meet with one of our senators, Kirsten Gillibrand.

In the meantime, I thought it would be fun to seek out the Senate cafeteria and have a bowl of the famous Senate bean soup. Fa had told me about it many times. He always made it a point to have a bowl when he went to Washington to see Senator Walsh. I wondered if it might still be the same. As I was going through the line with my tray, I noticed that the small woman in front of me was Senator Gillibrand herself. She gave me a friendly smile and I introduced myself: "Hello, Senator. I'm one of your constituents, and I happen to have an appointment with you at two o'clock."

She smiled again and asked, "Then why don't we have lunch together?"

When we sat down, I asked her if it would be appropriate to talk during lunch about the legislation. "My staff has already briefed me on that. Anyway, we can talk about all that at two. For now, just tell me about yourself."

I started with the unlikely coincidence that her father, Doug Rutnik, had been the assistant coach of my high school basketball team while he was a student at Boston College Law School. We talked about the Folger Shakespeare Library and the Archive of American Folk Song at the Library of Congress. We talked about the athletic rivalry between Holy Cross and Dartmouth, where she had been a student-athlete. We enjoyed our chat. And the soup was good.

The meeting in her office at two was genial and surprisingly substantive. Two of the members of our delegation were veterans, and Gillibrand listened with great interest to their employment horror stories. She asked us pointed questions about our expectations concerning enforcement if the provision were to pass. She pledged her support. Somebody took pictures and we adjourned.

I had two hours to kill before our group debriefing and decided on a long walk back to the Madison Hotel on 15th Street. The day was delightful, and I dallied for a while in the sculpture garden near the Museum of Natural History. The National Geographic Museum was near the hotel, so I decided to explore it. I was about a block away when I heard a voice behind me: "I got some friends who wanna meet you."

Anyone who hadn't been living in the Adirondacks for twenty-five years would have put their head down and walked away. Fast. But I thought the voice might belong to someone connected with the lobby days, so I made a rube's mistake. I turned and replied, "I'm sorry, but are you speaking to me?"

I was confronted by a menacing pair of eyes and a face that seemed distorted by some powerful drug. "Yeah, bitch. I'm talkin' to you. I got friends who wanna meet you."

I turned and walked as fast as I could down 17th Street. I could hear footsteps behind me. I didn't look back. I grabbed the Acme Thunderer police whistle I keep in my bag and was ready to blow it for all I was worth when I realized I was at the entrance to the Geographic building. I sprinted inside and saw a security guard. He was a portly, pleasant-looking man, about sixty-five, who looked as if he might be retired from the security force at some shopping mall. I rushed up to him, gesturing over my shoulder. "Can you help me?" I asked. "I'm being followed by a pimp." His jaw dropped and his eyes popped out like a cartoon character who had stuck his finger in a light socket.

After I had calmed down and it seemed that the crazed pimp had gone off in search of some other victim, I made my way toward the hotel. I stopped for a moment at a CVS for a bottle of water. As I was standing in the checkout line, I felt a tug on my sleeve and a voice behind me said, "You'd better come along with us, honey."

I reached for my whistle and whirled to confront my tormentor. Two benevolent-looking women in their seventies were smiling at me. *What kind of a crazy town is this? Even the old ladies are pimps?*

As it turned out, they had simply decided that I needed some beauty tips. They led me down the aisle where the shampoos and conditioners were and handed me a bottle of something. "You just got to try this, honey. It's a purple rinse. You have such nice white hair, and this will make it shine like silver."

Later, one of my friends came up to me as I walked into the hotel. She smiled and asked, "Well, did you have an interesting day?"

"You have such nice white hair, and this will make it shine like silver."
Taking a break outside the Senate Office Building.

74
Tracey

Not long ago, I sent my friend Tracey a slogan I had read somewhere: "Don't be afraid of being different. Be afraid of being like everyone else." She responded right away with one she had collected: "There is no greater burden than carrying an untold story." I've never been much of a sloganeer, but these ring true to me. When I do college, community and corporate outreach, and when I teach my Writing Your Transgender Memoir workshops, I build everything on two basic points. The first is that transgender experience is remarkably varied. For better or worse, every transgender person has to discover their own difference and define themselves by living it. It's an existential experience, without comfortable, heavily trodden pathways. The second is that transgender people, for our own health and the health of society, must be seen, must be heard and must be known. While I believe in these ideas, I admit they seem a bit smug when they're expressed as tidy maxims. Life isn't tidy. Oops, there goes another maxim...

Tracey and I became friends about fifteen years ago at a huge transgender event in Atlanta. We met again the following year at an international gender conference in Philadelphia. The conference was getting tedious, so we drove out to King of Prussia to have dinner and do some shopping. As relative newbies to venturing out, we were absurdly overdressed. Dinner took a long time, and we got to the mall about half an hour before closing. We parked hurriedly, opened the nearest door and scurried down an endless corridor with service elevators and doors with signs that read EMPLOYEES ONLY and WARNING: HIGH VOLTAGE. By now, Tracey was in full trot. I hadn't realized anyone could move that fast in heels. Finally, we found a door with a panic bar and pushed it open. We scampered up a flight of stairs, down another corridor, through another unmarked door—and right into the bridal salon of Lord & Taylor. The saleswoman looked at us in bug-eyed amazement. We managed a weak "Hi" and just kept moving.

Back at the hotel bar, we laughed for a long time about what must be on the videos from the surveillance cameras. Picture two guys in generic security guard uniforms, drinking coffee from Styrofoam cups in the basement of Lord & Taylor. One guy glances at the monitor. Then he grabs the other guy by the sleeve. "Hey, Charlie, you ain't gonna believe this!" I learned that night to enjoy Tracey's appreciation of the absurd and her talent for joking about herself.

Tracey and I have very different lives. She has a family and a real estate career that could be compromised if she went public. As things stand, she's pretty well closeted.[10] I don't have children or grandchildren, my faculty position with SUNY allows me free gender expression and my neighbors in Rhode Island are accepting of my difference. Yet in many ways, Tracey and I really are alike. Both of us have known what it feels like to get along in the world by living our lives in rigid compartments. This person gets to know this about me, that person gets to know something else. Nobody ever gets the whole picture—that would be way too risky. It's a strategy that becomes dispiriting and exhausting. We both know how difficult it is to tell someone you love that you kept part of yourself hidden because you were afraid of losing them. And Tracey and I both have marriages of long endurance—hers of more than thirty years, mine of more than twenty. Our marriages have been tested and tempered by our gender difference. Neither of us is complacent in marriage.

We were having lunch a few years ago and Tracey was having a bad day. I impulsively told her, "I just want you to fly." If she chooses, she can discover what that means for her and take flight in her own way. How? When? I don't know. But I do know that by being her friend, I've learned about myself.

75
Three Students

I never had the teaching career I intended to have when I finished my Ph.D. at Penn, in 1972, at age twenty-five. I was at the top of my fellowship class and had published in the journal of record in my field. It didn't matter. I looked for a job for four years. I had one interview, and that turned out to be a cattle call.

Finally, I gave up. I put aside my typewriter and picked up my guitar in earnest. I thought I would never teach again, and I grieved over that. Then, somehow, I found my way back to teaching and academic publishing in 1990. After a few years of classroom teaching at Albany-area colleges, I landed a position as a mentor at Empire State College. A specialized college of SUNY, the mission at Empire State is to guide students who have gotten derailed somehow, so they can complete their degrees. The average age of my students is about forty. For the most part, they are very highly motivated. I've worked with hundreds of students individually, and they often bring surprising and compelling stories to our encounters. Here are three of those stories.

Dorothy

Dorothy had been the wife of a dairy farmer for fifty years. She told me that she had always loved books and libraries more than anything else. Right out of high school, she had intended to go to college and became a librarian. "But I got married instead," she told me. "Once we were married, he wouldn't hear of me going to college. There was too much work on the farm, he said, and there were children to raise so we could keep the farm going. He even took my library card away. I had to hide books and read in secret. Then one day last year he keeled over in the barn. That was it. The day after the bastard died, I started to look at colleges."

She was a bright and dignified woman with both a dream and a burden of regret. She chose Empire State because of our history of helping students with unconventional life stories. I helped her plan a degree in Information and Communication, but I advised her that time wasn't on her side in terms of getting work as a librarian. "I know," she agreed. "I'll be seventy-two when I graduate. Who's going to hire a seventy-two-year-old librarian?" I didn't have a convenient answer, as much as I admired her pluck and determination. A few weeks later, she came back to the office. "I'm switching to Sociology," she announced. "I want to study why society wastes people like me."

Kamil

Kamil had been a hockey player for the Slovakian national team. He had been drafted by the Detroit Red Wings of the National Hockey League, was assigned to their minor league affiliate in Glens Falls and married a young woman from the town. The hyped-up local crowd made the Adirondack Red Wings games fun, and Kamil was making his mark as a punishing defenseman who could pass and score, as well as check an opponent. Then he had a devastating back injury. Without warning, his career was over. He showed up in my office with a fierce desire to learn and a very strange transcript from some two-year technical college in Slovakia. We worked up a program for his degree in Management.

One day, we got talking about the fascination that Eastern European intellectuals have had with Shakespeare. I told him about Kozintsev's brooding film adaptation of *Hamlet* in Russian. I showed him my old VHS copy. "I don't know of a subtitled version," I explained. That didn't faze Kamil. "No problem. They made me take Russian for ten years in school. I'll watch it." Then I told him about the Polish director Jan Kott's book *Shakespeare Our Contemporary*, which had inspired me to become an English major in college. "Inspiring to you? Then maybe inspiring to me, too. I know some Polish," he replied. Russian? Polish? Yes, and he also had some German. As it turned out, English (in which he was quite fluent) was Kamil's fourth or fifth language, depending on how you counted them.

We decided on an independent study of Shakespeare. Kamil kept a notebook on his reading. It took him a month to get through *Hamlet* and nearly as long to read *Richard III*. As he read, his notebook grew fat. He made lists of words over which he had puzzled. He wrote narrative sketches of individual characters. He came up with discussion questions about the conflicts between characters and about their motivations. He worked very hard. As his understanding of the plays evolved, Kamil increasingly viewed them through the lens of someone who had grown up in the Soviet Union. One of Kamil's particular strengths was his uncanny alertness to the cock-eyed power relationships in the plays—a sensitivity that was enhanced by his reading of Kott. Needless to say, *Richard* III was a carnival for him, and Claudius in *Hamlet* became a shadow Stalin. But Kamil's reading of *The Tempest* was the most refreshing surprise. "Prospero was a totalitarian! He even had his own secret police agent—Ariel!" he declared gleefully.

Cara

In early 2020, Cara was a student in my online history of ideas course on the Renaissance and the Reformation, studying Dante, Machiavelli, Luther and

Erasmus. At the beginning of the term, she had difficulty with the methodology of the course, so we had an email conversation to help her sort things out. During our exchange she mentioned that she was a pianist, and we got into the inevitable discussion about which of Gould's recordings of the *Goldberg Variations* we preferred, the 1955 or the 1981. She recommended a book, *A Romance on Three Legs: Glenn Gould's Obsessive Quest for the Perfect Piano*, which I read and found intriguing. Soon we were having email chats, mostly about Bach. I told her about a recent Handel and Haydn Society concert performance of the complete *Brandenburg Concertos*, during which I had wept actual tears of joy. In turn, she introduced me to Martha Argerich's recordings of the *Partitas*, which she described aptly as "beauty in motion." I enjoyed our exchanges and I was touched when she asked if it would be "proper" for us to continue as friends after the term was over.

In early April, she asked me to call her. She was concerned about maintaining her progress in the course. Her husband, a medical professional, had contracted the coronavirus and was isolating at home. Things were difficult and she was very worried. "He's always been so strong. And now he's so weak. I made him some soup, but I don't think he'll eat it." Then she told me their teenaged daughter had died unexpectedly two years earlier, and that completing her degree was part of her work to rebuild her life. I assured her we'd work things out about the course and closed with what had quickly become the universal valediction in those bad days: "Stay safe. Be well."

Three weeks later, I got an email after midnight: "Would you call me in the morning? Please." The word "please" jumped off the screen. I worried during the night that something awful had happened. It had. When she picked up the phone, she was struggling to talk. The words came out in pieces, but I understood enough to know that her husband was dead. "Maybe he had just seen too much," she sobbed.

I am writing this a week after that phone call—actually a month or so after I thought this book had been completed. A book. A life. What does it mean to be complete, anyway? I'm thinking of a strong man, weakened by disease, who had seen too much. Or perhaps simply seen enough.

Thinking of Cara, I listened a few minutes ago to the aria da capo of Gould's 1981 *Goldberg Variations*, recorded not long before his own death. In the liner notes to his 1955 recording, Gould had called this reprise of the aria that concludes the *Variations* a "benediction"—a blessing, as one bestowed upon parting. His final, fragile, courageous performance of the aria that I heard this morning, captured so close to death, is more than a benediction—it's an elegy for all of us.

76
Two Writers

Georges Simenon

Why am I so enthralled by the world Simenon created in his novels and stories about Inspector Maigret? On first read, it would seem that there really isn't that much about which to be enthralled. Simenon's is a Paris without the usual rhapsodic descriptions of chestnut trees in bloom and moonlight on the Seine. It's a Paris without adjectives. I don't know of any other writer, even Hemingway, who writes so economically, who leaves so much to the reader's imagination and at the same time provokes such an engrossing visual experience.

When I read a Maigret novel, I always have a map handy so I can follow him as he negotiates his way, seemingly by intuition, through the streets and along the boulevards of Simenon's sparse but emotive Paris. I have a book of Atget's photographs from the 1920s of a rapidly disappearing Paris, images that overlap the early career of the young Maigret. I also keep close by the photographs by the evocative Brassai and the wonderfully humorous Robert Doisneau of Paris street and café life from the 1930s through the '50s. A dram of Calvados at my elbow helps to complete the atmosphere.

In literature, economy of description and heightened imagination are often related, of course. One case in point: Apologizing for the technological inadequacies of his Globe Theatre, Shakespeare had his Prologue speaker at the beginning of *Henry V* urge the audience to "Think, when we talk of horses, that you see them." *Use your imaginations*, he is saying. *That's all we've got.* The next line shows us the way to do just that: "Printing their proud hoofs i' th' receiving earth."[11] Eight words. Yet, as the horses come thundering past in our imaginations, the turf is flying. We see them, we hear them, we feel the ground tremble.

Similarly, in a Maigret novel, I see the lights with their dim haloes glowing through the fog over some barge canal, I smell the cooking in the passageways of cheap apartment houses and feel the shiver on the back of my neck as I watch the glistening winter rain hit the cobbles of Montmartre. There is always the glowing coal stove in Maigret's office to take away the chill. It warms me, as it warms him.

Maigret's entire purpose is not so much to catch a criminal as to probe human motivations until the essentials are revealed: "It was up to Maigret to tear down that façade, to sniff around in the ruins and nose out at last the human beast."[12] More than a detective, Maigret saw himself as "a mender of destinies."[13] And I find the motto that Simenon gave to Maigret as a watchword as helpful as any I know in dealing with my fellow human beings in all of our wonderful vagaries: *Understand. And judge not.*

Jorge Luis Borges

Contrastingly, there are no photographs of Borges' world, and Borges himself is its only cartographer. Myopic, pedantic, squirrelly. These are surely not characteristics that would make any writer sound captivating on a dust jacket blurb. But there was no more powerful imagination in twentieth-century literature than Borges—and he was all three of those things.

Besides English, my languages are German and Latin; I have barely enough home-brewed French to laboriously read Simenon in the original with a dictionary at hand. I have not much Spanish beyond *Dos cervezas, por favor,* so I haven't even attempted Borges. But can he really be as elemental as he sounds in English? If so, that may be the key to his magic. The voice in his stories is given to the toneless narration of things that surpass the capacity of the imagination. This matches perfectly with the implicit narrative of many of his stories—the arduous navigation of a labyrinth, only to discover that the excursion has created an even more incomprehensible puzzle.

Time and space operate differently in a Borges story than they do anywhere else. This shouldn't surprise us, since when Borges organized a seminar in Buenos Aires to study English literature, the group started at the beginning by laboriously learning Anglo-Saxon. Time was no factor. In Borges' story "The Aleph," a small, luminous sphere in the basement of a dilapidated Buenos Aires house contains all of time and space simultaneously. In "Borges and I," he characterizes his work as "games with time and infinity."[14]

Borges wrote one of the most satisfying detective stories I know, "Death and the Compass." He also wrote one of the most illuminating essays on literature I have ever read, "Partial Magic in the *Quixote.*" In the essay, he ranges with supreme confidence from Cervantes' novel to *Hamlet* and the *Thousand and One Nights* to explore the magical potential of literature to render readers of fiction fictitious themselves. To me, one of his most intriguing writings remains the early *Evaristo Carriego,* a fragmented biographical study of a poet who wrote in turn-of-the-century Buenos Aires. Carriego's writings are a portal to Borges' meditations on the world of the gaucho, the tango and petty, knife-fighting hoodlums. But to what extent are the poet and his world even real? We learn to withhold such questions in the writing of Borges, who is the supreme fabulist. And rational thought isn't much help as a guide in this world. As the narrator of one of his stories says, "There is no exercise of the intellect which is not, in the final analysis, useless."[15]

These days, college bookstores sell mostly coffee mugs and sweat-shirts. They can't be blamed for the current realities of the marketplace. But fifty-five years ago, the bookstore at Holy Cross was a real bookstore, with a marvelous selection of titles by publishers such as Grove, Evergreen, City Lights, Penguin and Dover. My first day on campus I bought Jan Kott's *Shakespeare Our Contemporary*, Antonin Artaud's *The Theater and Its Double*, Simone de Beauvoir's *The Ethics of Ambiguity* and Borges' *Labyrinths*. Taking those four books to the cash register may have been one of the defining actions of my life. They are still among my most valued tools with which to challenge my mind.[16]

77
Reunion

About a year before my fiftieth college reunion, I started to get invitations in the mail to an entire weekend of reunion events. As the date got closer, the invitations became more frequent, more insistent and more lavish—three-panel foldovers with big color pictures of jolly families at barbecues and sophisticated couples at elegant dinner dances. Then, a couple of months before the reunion, I began to get weekly email reminders that I had gotten all those invitations and hadn't responded. The onslaught of mail spooked me. I realized that I really did want to see the people that I had lived with and laughed with for four important years of my life, so long ago. But those people had only known me as "Tom." How was I going to handle this?

As I puzzled over the question, I recalled the notorious ad for Holiday Inn that caused a furor when it played during the Super Bowl in 1997. In it, a glamorous woman in a clingy dress and killer heels makes an entrance at her class reunion. As she descends a staircase, she gets the heavy eyeball from everyone in the room. She smiles and approaches one fellow. He leers at her and smiles flirtatiously while he struggles to recall her name. Then a flash of recognition. His smug expression changes to dismay as he stammers, "Bob? Bob Johnson?" The ad launched the persistent cliché that a transgender person at a class reunion is a sure cause for embarrassment and dismay.

Some perspective. Holy Cross has always been one of the elite among Jesuit colleges, along with Georgetown, Fordham and Boston College. It produces phalanxes of doctors, lawyers, MBAs and college professors. But when I attended, Holy Cross was still an all-male institution. Twenty-five hundred young guys on a hill. You can imagine. Guys jumping off the roofs of dormitories into snowbanks in just their boxer shorts and a mad bomber hat. That sort of thing. It's not much of an exaggeration to say that the first time I saw *Animal House*, parts of it seemed like a documentary. Bluto, the joker in the film, reminded me of a classmate known as Hog. Hog was the organizer of manic road trips to women's colleges in places like Bennington, Purchase and New London. He had a silver whiskey flask, elegantly engraved with the slogan "Hog's Fuel." It got lots of use. I think he now has something to do with the World Bank. Which really is the point. Those crazy young bucks from the mid-sixties would now be professional men living in the suburbs or in retirement at the Cape, much more interested in visiting their grandchildren than engaging in impulsive, self-destructive behavior. Surely, they had changed. So why couldn't I?

Emboldened by that thought, I looked over the program for the weekend. A reception Friday night at the Worcester Country Club. Workshops and educational sessions during the day on Saturday. A gala banquet Saturday night in the ballroom of the Campus Center. Clearly this would require some planning.

To start with, I contacted the organizers and proposed a discussion circle for Saturday afternoon on the history and current status of LGBT at Holy Cross. I have a lot of experience doing outreach and education as a volunteer for SpeakOUT Boston, so I knew I'd be on confident ground and I hoped that the session would give at least a few people a chance to get to know Connelly. For some reason, Friday night seemed manageable—cocktails, hors d'oeuvres and schmoozing. Maybe I could dress down a bit for that. But the shindig on Saturday night was a gala—everyone dressed full tilt. No hiding in the woodwork then.

My reunion rescue party—Hugo, Brian and Richard

I'm in the silly habit of buying beautiful, unusual clothes at thrift shops and clearance sales that I will likely never wear anywhere. I just like browsing the sale racks and discovering something with a striking color or a beautiful fabric. So what if I spend twelve bucks and it hangs in the back of the closet? I still have the fun of the treasure hunt and the find. Susanne helped me go through these half-forgotten bargains to unearth some appropriate clothes. For Saturday night, we discovered a black-and-silver geometric print cardigan and a very sleek black-and-silver necklace. It looked classy and felt comfortable.

We got to the Friday night gathering early, grabbed drinks and a plate of appetizers and stood off to one side, waiting for something to happen. As my classmates filtered in, I had the odd realization that I didn't recognize them any more than they appeared to recognize me. I was relieved when a rescue party crossed the tent in our direction: Hugo, who started life after college as a lobsterman and became a maxillofacial surgeon; Richard, my friend since the seventh grade, who left a law career to become a successful actor in New York; Brian, who was always running around campus with a Nikon slung around his neck and is now a cinematographer who travels the world, shooting mostly from helicopters. Like mine, their life stories had cracked the mold. We talked for a moment and Richard grabbed the arm of Michael, another old friend of ours who was standing nearby and said, "You remember *Connelly*, of course?" Michael, who had been the best man at my first wedding, looked a little bewildered, but gathered himself quickly and smiled, "Oh yes, Connelly! Of course!" Then he spontaneously gave me a hug. Soon we were all at a table, laughing and telling the old stories.

The organizers of the reunion had been skeptical about the Saturday discussion circle. What if only a handful of people came? We arrived early to set up the room and discovered one alumnus sitting patiently in a chair. As Susanne went over to greet him he said, "I'm just so happy to be here. I've been waiting fifty years for this." As it turned out, we had an energetic, candid discussion among forty people, including several of my classmates and their spouses.

By Saturday night, word was definitely out—and therefore so was I. I was still intimidated by the scale and glamour of the event, but my trio of allies stayed close by. And everyone was drawn to Susanne, who was in high spirits and looked beautiful. I felt proud that we were there together.

Earlier, Susanne and I had a cordial, relaxed conversation with my former basketball teammate Orion and his wife. Orion is quite a serious character. He's now a Georgia state judge and carries himself with appropriate gravitas. But fifty years ago, he had an impish sense of humor. He'd always have a sardonic comment to make as we were riding through the night on

La Vie en Rose, with Orion

the team bus. Now, as the Saturday evening event was winding down, he came over to say goodbye. I was happy to see him walking my way. I was always fond of Orion, but I was having the disconcerting thought, *I'll never see this person again*. Something in the expression on his face told me that the Orion I knew as a teammate was about to emerge from the judicial veneer. As he extended his hand to Susanne he gestured toward me and told her, "You're a saint!" That made us laugh. Then he grabbed my hand in the kind of soul brother shake we used to share in the '60s, put his arm around my shoulder and said in a stage whisper, "Don't take this the wrong way, sister, but you've got a lot of balls."

Flow

The old aphorism from Hippocrates says, *"Ars longa, vita brevis."* I am in my seventy-third year as I write this, and there are certainly days when art does seem long and life does seem short. There still seems to be so much to do. I'm bewildered by friends who talk to me about this or that television series they watch, or which football team they follow every Sunday. I'm not a TV snob; I just can't imagine where they find the time. Maybe I need to read one of those time management books, but I feel as though I'm always in a scramble to complete something before it's time to go to bed.

I have always been captivated by Paul McCartney's song "When I'm Sixty-Four." He nailed the music hall idiom perfectly; it's homage as much as it is parody. And when the song came out, who could even imagine an old Beatle? So when I turned sixty-four myself, I played the song, sang along and used it as an excuse to do some self-assessment. One of the questions I asked myself was whether I had anything left to say, musically. I'd had a very nice run with Neil, playing concerts and recording old-time music, ragtime and zany vaudeville songs for about ten years, but that seemed to be winding down. He and I agreed that the last thing we wanted to be in our golden years was a Tom and Neil tribute band. I had some original songs that I had performed for years that had never made it beyond the demo stage. I thought I would like to hear finished versions of those. Then I took my guitar to Ontario for a week of vacation. By the end of the week, I had written three new songs. They seemed promising, worth bringing into the studio.

So I started to record. I've had experience as an engineer and producer, and the technology has become increasingly accessible. I fired up my little studio and laid down a rhythm guitar track for "Blue Line Boogaloo." Then a bass line. Then, after dinner, a scratch vocal. I listened to it after breakfast and decided to redo the bass part. A few days later, I added a slide guitar—but redid that a week later. And so it went, in bits and pieces, for nearly five years. The project grew organically, like Marvell's "vegetable love" in "To His Coy Mistress." The record ultimately declared itself to me—what it was about, and what its boundaries needed to be.

I invited some of my favorite singers and players to be part of it, and they trickled in when their schedules allowed. I insisted that we go for whole performances, even if they were overdubbed. No punching in this phrase or that, no editing chicanery. I wanted this record to sound like real people playing actual music. As Jerry Douglas famously advised, "Leave a little of the bark on." This led to a few cases of "microphone fever," when a good take is going and the little voice inside takes over: *Great so far, but just don't fuck it up.* The second guitar solo on "Don Quixote" is a case in point. The first solo is supposed to represent the censorious voices of everyone who does not appreciate Don Quixote's splendid madness. Scorn came easily; I did that in a couple of takes. The second solo had to start as his mocking parody of their scolding and then escalate into the musical expression of Quixote's triumphant, manic laugh. I'd tried a lot of approaches and concluded I was just making things impossible for myself. Before I hung it up for the night, I hit RECORD one more time and just played without thinking. Halfway through the take, the inner voice began to squeak: *This is your only shot. It's your "Shoot Out the Lights" moment. It might be the best thing you've ever played. But I know you, you'll self-destruct!* I blocked out the voice and went for an ascending, hysterical phrase I couldn't play again to save my soul from perdition. But in that moment I did, somehow.

I discovered the theme of the project when I wrote the title track, "Flow." My friend Joey was visiting from London; he's a bassist whose Sermon on the Mount is the synthbass line from Stevie Wonder's "Superstition." Joey started to play a funky bass riff that gave a shot of energy to the percussive guitar track I had laid down earlier and nearly forgotten. Joey's riff turned it into a song. All of a sudden, I needed words:

> Water keeps flowing to the sea
> Music keeps flowing over you and me
> Time keeps flowing
> That's the way it's gotta be

As I wrote these lyrics, I realized that I had spent a lot of my life's energy trying to make things different than they were. Perhaps it was time to let a little of the *Tao* in:

> If you realize that all things change,
> There is nothing you will try to hold on to.[17]

The song became my affirmation that this world has its own inevitability. After the album came out, an NPR interviewer asked me what I had learned in the process of making the record. I surprised myself with my answer: "That it's good to be sixty-eight years old."

After "Flow" was written, I began to like the project very much, and to believe it was the musical statement I had wanted to make for a long time.

I put together a rough mix of the whole album and took it to my friend Joel for a listen. He's a very musical person and a superb engineer. When it was over, he simply said, "You've got a record here."

The title came easily. Susanne and I have had many conversations about the "flow" experience—the sense of timelessness and selflessness that gives such immense pleasure when we engage our consciousness fully in anything. I knew it when I was playing basketball. I would become oblivious to the crowd noise of five thousand people, but acutely aware of the staccato music of the squeaking sneakers on the polished maple floor, the playing of the pep band sounding like a toneless drone of distant thunder, the sense of things happening very rapidly but in slow motion at the same time. And then the jarring referee's whistle, calling me back to reality. It's what I've sought in lovemaking, more than physical sensation—and perhaps even as much as emotional or spiritual connection, if the truth be told. And I think it's why I play music. I love the sensation of becoming lost in the trance state of playing and singing a song. For me, music is a gateway to *flow*.

Susanne and I chose the cover photo from among photographs we had taken on vacation. It shows our two little solo canoes on the shore of vast Lake Ontario. An island is in the distance, waiting. To me, the picture says: *Venture. Abandon yourself. You are not alone. There is a place to land.*

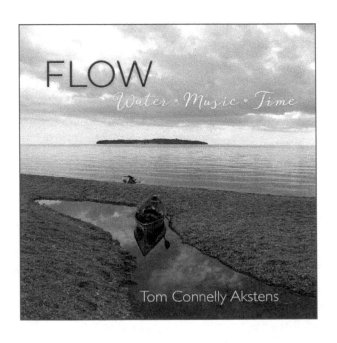

79
Beachcombing

Susanne and I love to walk the beaches of Rhode Island. We always come home with our pockets bulging with scavenged treasures—a per-

fect little scallop shell, smooth crescents of quahog shell that in our dreams will be turned into jewelry, smooth black rocks, smooth white rocks, smooth dappled rocks. All kinds of rocks. One of my favorite memories of Susanne is sitting for an hour on the sand, listening to the breakers and watching as she combed through a mass of pebbles no larger than peas, looking for the perfect colors and the perfect luminosity.

Susanne with beach rocks, 1996

After one early morning walk, we went to our favorite breakfast spot. While we waited at our outside table, Susanne began to stack the rocks and shells from our pockets, building a cairn. How high could they go? Could I make a cairn as tall as hers? Could I make one with as many rocks and shells? Could we make a taller and more complex cairn if we collaborated?

I often walk the beach alone, as well—usually with a surf rod or a camera in my hand. One early December day, I came across the carcass of a gannet. Ted Hughes once wrote a meditative and rather grim poem called "Relic" that begins: "I found this jawbone at the sea's edge…"[18] I thought of that poem as I stood, looking at the gannet. There was noth-ing sad about the dead bird. My conscious-

Susanne building a cairn with our beachcoming treasures, 2016

ness was filled with how beautiful it was. Its sleek head was shaded with soft russet. Dramatic markings traced the edges of its bill and outlined its eyes. I had never seen a gannet up close. I had only seen them a hundred yards or more offshore in the late fall and early winter when the sea herring run is on. They attack the schools of herring in flocks of dozens, diving from a hundred feet in the air, folding their wings into a torpedo shape, rocketing through the waves at sixty miles per hour and grasping a fish underwater. It's an

The gannet

exciting show. Gannets are big, powerful, pelagic birds with a wing-span of six feet. In death, this gannet was a relic of the vibrant wildness of its species, now revealed in its ulti-mate fragility.

Sometimes, when life is bur-densome, Susanne and I walk the beach at dawn just to be in contact with something much larger than ourselves. It gives me great comfort, in the increasing awareness of my own mortality, to know that when I am no longer alive to walk these beaches the breakers will simply roll on, without notice or concern.

> We are such stuff
> As dreams are made on; and our little life
> Is rounded with a sleep.[19]

Epilogue: At the Vernal Equinox, 2020

As I write this epilogue, the coronavirus is tightening its grip on the world. I'm frightened. I've noticed that my senses are highly alert to anything that might take me out of my fear—the woody sweetness of fresh ginger, the brittle sound of a harpsichord on the radio, the rough comfort of my old sweater…and the lovely dodging and fluttering of the finches at the feeder outside our dining room window.

They remind me that when I was a young child I would hear song sparrows calling in my grandfather's front yard at Falmouth Heights. Their little trills charmed me then. Yesterday morning, seventy years later, my old friends were back, singing for me in our front yard in Rhode Island, charming me all over again.

Perhaps they simply wanted to remind me that while some things change, some endure.

Swans flying down the Potowomut River behind our house.

Acknowledgments

Susanne kept asking, "Why don't you write a book?" Eventually, I did. I don't think I ever would have done so without her encouragement. I treasure her patience—she's heard most of these stories many times and still asks me to read them aloud for visiting friends. And her marvelous graphic design made this book what it is.

Peter Kaminsky has been my most trusted reader. I thank him for reading the whole thing through with a critical eye and giving me forthright encouragement over cocktails at the swanky Campbell in Grand Central Station.

Betsy Folwell has been my editor at *Adirondack Life* and has encouraged my writing for more than thirty years. She still has an infallible ear and responds with unvarnished candor to anything I send her.

Chris Jerome edited my manuscript with patience and surpassing judgment; she will doubtless be gratified that I didn't spell it "judgement."

David Shiang took an early interest in this book and gave me valued suggestions about how to make it better.

Many of my other friends have read or listened to this book at various stages and offered criticism and encouragement. I want to thank them all for their generosity of time and goodwill: Pat Alger, Peter Bien, Sophie Carlhian, Diana Christie-Robitaille, Dan Crane, Cynthia Darlow, Richard Ferrone, Jack Fitterer, Taff Fitterer, Joanna Frost, Karen Garner, Kathryn Guare, Elaine Handley, Alan Hawkridge, Patricia Hawkridge, Brian Heller, Keith Hochstein, Mary Imbornone, Michael Imbornone, Mindy Kronenberg, Karen LaBarge, Naton Leslie, Barbara Malagraph, Alan Mandell, Andrea Masters, Tracey McKenna, Stacy Parks, David Paul, Bruce Piasecki, Robert Pinsky, K. J. Rawson, Susan Ritz, Jim Rooney, Neil Rossi, John Stacey, Mary Staulo, Bonnie Sullivan, Jeff Sullivan, Chrissy Testani, Happy Traum, Dorothy Wang, Sylvia Jane Wojcik and Meg Woolbright.

Special thanks to Brian Heller for the photos of Holy Cross basketball and John Walsh, to Martine Gaudet for the photo of La Duchesse Anne, to Andrzej Pilarczyk for the photos of me at Caffè Lena and Artie's last concert, to Nancie Battaglia for the photo of me with Billy and the red guitars, to Gerald McCarthy for the photo of Rufina and her father in Ireland, to Andy Spence for making available Bill Spence's photos of Big Trout Radio, to Jim Rooney for the archival Club 47 material, to the Boston Public Library for the Ringling Brothers circus poster, to Kevin Hewitt for preparing some of the photos for publication, to Rob Houllahan for shooting the *Richard II* video, to Katherine McKay, Abigail Stambach and the College of the Holy Cross

Archives and Special Collections for the old yearbook photo of Father as a gangster, to the Michael Ochs Archive and Getty Images for the Bo Diddley photo, and to Evan Stover, Jerry Oland, Robert Pool and Fred Robbins for the photo of Evan and Dan Del Santo.

I owe my greatest debt to the remarkable characters who populate this book. If you are one of them, I trust that you will recognize that my portrayal of you and of those times when our lives touched each other has been done with affection and appreciation for the ways in which you made my life richer.

Notes

1   Lao-tzu. *Tao Te Ching*. New York: Harper, 1988, p. 70.

2   Peabody, Marian Lawrence. *To Be Young Was Very Heaven*. Boston: Houghton, 1967, pp. 155–56.

3   Joyce, James. "Araby." *Dubliners*. New York: Penguin, 1988, p. 30.

4   Frank, Elizabeth. *Louise Bogan: A Portrait*. New York: Knopf, 1985, p. 200. As her mentor, Rufina's father actively fostered these traits in his daughter. Their relationship is explored, using unpublished letters, by Paula M. Kane in *Separatism and Subculture: Boston Catholicism, 1900–1920* (Chapel Hill, U of North Carolina Press, 1994). Writing to Rufina about some deficiencies in her grade report from Elmhurst Academy, McCarthy showed the humorous side of their relationship: "As to 'order' and 'diligence in study,' you'll have to develop them without much help from heredity" (174). Kane also recounts that Uncle Denis met with William Butler Yeats in 1911 and subsequently told the *Boston Sunday Post*, "I don't understand many of the things [he] says" (p. 256).

5   Limmer, Ruth, ed. *What the Woman Lived: Selected Letters of Louise Bogan 1920–1970*. New York: Harcourt, 1973, p. 241. My sincere thanks to the Amherst College Library Archives & Special Collections for generously allowing me access to the Bogan correspondence.

6   Shakespeare, William. *King Lear*. Ed. R. A. Foakes. London: Routledge, 2000, p. 292 (3. 6. 74–75).

7   My song "The Yellow Mailbox" on the *Big Trout Radio* album is about the spirit and fragility of that time and place:

> Tying flies on the old front porch
> Let's follow the river around the bend
> Guess we'll be home about half-past dark
> This won't last forever, my friend

8 "Raymond Saville Conolly de Montmorency Lecky-Browne-Lecky of Ecclesville 1881–1961." http://mcclintockofseskinore.co.uk/Raymond%20Browne-Lecky.html

9 My gardens were featured in *Gardens, Adirondack Style*, by Janet Loughrey (Camden, Maine, Down East Books, 2006).

10 I use the term "closeted" only because it's current. I dislike it because it's part of the rigid "closeted" / "out" binary construct that fails to account for the diversity of transgender experience and the complexity of our relationships. After so many decades in the shadows it suits me now to be known but, for many reasons, it didn't suit me earlier. David Mamet, the playwright, has written about the transformation of the tragic hero in drama in terms that resonate for me with shedding the fear of consequences and becoming known: "[Life] can be led truthfully, without either shame or anxiety, *as one no longer fears discovery.*" ("The Code and the Key," *NR Plus Online Magazine*. June 1, 2020 issue).

11 Shakespeare, William. *Henry V*. Ed. T. W. Craik. London: Routledge, 1995, p. 121 (Prologue 26–27).

12 Simenon, Georges. "The Old Lady of Bayeux." Trans. Anthony Boucher. *The Short Cases of Inspector Maigret*. New York: Ace, 1959, p. 124.

13 Simenon, Georges. *Maigret's First Case*. Trans. Ros Schwartz. New York: Penguin, 2016, p. 85.

14 Borges, Jorge Luis. "Borges and I." Trans. Andrew Hurley. *Collected Fictions*. New York: Penguin, 1998, p. 324.

15 Borges, Jorge Luis. "Pierre Menard, Author of the *Quixote*." Trans. James E. Irby. *Labyrinths*. New York: New Directions, 1964, p. 43.

16 One dark assertion of Kott's has haunted me for decades as I have sought to discover myself and puzzled over what it means to live an authentic life: "To be oneself means only to play one's own reflection in the eyes of strangers." *Shakespeare Our Contemporary*. New York and London: Norton, 1964, p. 270.

17 Lao-tzu. *Tao Te Ching*. New York: Harper & Row, 1988, p. 74.

18 Hughes, Ted. "Relic." *New Selected Poems*. New York: Harper & Row, 1982, p. 41.

19 Shakespeare, William. *The Tempest,* Ed. Frank Kermode. London: Routledge, 1990, p. 104 (4. 1. 156–58).

WITHDRAWN

4/2022

$29.95

CPSIA info
at www.IC
Printed in t
BVHW05
627987B

781736 4379